$\mathcal{F}$ROLICS *in the* $\mathcal{F}$ACE *of* $\mathcal{E}$UROPE

FROLICS *in the* FACE *of* EUROPE

SIR WALTER SCOTT, CONTINENTAL TRAVEL AND THE TRADITION OF THE GRAND TOUR

IAIN GORDON BROWN

FONTHILL

To the memory of my mother and father,
who first took me, at the age of eleven,
to the great cities of Italy:
a 'Grand Tour' that formed my taste

www.fonthillmedia.com
office@fonthillmedia.com

First published in the United Kingdom
and the United States of America 2020

British Library Cataloguing in Publication Data:
A catalogue record for this book is available from the British Library

ISBN 978-1-78155-809-6

Typeset in 10pt on13pt Sabon
Printed and bound in England

Preface

Two major concerns of my scholarly career have been (on the one hand) the study of the Grand Tour and (on the other) the life and world of Sir Walter Scott. In this book I have attempted to combine both themes in a way that is novel, and one that will, I trust, be found interesting.

This work is a contribution to the celebration of the 250th anniversary of Scott's birth, which will be commemorated in August 2021. By chance, publication coincides with the 350th anniversary of the coining of the term 'Grand Tour' itself. It was first used by Richard Lassels in *The Voyage of Italy* (1670), an enormously influential work and one of real importance in the history of travel: in an early manuscript incarnation this had been written as a guide for a Scottish nobleman.

Walter Scott did not *quite* make a 'Grand Tour'. That distinctive genre of travel—a cultural phenomenon which, in earlier days, exerted a profound effect on British society and taste in the arts—had all but ceased to exist before Scott at last reached the Mediterranean late in 1831. Arguably the Grand Tour was already dying out even before Scott first contemplated a European venture of any kind, for the long wars with France had effectively sealed the Continent to would-be travellers from the British Isles. Nevertheless, elements of the old tradition still endured, however much its *raison d'être* and its defining characteristics might largely have been confined to history, to be replaced after 1815 by a new kind of 'Romantic' travel.

These surviving manifestations of a past tradition certainly remained vivid to Scott, even if he did not feel an overwhelming compulsion to sustain them, or to provide his own gloss upon them. Scott's rich imagination had already done much vicarious travelling. To be, or to have been, a 'Grand Tourist' of the classic type was to exhibit concerns, tastes and interests that Scott really did not share. Certainly, he *travelled* in Europe, but on three occasions only: all of them were for specific and limited needs, circumscribed by other priorities at home or (in the case of his last journey) by failing health. Thus none of these three episodes properly constitutes a 'Grand Tour' in its tried and tested guise. All, nevertheless, are full of interest and have a great deal to tell us about Walter Scott, about the ideas and actualities of contemporary travel, and about Scott in relation to travel. With his death in 1832, the era of the institutionalised Grand Tour, the extended Scottish Enlightenment, and even the 'long eighteenth century' itself, may all be said to close.

This succession of Continental adventures—whether achieved or merely imagined—has never been considered as a discrete aspect of Walter Scott's life and thought. My approach differs from that of the late Dr Donald E. Sultana, a meticulous scholar who wrote three enormously detailed works on Scott's travels to Paris and Malta. My purpose is more limited but at the same time more wide-ranging in its chronological scope. This book deals as much, if not more so, with the 'Grand Tours' Scott *never* made as with those trips he did manage to complete, for he thought and wrote of many other European journeys beyond those he actually accomplished.

The origins of this study go back to 2011, when I first became seriously interested in the topic. Indeed, I was due to speak on this subject in Germany— at the Old Castle of Schönburg on the Rhine, and thus in a setting Scott himself would have relished—having been invited to do so by Dr Sigrid Rieuwerts on the occasion of the inauguration of the Society for Scottish Studies in Europe. An outline of my proposed paper had actually been published in the conference literature issued by the Johannes Gutenberg-Universität Mainz when an impending hospital operation obliged me to withdraw. The research, only just started, was then set aside in favour of the other work that has filled the intervening years. I resumed it only in late August 2019.

In picking up the threads again, I first envisaged merely an article—albeit a substantial one—on the subject which now forms this book. As I read widely in the sources, however, and then began to arrange the rich material that was being amassed, it became clear that no scholarly journal could cope with something as extensive as that forming in my mind. Moreover, no one academic journal appeared to offer a completely suitable forum for publication of the sort of study I found myself preparing.

This book is really an extended, discursive essay. Scott might have described it as 'dumpled'—that is, filled out and rounded. It does not tell the story of Scott's Continental travels in every last detail. The standard biographies, notably the fundamental life by J. G. Lockhart, and the fullest of the more recent studies—that by Edgar Johnson—remain generally (if not entirely) trustworthy guides to the minutiae and chronology of Scott's journeys. Though based on extensive research and a thorough examination of all the available evidence, my work is episodic, allusive and rather in the nature of a series of pen-portraits or vignettes illustrating aspects of Scott's travelling experience. My book links events, places and personalities, often in different and unlikely ways; it makes connections—social, literary, artistic—and looks at Scott's travels from, I think, an imaginative viewpoint. It investigates what some would see as unfashionable aspects of an unfashionable man, for Scott's is not a name that would immediately attract the attention and interest of contemporary academics who approach the Grand Tour as an aspect of 'cultural history' or 'cultural studies'. Scott's 'Grand Touring' experience might not lead him to stand as an obvious representative of—to quote an amalgam of phrases used by several recent scholars—those 'privileged socio-economic protagonists' for whom European travel had established a 'technology of the self' in the 'transformation of personhood' during a 'critical period of geographical and social passage' on 'a stage for the performance of elite masculinity'.

The title of the present book is appropriated from a phrase in a letter of Scott's of 1824. I myself began researching the vicissitudes of his 'Grand Touring' predilections during the United Kingdom's extraordinary 'Brexit' autumn of 2019: this chronological coincidence has given added piquancy to my work. The book was written during the febrile 'Brexit' winter that followed. Composition has, therefore, been carried out at an unsettling period in national life, when confused and widely divergent ideas of what Europe means to the British became the common currency of every social gathering. On 20 October 1831, as he made ready to leave London for his voyage to the Mediterranean, Scott wrote in his journal of a country beset by political uncertainty on the eve of Reform: 'It seems to be in one of those crises by which Providence reduces nations to their original Elements.' Scott might have recognised another such moment had he seen the condition, or felt the mood, of a disunited kingdom between August 2019 and the end of January 2020— and after. It is a whimsical conceit that, as a nation trapped in the 'Brexit' quagmire, Britain has been guilty of committing its own modern 'Frolic in the face of Europe'. Government, Parliament and people have indulged in this without ever having had recourse to Scott's evocative phrase. Even without benefit of his telling terminology, we have surely been able to recognise today—albeit in another context, and in an altered setting—something of what he implied.

My book has been completed in the shadow of the Covid-19 Coronavirus pandemic. The circumstances of 2020 would be familiar to those who travelled in the age of the Grand Tour, with contagious disease always a danger, and cholera a particular threat in the early nineteenth century. To read of Walter Scott's Mediterranean voyage being interrupted by such health scares is to be aware of a constant hazard of foreign travel in his time and in that of his predecessors. Scott was unable to disembark at Gibraltar, and even his letters could not be sent ashore; he underwent quarantine both at Malta and off Naples. From Malta, he wrote to a friend that 'It is in the capacity of Quarantine prisoners that we now inhabit the decayd grandeur of a magnificent old Spanish palace', where they were watched over by sanitary officials in yellow-collared uniforms. Words such as 'captivity', 'confinement' and 'imprisonment' in the lazaretto, as used by Scott in his journal and his correspondence, have a resonance today, and will be readily intelligible to citizens of the world of 2020. Scott practised 'social distancing' at Fort Manoel in Malta, his visitors having to remain beyond a barrier. One of these, the daughter of an Edinburgh legal friend of Scott's and married to a doctor on the island, recorded that 'a quarantine is a notably uncomfortable thing'. *Plus ça change.*

Iain Gordon Brown
Edinburgh
8 May 2020

Acknowledgements

The dedication records a debt I feel wholly unable to repay. My parents set me on a literary and historical path, and to them I owe more than I can say. This book is for them, in memory—and in memory, too, of Italian, Greek and French days long ago.

My wife, Dr Patricia Andrew—herself a scholar of the Grand Tour and of the British in Italy in the eighteenth century—has been customarily generous with the time she has spared from her own research and lecturing activities to listen to my ideas as they evolved. Her immensely helpful, constructive and practical criticism—not to mention her love, care and patience—at every stage has been invaluable, as has her wise and perceptive advice on the shape and balance of the book. She has enabled me to keep going in the traces of the 'diligence' as it has rumbled forward over the rutted roads of the old Grand Tour.

As a result of conversations when I was on the point of taking up my research in a determined way after some initial consideration of the subject, Professor Peter Garside encouraged me to pursue the topic.

In addition to allowing me to reproduce several illustrations from works in his possession, Dr Murray Simpson very kindly read the manuscript and commented in detail on the text at an advanced stage, having previously looked over an early version before much new material was incorporated. I am enormously grateful to him not just for his insight and advice on specific points, but for his general interest in the project and for his great support and friendship throughout.

I am especially indebted to Professor Cedric Reverand and Dr Michael Edson, respectively Editor and Associate Editor of the admirable journal *Eighteenth-Century Life*—to which I have been privileged to be a contributor—for helpful and generous advice on how best I might configure a mass of material when it became clear that it could not easily be comprehended within the confines or structure of their, or indeed any, periodical.

In Alan Sutton I have been fortunate to find a publisher personally interested in the topics I bring together in this book. He has been immensely helpful and supportive, and much more tolerant of a growing manuscript than I had any right to expect.

Dr Michael Heafford and Dr Nicholas Stanley-Price supplied scholarly first-aid at important moments, and Professor Joseph Farrell provided a significant reference in a place I might not have looked for it. Dr Harriet Harvey Wood kindly furnished me with a copy of her recent privately-published book on J. G. Lockhart.

I am most grateful to the Earl and Countess of Rosebery for permission to describe and discuss in detail, for the first time, a document which I identified some years ago in the library at Barnbougle Castle and also for authority to reproduce it here, again for the first time.

The resources of the National Library of Scotland have been, as ever, essential and invaluable. Closure of the Library due to the Covid-19 pandemic has, undeniably, caused problems, and I have been unable to gain access to several manuscripts which, at a late stage in my work, I found that I would have liked to consult.

The exemplary catalogue of Scott's own library at Abbotsford, maintained by the Library of the Faculty of Advocates, has proved extremely useful. Kirsty Archer-Thompson of the Abbotsford Trust kindly provided a photograph of a drawing at Abbotsford when circumstances were difficult.

I have been informed and inspired by much Scott conversation over the years with my colleagues on the Faculty of Advocates Joint Abbotsford Advisory Committee: Professors Ian Campbell, David Hewitt, Alison Lumsden and Gerard Carruthers; Drs Stuart Allan, Lindsay Levy and Ralph McLean; Ian Gow and George Dalgleish. Other Scott scholars whom I should like to acknowledge from times past include the late Dr Donald Sultana, Professor Andrew Hook, Dr J. H. Alexander, Professor Claire Lamont and the late Professor Douglas Gifford, sometime Honorary Librarian of Abbotsford.

As the moment of the Scott 250th anniversary draws near I remember especially, with gratitude and affection, four friends and colleagues who have made major contributions to Scott studies: Patrick Moubray Cadell (d. 2010) and Alan Scott Bell (d. 2018), both formerly of the National Library of Scotland; Professor Jane Millgate (d. 2019) of the University of Toronto; and Sir William Eric Kinloch Anderson, KT, who died as this book was being completed. I like to think that they might all have found in it something to interest and instruct, and perhaps—just occasionally—to amuse.

A Note on Sources

Because the notes and references at the end of this book are full and detailed, the decision had been taken not to provide a bibliography.

Quotations from Walter Scott's letters are taken very largely from the twelve-volume edition by Sir Herbert Grierson, assisted by Davidson Cook and W. M. Parker (London: Constable, 1932-37). Spelling and punctuation—which does not always make for an entirely easy or an initially comprehensible read—have been retained. Scott wrote fast, and frequently with a minimum of punctuation. Where a misspelling or an odd usage really jars, I have drawn attention to the fact by inserting [*sic*]. On occasion the printed texts have been corrected by reference to the original manuscripts. Grierson's edition, though monumental, was not well planned: it is, frankly, inadequate. Many letters, the texts of which were known and which had been transcribed and typed, were omitted on an almost arbitrary basis when they should really have been included in their proper sequence. Furthermore, Grierson's volumes were published without an index. The *Notes and Index* to Grierson's edition, compiled by James C. Corson (Oxford: Clarendon Press, 1979), makes effective use of the Grierson volumes possible for the purposes of research like that which underlies a book such as the present one.

The Millgate Union Catalogue of Walter Scott Correspondence, compiled by Jane Millgate and available through the National Library of Scotland website, now provides records of over 14,000 letters by or to Scott which are known in collections worldwide.

The Walter Scott Digital Archive, maintained by the Centre for Research Collections at Edinburgh University Library is a first-class resource.

Quotations from Scott's great *Journal* are taken from the edition by W. E. K. Anderson (Oxford: Clarendon Press, 1972).

Bibliographical queries, and very many biographical and literary questions besides, will almost certainly be settled by consultation of the magisterial work of William B. Todd and Ann Bowden, *Sir Walter Scott: A Bibliographical History 1796-1832* (Oak Knoll Press: New Castle DE, 1998).

Contents

1

Fairy-Lands and Regions of Reality

By the Spring of 1826, Sir Walter Scott had been toying for a decade with the notion of making a Continental tour which would, very possibly, have had Italy as its goal. His ideas for this venture advanced and receded in his mind, and his enthusiasm varied with his mood and the pressures of a life which had entered a period of profound crisis. In January he had discovered that he was facing utter financial ruin; in May his wife, long unwell, would die. In the cold dawn of realisation of the extent of his ruination and the enormity of the crippling debt he had incurred, he mused to his journal that, as an alternative to drinking grog or taking laudanum, he 'should like methinks to go abroad

"And lay my banes far from the Tweed."'

But this was merely a fleeing thought and a passing conceit. His real determination was to work off the debt; and the same day's journal entry includes the famous statement of resolution that 'My own right hand shall do it.'[1]

At this juncture he received a letter from Charlotte Eaton (*née* Waldie), a travel writer and would-be novelist who had enjoyed some real success in the former field, and who was now seeking to revive an early ambition in the latter by publishing a work which combined both travel-writing and fiction in a somewhat uneasy way. Her new book was to be called *Continental Adventures*.[2] She wrote to Scott anonymously. Her gender, however, was not in doubt; and some clues she supplied might well have given him an inkling of her identity. But whether or not he actually realised this must remain a matter for conjecture. He docketed the letter simply with an endorsement giving its subject but not the writer's name, a fact strongly suggesting either that he genuinely did not know, or that the clues she had supplied were not sufficient to stir his memory or prompt his curiosity.[3] She declared that she had 'enjoyed the delight of his society'. Should Scott have been able to work out who she was, then he would have been aware of a connection: in truth he had been acquainted with her Borders family since childhood, and he knew and admired some of her other writings on themes connected with various aspects of European travel. In that sphere he would correspond with her again in the summer of 1831 before he went, at last, to the Mediterranean.

Charlotte Eaton's correspondence with her publishers records a world of indecision on the writer's part about what the precise title of the work should be.[4] (By coincidence, but in ways too complex and irrelevant to be discussed here, that same publishing house—Hurst, Robinson & Co., of London—was instrumental in the extreme financial discomfiture of Scott himself.) Anyhow, she was now seeking Scott's blessing for her to dedicate her travel-novel to him. Her letter was fulsome, not to say fawning. She herself hoped it would not appear, as she expressed it, 'hyperbolical'; but that is precisely what it was. Her proposed dedication, a draft of which she appended, ran thus:

> To him, whose genius has formed a new era in literature—whose works, which would alone suffer to perpetuate the language in which they are written, have become the Library of the World & will be coeval with the world itself ...

Disingenuously—but also displaying some evident knowledge of the customs and the art of the Continental Europe about which she wrote—she protested to the recipient of her epistle that she bore

> no latent hope, that as the saints in Catholic churches are represented flying up to Heaven & bearing a few lucky sinners clinging to their skirts, so she may contrive, by attaching herself to him [that is, Scott] to soar into the Heaven of popular favor ...

Doubtless embarrassed, annoyed even, by what was proposed, he declined her proffered dedication. Such a tribute, he told the putative author curtly, was 'infinitely beyond my merit'.[5]

Scott's decision to refuse Mrs Eaton's tribute may reflect his pervasive unease when it came to the subject of Continental Adventure. Charlotte Eaton had travelled widely; his first-hand knowledge of Europe was very much more limited than, and inferior to, hers. There is, indeed, a measure of irony in what occurred in April 1826. For here was possibly the most famous writer of the age—and one of most celebrated individuals of the day both in Britain and in Europe—who talked much about travel abroad, but who in fact accomplished comparatively little in that regard. The more we examine the subject of Scott and European travel and the residual tradition of the historic Grand Tour, the more intriguing it seems that he should have been offered such a dedication; and the more appropriate, or expedient, it should have been for him to refuse the accolade.

Disinclination to accept the book's dedication apart, Scott did not know that Charlotte Eaton had shared with her publishers a worry that his own forthcoming novel, *Woodstock*, might appear at the same time as her *Continental Adventures*. Such a coincidence might result in her efforts going unremarked, being outsold in the shops, or out-publicised in the press. As she put it charmingly to her publishers—using a metaphor from the world of travelling in so doing—'His (Sir W.S.'s) thundering Coach & Four wd instantly run down my poor donkey cart.'[6]

But, beyond all this, Scott can little have imagined how Charlotte Eaton's narrative would open. The irony becomes even stronger when we realise that, although her *Continental Adventures* may lack a dedication to Sir Walter, her actual allusions to him—'tribute' would be a word loaded with implications beyond what the context warrants—are rather more subtle and more pervasive. First, in her address to her readers, she justified her anonymity (which she called her 'unambitious domino of—The Author': itself a reference to the Venetian carnival costume known to all Grand Tourists) by citing three of Scott's own literary aliases, and calling them facetiously 'my distinguished friends'.[7] Second, in an audacious move, she appropriated some of Scott's own most famous lines on Scotland and turned them into an epitome of the magic of Italy. A man who was so intimately connected, in the mind of the reading public, with Scottish history and Scottish landscape, thus appears, under the pen of this minor female writer, to become an ambassador for a version of the old 'Grand Tour' experience adapted for the romantic sensibility of the young ladies of England.

Two such fictional representatives of the type, Georgiana and Caroline, are encountered in a country-house drawing room. Idling away an indolent hour, one is sketching; the other looks at a book, 'one of the innumerable new "Travels in Italy"' (this is itself an allusion to the contemporary rash of travel-writing, both factual and imaginative, that catered for the new breed of British visitors let loose upon the Continent in the years immediately following the battle of Waterloo). It is to Italy that Caroline, Eaton's heroine, is anxious to go. In a swoon of Mediterranean rhapsody, a spontaneous verse trips from her lips.

> Breathes there *a girl*, with soul so dead,
> Who never to herself has said,
> *I'd like to see some foreign land* —
> Whose heart has ne'er within her burn'd,
> *As fast the chariot wheels have turnd,*
> To bear her to a distant strand? ...

Her sister, Georgiana, exclaims: 'Why Caroline, how can you, of all people, attempt to parody these beautiful lines that I have heard you repeat a hundred times, with such enthusiasm—spouting after them

> O Caledonia! stern and wild,
> Meet nurse for a poetic child!
> Land of brown heath and shaggy wood,
> Land of the mountain and the flood,
> Land of my sires! ...'

'No', interjects Caroline; and refining her preferred southern destination, she declares that she would now exclaim

> O Italy! serene and mild!
> Meet nurse for a romantic child!
> Land of the classic field and flood!
> Land of the great, the brave, the good!
> Land ...

Breaking off, Caroline adds the qualification: 'Not of my sires—but of my desires.' No contemporary reader, encountering these passages, could have failed to spot the parody, in the first and third verses given above, of celebrated stanzas in the Sixth Canto of Scott's *The Lay of the Last Minstrel* from which a famous quotation appears between.[8]

Charlotte Eaton's novel combines a part-factual travel narrative within a wholly fictional framework. (She was to write in a similar fashion again in 1831, when she revived an incomplete novel—begun in 1814, and abandoned because it appeared, in some ways, too similar to Maria Edgeworth's *Patronage*—and published it as *At Home and Abroad*. A copy of this she was very anxious to send to Scott.) But the story of *Continental Adventures* leads us through France, Switzerland and the Alps, regions that occupy more than a whole volume containing some very good topographical description. Her characters finally arrive in Italy—a travelling dream realised—with volume three. Italy,

> that Queen of the Earth, that favoured daughter of nature, adorned with her choicest gifts, crowned with the spoil of all ages and nations,—to whom the arts, the sciences, and the graces, offered their earliest trophies and their latest fruits;—beneath whose favouring smile sculpture, painting, poetry, and music, in ancient times, reached their full maturity; and having slumbered in their chrysalis state through the winter of the dark ages, again burst forth in the second spring of morn, in renewed and youthful existence.[9]

The other side of the Grand Tour mentality is seen in the reaction to Rome of one of the characters in the novel, Lord Melfort, who has been there and who does not care for it.

For my part, when I have seen the Coloseum and the Pantheon, and looked at a few broken columns and brick walls, which I am content to believe any thing any of the antiquaries choose to call them—for they call them by different names, and none of them know any thing about them,—I begin to tire of Rome, and find out that it gives me the vapours; for the place is so superlatively dull and dismal, that actually the very sunshine looks melancholy.[10]

Here Charlotte Eaton deliberately presents a view of Rome that was very much at variance with her own, for she knew the city intimately. Before her marriage she was the (anonymous) author of a disarmingly frank and opinionated, but nevertheless comprehensive and celebrated, three-volume guide—*Rome in the Nineteenth Century* (1820)—which Walter Scott, who had never been there himself, enjoyed presumably because it presented the delights of the place digestibly and appealingly to the reader. John Gibson Lockhart, Scott's son-in-law and biographer, remembered Scott's pleasure in reading this 'ingenious' work late in life, and therefore perhaps on the eve of his one and only visit to Rome, specifically the book's 'delineations of the high places of Popery.'[11] The author prided herself on having arrived in Rome in a state of blissful ignorance of the city, but equally on the fact that she had since accumulated so much knowledge that she regarded herself superior, not just to the local *ciceroni* and antiquaries who peddled their inaccuracies to the tourists, but to several other British authors of the 'standard' and more overtly scholarly guides. This knowledge she intended to impart to would-be tourists in advance of their visits, so that they would not emulate *her* initial state of ignorance with regard to topography and history.[12] But one suspects that Scott's own view of Rome—either in his imagination, before actually setting foot in the Eternal City, or when he indeed accomplished this most essential step in the *cursus honorum* of the long-established 'Grand Tour' travelling experience—might well have tended to side with Melfort and against Mrs Eaton's young and enraptured enthusiasts.

Scott had recently published his life of Ann Radcliffe, a writer who (like himself) had not been to Italy, but who nevertheless set her most successful romances in the south of Europe.[13] Mrs Radcliffe, wrote Scott, did not intimately understand the language and manners of Italy, but she knew well and instinctively how to 'paint Italian scenery, which she could only have seen in the pictures of Claude or Poussin.' Thus, for example, her pen-portrait of the Bay of Naples constituted 'a splendid and beautiful fancy-picture'. And even if it were true that she 'rather walks in fairy-land than in the region of realities', she was still able to convey 'beautiful descriptions of foreign scenery, composed solely from the materials afforded by travellers, collected and embodied by her own genius...'.[14] This is what Scott himself (as we shall see) was largely content to do, and to do very effectively. 'Travelling' at one remove was his preferred kind of European experience. Moreover, his view of the South was coloured by his own prejudices as much as it was informed by the first-hand knowledge of others. These traits are evident in this passage from his life of Ann Radcliffe.

> She has uniformly selected the South of Europe for her place of action, whose passions, like the weeds of the climate, are supposed to attain portentous growth under the fostering sun; which abounds with ruined monuments of antiquity, as well as the more massive remnants of the Middle Ages; and where feudal tyranny and Catholic superstition still continue to exercise their sway over the slave and bigot, and to indulge to the haughty lord, or more haughty priest, that sort of despotic power, the exercise of which seldom fails to deprave the heart, and disorder the judgment.[15]

It was to be some half dozen years before he was able to see for himself something of this world about which he appeared, in the mid-1820s, to be both so very knowledgeable (at second hand), yet also (at the same time) so relatively unreceptive.

*   *   *   *   *

Walter Scott was never fated to make a conventional Grand Tour, that *voyage de gentilhomme* designed to give a man 'parts'; 'to polish his conversation and manners, deepen his experience of the world, sharpen his judgment of art, habits and character, and, not least, provide him an easy fluency in foreign languages'.[16] Lack of opportunity and absence of inclination combined to deny him this cultural experience in the full sense of the term, or in the traditional style of a custom admittedly well past its prime but still, in some measure, clinging to life in a world that had changed and moved on in respect of the requirements of the new travelling classes. A young man of the middling rank of society into which he was born (the baronetcy, offered in 1818 and finally gazetted in 1820, was a remarkable honour for a man of letters) might not normally have been expected to undertake such a traditional, predominantly upper-class, educational and cultural venture. Besides, unlike some contemporaries and many 'Grand Touring' predecessors, he had a professional career to forge in Edinburgh. He was not an artist who needed to go to Venice, Florence, Rome or Naples as part of his training. Nor was he a classical scholar on whom Joseph Addison's 'classic ground' of Italy exerted its siren call: Scott was not, in fact, classically-minded, so the seeing of Rome was not of critical importance. Childhood ill-health led to his being considered delicate and, although youthful difficulties gave way to a robust early manhood, he subsequently suffered many bouts of crippling illness, and the Grand Tour at its most extreme was not for the feeble or the faint-hearted. In addition, Scott increasingly had to make time for the literary avocations which, from the age of 25, competed with the demands of his professional development as a lawyer. In the 1790s, too, a good deal of nervous energy was spent on finding a wife; and, as French invasion threatened, much time was occupied by near-obsessional involvement in the life and duties of the local volunteer cavalry.

Of course there were literary and educational pundits who did not recommend a man to travel abroad when young—or indeed to travel at all, if he could not benefit from the experience. Vicesimus Knox was the accepted arbiter in such matters for Scott's generation. Only those 'possessed of parts' should ever do so. To journey too early would lead a youth to be 'struck by and captivated with vanity and trifles'. Europe was no place for 'empty coxcombs'. Assuredly, 'He who goes out a fool … will return insufferable.' The corruption of the British state was greatly increased by 'our too frequent intercourse with France and Italy'. Continental travel should be for mature men, 'after they are settled': married, established in their professions, secure in society. Such stalwarts, 'who, during the intervals of business, and those recesses which are allowed', might profitably 'make a voyage to another country', for then they would benefit from their maturity. They should 'go as philosophers', argued Knox; not as the rakes or boobies of the popular literary or visual satire with which Scott will have been familiar. Knox reckoned that between thirty and forty was the ideal age to go abroad. His paragon would 'then search for gold, and find it in abundance; while, at a boyish age, he would have been fully employed and sufficiently fascinated in procuring dross or tinsel, instead of bullion.'[17]

Such was the theory; and wise it was. However, once increasing literary fame and fortune had come to Scott, the French wars had cut off nearly all opportunity for civilian travel to and on the Continent. Jean-Bernard, l'Abbé Le Blanc had observed cynically that the British 'look upon their isle as a sort of prison; and the first use they make of their liberty is to get out of it.'[18] This Scott and most of his friends could not do.

A fantasy that he might go to embattled Portugal and Spain was never really a serious proposition. Two trips to Belgium, northern France and Paris would eventually follow, but these only touched on places where many a traditional Grand Tour had begun; Paris trips alone were not the stuff of real European touring. German lands attracted him, but no specific travel programme there—beyond his journey home in 1832—actually came to fruition. Other travelling schemes came and went in a mind overburdened with literary work, private financial and property-related concerns, and public duties. Despite his thraldom to literary work, he was in fact—as A. N. Wilson has reminded us—never a full-time writer.[19] There were periods when, quite genuinely, and without having always to shelter behind some excuse or other not to make the move, he could not simply abandon his other commitments and dash overseas. Italy—the great goal of the Grand Tourists of past aristocratic cultural tradition—claimed Scott only very late in life, when a voyage in a British warship as the Admiralty's guest offered him the chance he had never before enjoyed of seeing 'the shores of the Mediterranean': that experience without which Samuel Johnson declared a man must always be conscious of an inferiority, 'from his not having seen what it is expected a man should see.'[20] But Scott was now seriously unwell and unable to appreciate to the full the prospects at last opened to him. Circumstances made the actual business of travel, and the absorbing of ideas and impressions, too taxing. Yet notions of Greece, and beyond, tempted him even then. Physical and mental decline, however, supervened, and he could think only of returning, as quickly as possible through central Europe and the Rhineland, to Abbotsford. His fear of dying abroad was obviated, and his wish to breathe his last at home was granted.

*   *   *   *   *

On several occasions Scott called the experience of European travel, rather dismissively, a 'frisk'—once or twice qualifying this somewhat derogatory term as either 'little' or 'sudden', so as to suggest a thing of trifling importance, or else one born of impulse. Indeed, in describing spurs towards, or actual episodes of, travel by such slighting epithets as 'frisks' or 'frolics', Scott may have been concealing a deep unease or embarrassment stemming from the realisation that he should have travelled more than he had done. His last known letter, in fact his last written words, includes a self-deprecating mention of the 'little tour' which was even then drawing to its pathetic close.[21] Defensively, he confessed to himself in his journal in October 1826 that 'One knows nothing of the world if you are absent from it so long as I have been.'[22] Should we therefore consider Scott not as one of the significant European 'Grand Tourists', but merely as a man for whom the Continent was a place of temporary diversion, coming in his interests and affections a long way after his own 'Caledonia, stern and wild'?

A recent comprehensive reference work on the literature of travel fails to mention Scott as a traveller in his own right, though—significantly—Scott does rate mention, in an essay on Scotland, as a promoter of that country as a destination.[23] As indicated above, Scott may have been perhaps the most widely read of contemporary writers in Europe but in fact he knew the Continent but little from personal experience, however much he might be familiar, through his voracious reading, with the histories, topographies and literatures of European states and regions. His factual reading informed the settings of his fictional characters and plots: of *Quentin Durward*, for example (Flanders, Touraine, etc.), of *Anne of Geierstein* (Switzerland, Burgundy, Provence), or of *Count Robert of Paris* (Constantinople). The novelist who wrote of so many adventures travelled widely only in his imagination. Yet his one completed foray into the genre of foreign 'travel book' writing—*Paul's Letters to his Kinsfolk* (published January 1816)—shows how successfully and easily he could master a mass of historical, geographical, political, social and cultural information and present it for a beguiled readership. He once said that, in the matter of learning, Scotland resembled a besieged city where every man has a mouthful but no man a bellyful:[24] so it was with Scott the European traveller, with his very limited horizons. Yet his idea of the residual Grand Tour—accomplished or not according to the traditional rubric, and achieved in some slight measure and in whatever form—remains an interesting conceit, and a subject worth considering as a journey both in actuality and in the realm of the imagination and the might-have-been.

Walter Scott has never been discussed, even in passing, in any survey of what might be termed the traditional or classic Grand Tour. Nor, rather more surprisingly, has he figured in critical accounts or interpretative studies of the rather different kind of Continental travel that supplanted the established Grand Tour, beginning with the rush to the Continent in 1814 and then (after this false start) again in 1815 following the final conclusion of the wars with France.[25] This period, extending to about 1830, might well be designated the Indian Summer of the Grand Tour.[26]

The change in mentality, aesthetics and sentiment which now governed the new kind of travel involved a rejection of what James Buzard, in a perceptive study (though one that omits mention of Scott), has called 'the repetitive ritual of classicism'; the 'process of cultural accreditation through Continental touring was seen to have changed significantly.' The 'Romantic' tourists, post-1815, objected to the 'tired classical associations of the tour' and they 'chafed at imitation and repetition as such … The very sign that someone had preceded them, laying down preferred routes, establishing a hierarchy of attractions to be seen, fostering conventions of response, unsettled new tourists, much of whose behaviour was driven by the need to demonstrate uniqueness.' Tourists after 1815 would now adopt the sentiments and ideals of Romanticism, with its 'heightened sensitivity and exquisite emotions'. They could aspire to 'appropriate some of the pathos and power of Romantic figures' in a process of what Buzard terms the adoption of 'an aristocracy of inner feeling, the projection of an ideology of originality and difference'.[27]

In another influential work, John Urry characterises this change in taste and attitudes as a shift from 'a scholastic emphasis on touring as an opportunity for discourse, to travel as eyewitness observation. There was a visualisation of the travel experience, or the development of the "gaze"…'. Emphasis altered from 'the emotionally neutral recording of galleries, museums and high cultural artefacts, to the nineteenth century "romantic Grand Tour" which saw the emergence of "scenic tourism" and a much more private and passionate experience of beauty and the sublime.'[28] Hartmut Berghoff and Barbara Korte have assessed this new Romantic type of travel as ideally and essentially for the enjoyment of nature and landscape: this 'mechanism of cultural construction' led, for example, to the Alps becoming a desirable destination. Chloe Chard defines the new Romantic tour as 'an adventure of the self'.[29]

Underlying all these comments is the earlier work of John Towner, who recognised and categorised clearly and concisely the two distinct periods of the Grand Tour as a whole: the 'Classical Grand Tour'—when interest in the ancient classical world and its rediscovery was reaching its zenith; and the 'Romantic Grand Tour'—'when romantic and picturesque sensibilities dominated the taste of many tourists and the Grand Tour was enjoying its Indian summer.' The former tour-pattern had included areas of Europe most associated with continued education—Holland, for example, or the Loire valley—whereas the latter tour-pattern is best viewed in terms of 'scenic tourism': travel with a concentration on the mediaeval in architecture and townscape, wild nature, sublime and picturesque mountains, and so on. Towner's concise account of the change that came over the institution of the Grand Tour, with 1800 as a rough dividing line, is worth many more recent and more self-consciously intellectual analyses of the topic.[30]

Michèle Cohen has further suggested that, as 'a means of producing the gentleman', the Tour had outlived its usefulness. A liberal education at home was often thought to be more desirable. The old Tour had led to what she calls 'over-shining': over-display, over-ostentation.[31] Something of these dislikes is evident (as we shall see) in Scott's reaction to Paris.

As a traveller, Scott should have been happy and at ease with the general changes in ethos and sentiment from Classical to Romantic. But in fact he falls between worlds: that of the old Grand Tour proper (as described and analysed by, for example, William Edward Mead, and more recently by Christopher Hibbert, Jeremy Black and Rosemary Sweet) and that of the proto-Victorian upper-middle-class traveller in the new age of more comfortable but less structured tourism, itself increasingly reliant on the steam-ship and later the railway (a travelling realm ably discussed by John Pemble and Robert Holland).[32] Scott's travelling experience—whether marked in actual and accomplished journeys, or in those many jaunts merely wished for—might well have furnished valuable evidence and telling examples in terms of manners, moods and mores for any historian of the old Grand Tour or the rather different age of travel that followed. He inhabited both the 'old' Grand Tour and the 'new': that period in which, as Rosemary Sweet had suggested (though without referencing Scott), the classical vision of Italy was evolving into that of *Italia romantica*, and when travellers began to 'feel and articulate an emotional response to Italy…that displaces the didactic intent of earlier narratives'.[33] While I was writing this present book, the suggestion was made (in a work published late in 2019) that 'more needs to be said about [Scott] as a consumer, as well as a contributor to mass tourism'.[34]

In his study of the way that the Mediterranean played a significant part in the British way of life (and, indeed, the British way of death) in the earlier nineteenth century, John Pemble might have cast his fishing-net over the floundering form of Walter Scott. Sir Walter might, indeed, have formed a starting-point for Pemble's excellent book. Scott's ultimate journey to Italy in quest of health and restoration of bodily and mental vigour was characteristic of a general British tendency to seek the lush, genial, welcoming and smiling 'warm south'. But in chronicling the hazards and difficulties faced in Italian climes, which were not always so beneficent as we may like to suppose, Cecilia Powell has observed shrewdly that 'the pursuit of health had a very high failure rate'.[35] Byron may have lauded Italy lyrically as the 'Garden of the World' in *Childe Harold's Pilgrimage*, Canto IV, stanza xxvi; but, as innumerable monuments to British travellers testify, it was also the grave of many hopes and dreams.

Maybe, for drama, emotional effect and posterity's regard, Scott should really have died in Italy. As Pemble perceptively observes, the lives and works of Byron, Shelley and Keats had enhanced the Mediterranean in the British imagination, and given a special slant to the Victorian vision of Italy and Greece. The Romantic poets had filled the Mediterranean landscape (the actual landscape, that is, but also the metaphysical, metaphoric, imagined 'landscape of the mind') with 'associations of noble purpose and tragic death.' Byron's death in Greece, and those of Shelley and Keats in Italy, 'sanctified these Mediterranean lands and suffused them with elegiac reminiscence…'.[36] Yes: the nobility of Scott's later life, with its unceasing literary toil in the face of adversity, and his famously heroic struggle to clear his vast debts by the exertion of his 'own right hand', might actually have been more greatly enhanced in the national psyche if he had expired of exhaustion in Naples or Rome. His failure to die there, and the fact that he was carried home in a pathetic state to Abbotsford, has actually rendered him somehow less worthy of study as a tragic hero emblematic of the last guttering flame of the Grand Tour. Furthermore, his late dreams of travel in the Aegean seem to have been almost wholly overlooked: they too, might have enhanced what one could perhaps call his emotional credentials as a Romantic traveller in the South. Thus Robert Holland finds no space for Scott, even as a passing reference, in his otherwise comprehensive Chapter 3, 'The Distorted Mirror. The South in British Culture during the Age of Byron 1800-1830'. Instead we have Byron's travels from 1809 onwards, and the conclusion that this 'uncommon turnpike might be taken as the last authentic tour in the grand eighteenth-century manner'. After Byron's actual travels, and his reiteration of them in *Childe Harold's Pilgrimage*, other such travels could only be, as Holland argues, 'mimetic'.[37]

Nor has Walter Scott been considered in recent literature on the aesthetics or the mechanics of travel. Some modern commentators might be uneasy or dissatisfied with Scott's comparatively simple motives for travel, and unsettled by his somewhat insouciant description of his attitudes and feelings. Contemporary academic scholarship might well consider that a study of Scott's European travels affords all too little opportunity for assessment of 'the discourses of travel in terms of a hierarchical opposition between the serious and the frivolous', but instead merely conclude that, in his case, there is scope only to 'assign visual and verbal representations that refer to the imaginative topography of the Grand Tour to a category of trivial frivolity...'.[38] Yet Scott does indeed offer a most interesting case-study of someone's 'imaginative geography' which was 'entered and traversed'.[39] It is for this reason that I have set out to assess all the evidence, and to offer this essay as a further contribution to the broader study of the Grand Tour as the history of that cultural phenomenon drew to its close.

2

Milordi Scozzesi and Home-Keeping Youth

Robert Burns, whom Scott called that 'inimitable genius', provided him with phrases that captured—as he once said—many a sentiment that he wanted to express.[1] Thus in Burns's 'The Twa Dogs. A Tale', Scott, himself a dog-lover of no mean order, might have found a witty epitome of the Grand Tour as it had affected Scottish society. This is a dialogue between the common dog, Luath, and the gentry hound, Caesar. Caesar sports an inscribed brass collar (such as was in reality worn by the Duke of Hamilton's hound in Gavin Hamilton's celebrated Grand Tour portrait of the Duke with his tutor, Dr John Moore) that marks him out as a canine *'gentleman* an' *scholar'*. Caesar's own master has quite possibly made the Grand Tour, as rite of passage of his kind and class; if not his master, then one of his owner's friends or relations:

> … Or maybe, in a frolic daft,
> To HAGUE or CALAIS takes a waft,
> To make a *tour* and take a whirl,
> To learn *bon ton* an' see the worl'.
>
> There, at VIENNA or VERSAILLES,
> He rives his father's auld entails;
> Or by MADRID he takes the rout,
> To thrum *guittarres* an' fecht wi' *nowt*;
> Or down *Italian Vista* startles,
> Wh-re-hunting amang groves o' myrtles:
> Then bowses drumlie *German-water*,
> To make himself look fair an' fatter,
> An' clear the consequential sorrows,
> Love-gifts of Carnival Signioras.
> *For Britain's guid!* For her destruction!
> Wi' dissipation, feud an' faction!

Burns captures here something of the essence of the Grand Tour and does so without himself ever having been abroad, let alone having followed the track of the *milordi scozzesi*. The Tour, with the tradition of which Burns was familiar, was clearly a mixed blessing, and an inheritance of questionable cultural value. Far from conferring an acquaintance with true *bon ton*, it was often merely an excuse for a 'frolic daft'. Scott must have set this shrewd assessment against the romance, the dream and the real opportunity for 'improvement'.

The Jacobite heroes of Scott's imagination—though not exactly 'Grand Tourists' *per se*—would very probably have been all too familiar with France and Italy in their years of exile and attainder. 'Real' Grand Tourists, however, were certainly not unknown to the young Scott. His early and intimate friend William Clerk, for example, came of a family—the Clerks of Penicuik—with a particularly significant tradition of European cultural connection. The line of his Buccleuch 'chief' boasted many European travellers, one of whom had employed Adam Smith as a travelling 'governor'. Sir William Forbes of Pitsligo, father-in-law to be of Scott's first love, Williamina Belsches, made a significant European tour with his wife and daughter in 1792-93, meticulously recorded in a very extensive series of journals.

Scott's Abbotsford neighbours, the Haigs of Bemersyde, spent nearly five years in Italy as a family in the 1820s, a daughter of the house becoming proficient in Italian music. The laird of Bemersyde, James Zerubabel Haig, had earlier been to Paris and Versailles in 1783, and thereafter to Florence, Rome and Naples in 1784-85. Roxburghshire neighbours, the Elliot Murray Kynynmounds, Earls of Minto, were familiar with most of Europe, including its central and eastern realms, whether through private travelling or public duty: Italy they knew well, and Switzerland and the Alps particularly attracted the second Earl.

Other Borders gentry, the Waldies of Hendersyde Park, sent three siblings several times through Europe: Charlotte (Waldie) Eaton's literary legacy of her Grand Touring days has already been discussed; Jane (Waldie) Watts would also write much on Italy; their brother John Waldie really got an incurable travelling bug, and wandered all over the Continent for many years, idly collecting here and there, and extending his expeditions to Greece and Asia Minor. Successive generations of the Halls of Dunglass, on the East Lothian-Berwickshire border, had travelled extensively in Europe and had written copiously about their experiences in other fascinating series of detailed travel diaries and memoirs.

Scott's legal contemporary Henry Cockburn (younger by eight years) waited a long time before he succumbed to the delights of Europe, going, at last, to Venice in 1823. Their mutual friend John Richardson had been urging just such a tour on 'Cocky' at least five years previously, conscious of the Dante-esque *mezzo del cammin* of a man's life. Cockburn, though dilatory in this regard, and over-worked at the Bar, was in fact longing to go abroad, and in 1817 confessed to being 'inflamed' by the desire of doing so: the Swiss Alps were exerting a mental hold, and he implored another busy legal friend thus: 'I should delight to pass a long vacation there. Do let us get green jackets, strong shoes, light hats and long poles, and set forth. I shall put on my very best Arcadian temper...'.[2]

James Skene of Rubislaw, some four years Scott's junior, was a particularly close friend whose wide travels through Europe were in marked contrast with Scott's own stay-at-home existence. Scott—in theory, at least—would like to have gone abroad with Skene as experienced companion, but whether he could or would ever have matched a traveller who was familiar with Germany, France, Italy, Sicily, Malta—and later with Greece—is unlikely. George Ellis, Scott's senior by eighteen years and a dedicatee (like Skene) of one of the cantos of Scott's *Marmion*, was familiar with the life of Versailles, had been involved with diplomacy in the Netherlands, and had made tours of Germany and Italy. His travels had taken him across the Alps. On a mountain route he once encountered the Scottish antiquary, General Robert Melville, who was tracing Hannibal's route: becoming so involved with his theories, and concerned at the impracticality of taking elephants over the passes, Melville seemed to imagine that he actually had the beasts with him.[3] Scott's friend William Stewart Rose spent some four years in Italy. He described his crossing of the Alps and his travels through the north of Italy to Venice—on which city, and its hinterland, he had a great deal to say, and to it say well in a series of delightful 'literary' letters written (as he quaintly put it) 'as I should speak, were it unfortunately the fashion to speak octavos.'[4]

John Bacon Sawrey Morritt of Rokeby, Scott's exact contemporary whom he met in 1808 and who became a great friend and correspondent, had by the time of their first acquaintance accomplished an early, extensive and exotic Grand Touring experience of the sort of which Scott could only dream. These travels had taken Morritt to parts of Central Europe, the Balkans and Asia Minor in addition (of course) to Italy. Morritt became a pillar of the Society of Dilettanti, and a founding member of the Travellers Club. When first they met, Scott could boast merely of having been to London, Bath, the Isle of Wight, Windsor, Oxford and a handful of other places mostly in the north of England, and must have felt decidedly homespun with a travelling account otherwise confined to limited parts of Scotland, and not even to the more romantic isles at that.

※   ※   ※   ※   ※

In domestic tourism, however circumscribed, Scott took great delight. The French Revolutionary and Napoleonic Wars restricted all but a handful of British subjects to their own country for the duration of a conflict, lasting from 1792 to 1815 (with intervals of interrupted peace) that shut off the Continent, and which made travel by sea through the Mediterranean even more hazardous than ever it was in face of Barbary corsairs, privateers and the elements themselves. Confined largely to Scotland, a 'Grand Tour' for Walter Scott meant a Highland tour. It was as a youth, delegated by his lawyer father to conduct some business with a Jacobite client in his remote fastness, that Scott had first encountered the wild scenery of Highland Perthshire, where was to be found 'Beauty lying in the lap of Terror'. Reining in his pony above Perth, he had gazed upon the Highland mountains

> as if I had been afraid [the scene] would shift like those in a theatre before I could distinctly observe its different parts, or convince myself that what I saw was real ... the recollection of that inimitable landscape has possessed the strongest influence over my mind ...[5]

Such early experiences of travel were ones he would describe as seeming to be 'in *high relief* engraved on my memory' in all their 'freshness and vivacity', even when more exotic scenes were at last opened to him in Europe.[6] But the fact was that by 1810 even the Highland Tour, along by then well-trodden routes, seemed somewhat passé, as Scott himself remarked:

> ... the harvest of glory has been entirely reaped by the early discoverers; and in an age when every London citizen makes Loch Lomond his washpot, and throws his shoe over Ben-nevis, a man may endure every hardship, and expose himself to every danger of the Highland seas, from sea-sickness to the jaws of the great sea-snake, without gaining a single leaf of laurel for his pains.[7]

Tourists had been visiting Scotland, notably the central and western Highlands, in increasing numbers since the suppression of the final Jacobite rising in 1746. Many were the English travellers who recorded their experiences and opinions. They came with an almost anthropological curiosity after the inhabitants of the country, or in pursuit of its natural curiosities and its historical sites; they came increasingly on account of literary associations, notably those of the Ossianic poems; and they came in the wake of the revolution in taste that endowed the landscape with the appeal of the Sublime and the Picturesque. As Christopher Smout put it: 'the age had arrived of the connoisseur tourists going on the Grand Tour of Nature's picture galleries and the ruins of historical association.'[8] And yet, in some ways, the greatest days of the Highland Tour were still to come; and for them Scott himself was in large measure responsible.[9] Although it is true to say that the tree-hung Trossachs and lovely Loch Katrine were already on an established visitor route by 1810, when he published his hugely successful *The Lady of the Lake*, Scott's verse made the region a major tourist destination; the landscape of the poem became as fashionable a place of resort as the Wye Valley or the English Lakes. When a perceptive Polish visitor credited Scott's genius with having 'taken these places out of oblivion, deserted and unknown beforehand', he was exaggerating somewhat, and certainly contradicting historical fact. But he was perfectly correct when he went on to write of these same locations—improved and 'sanctified', one might almost say, by Scott's descriptive power—as now 'swarming with people who come from many distant parts, anxious to see their beauty.'[10] Even in 1810 a local doctor wrote of the 'mania' for the Trossachs he observed as he witnessed the influx of coaches and their eager occupants.[11] Indeed, the process of getting to the territory of Roderick Dhu, the fair Ellen and Malcolm Graeme was more taxing than that of reaching some other 'picturesque' destinations; and such travels to the land of the 'Harp of the North' perhaps made those denied the adventure of Continental touring feel somewhat less bereft of the excitement of the experience than they might otherwise have done. It was said that *The Lady of the Lake* and later *The Lord of the Isles* furnished the best guidebooks to the Highlands. Tourists 'did not go to commune with nature, but to commune with the spirit of Scott communing with nature and with romantic history.'[12] Walter Scott 'effectively wrote the script for the promotion of Scottish tourism through the nineteenth and twentieth centuries.'[13] Scotland became 'Scott-land': it was an American who called it so, in 1844.[14]

Eight years after Scott's death, William Howitt acknowledged his contribution to the promotion of domestic tourism. Howitt did not actually advance the case for home travel as either an alternative to Continental tourism or as something superior; but the implication of its comparative worthiness is implicit in what he wrote, specifically with reference to Scott's verse:

> ... no poetry so thoroughly imbued with that species of beauty which every summer leads so many thousands to the Scottish highlands, as that of the man whose very name seems to designate him, *par excellence*, THE SCOTT.

And Howitt continued:

> See what he has done for Scotland. See every summer, and all summer long, what thousands pour into that beautiful country, exploring every valley, climbing every mountain, sailing on every firth and loch, and spreading themselves and their money all through the land. And what roads and steam-vessels, what cars

[light carriages] and coaches, are prepared for them! what inns are erected! …
so rapidly does the spirit of the poetical and picturesque spread—so wonderfully
do the numbers of its votaries increase, seeking a little easement of their swollen
purses, a little outlet for their taste and enthusiasm.[15]

There remained a great deal of Scotland for Scott himself to discover. He
explored some of the Hebrides in 1810, pontificating thereafter of that 'taste
for the beauties of nature which as it is one the most attainable is also one
of the most certain sources of enjoyment which life offers us.' Acquisition
of that taste was a direct and consequential benefit of travel: 'The grandeur
of the scenes which the islands afford is a little qualified by the sombre and
strange state in which it is expressed.' In contrast to the well-wooded and
generally kinder aspect of the west coast of the mainland, the Hebrides were
characterised by lack of trees, barren hills and wild torrents 'where the waters
bear no more proportion to the excavations and ravines which they tear out
of the bosom of the hills than human passions do to the consequences of
their indulgence.' It seems appropriate that this somewhat melodramatic and
theatrical assessment of the prospect before the traveller, and the metaphysical
musings prompted by Scott's personal discovery of the landscape, should be
shared here with an actress whom he admired.[16]

Even before he had fully discovered the Highlands, Scott was advocating
the beauties, historic sites and literary associations of his beloved Borders
as the stuff of travelling heaven, and was doing so unashamedly to friends
and acquaintances who themselves had seen further shores. An example of
the kind of experienced foreign traveller whom Scott hoped to convert into a
domestic one was Patrick Murray of Simprim. In September 1793 Scott wrote
to this Perthshire laird (despite owning land in Berwickshire he actually lived
near Meigle) in the hope of enticing him to Kelso, and in doing so deployed
a number of allusions to travel as a Grand Tourist might have recognised it.

I would have let fly an epistle at you long ere this, had I not known I should have
some difficulty in hitting so active a traveller, who may in that respect be likened
unto a bird of passage. Were you to follow the simile throughout, I might soon
expect to see you winging your way to the southern climes, instead of remaining
to wait the approach of winter in the colder regions of the north. Seriously, I
have been in weekly hopes of hearing of your arrival in the Merse, and have been
qualifying myself by constant excursions to be your Border *Cicerone*.
   … I have got by heart … a reasonable number of Border ballads … which
I intend to throw in at intervals, just by way of securing my share in the
conversation. As for *you*, as I know your picturesque turn, I can be in this
country at no loss how to cater for your entertainment, especially if you can
think of moving before the fall of the leaf. I believe, with respect to the real

To Kalon ['the beautiful', 'the right'or 'the noble' in Greek, but transliterated by
Scott in English characters], few villages can surpass that near which I am now
writing; and as to your rivers, it is part of my creed that the Tweed and the Teviot
yield to none in the world, nor do I fear that even in your eyes, which have been
feasted on classic ground, they will greatly sink in comparison with the Tiber or
Po.Then for antiquities, it is true we have got no temples or heathenish fanes to
show; but if substantial old castles and ruined abbeys will serve in their stead,
they are to be found in abundance...[17]

*   *   *   *   *

Temporary cessation of hostilities with France made travel in Scotland and
domestic Scottish scenery rather less attractive, as Scott expressed the matter,
to 'our Suthron freinds [*sic*] than they were before the avenues were opend
to Paris ...'.[18] At the peace of 1801 and with the Treaty of Amiens of 1802,
which endured for less than a year, hordes of eager British would-be tourists
flooded across the Channel, 'to feed at the banquet and appease' (as John
Pemble has recently put it) 'with one gargantuan gorge, appetites starved by
ten years' enforced abstention from the Grand Tour.'[19] Writing rather nearer
to the actual time, and seeking a simile for the extraordinary rush of British
tourists across the Channel, Mary Shelley hit on the somewhat tasteless one
of Norwegian rats which hurled themselves into any streams encountered so
that others in their pack might eventually cross over their drowned bodies.
This 'substratum', as she put it, allowed travellers who came later to enjoy
better times and improved travelling conditions.[20]

James Skene seized the chance at that time to visit Germany, Switzerland,
Italy, Sicily and Malta and returned safely through France before the door to
the Continent slammed shut once again. Less fortunate by far had been Joseph
Forsyth, who was to become a household name among British travellers as
author of the celebrated *Remarks on Antiquities, Arts, and Letters During
an Excursion in Italy in the Years 1802 and 1803*, a work which Walter Scott
owned in its second edition of 1816. So eager had the 38-year-old Forsyth been
to go abroad that, on hearing of the preliminary discussions for peace—just
discussions about a truce, not the concrete fact of a peace treaty itself—he
needed only five days to pack his bags and make ready to leave Elgin, and then
he was off like a shot to Paris and thence to Italy. His actual sojourn in Italy went
perfectly well; but he was apprehended by the French in Turin on his return
journey, and was obliged to spend the next eleven years as a prisoner, first in the
remote fastness of the Vosges, then at Verdun, and finally in Paris. He was able
to write his book in gradually improving conditions of close confinement, and
his manuscript was somehow conveyed from Paris to London where it was first
published in 1813. Released and repatriated in 1814, he died the next year.[21]

But Scott himself did not go to the Continent in 1801-02, not even as far as Paris. He clung still to Scotland and betrayed no great wish to see further. There were excuses a-plenty, both at the time and retrospectively, for this: his family, his legal career, his literary work; then, rather later still, the need to deal with matters connected with the development of his new house of Abbotsford, and the increasing estate (or 'policies', in Scottish terminology) he came to own there. But one feels that, if he had really wanted to go, he would have found time, money and opportunity to do so, even if his jaunt had been but a speedy one. Scotland, however, remained firmly his focus. Almost a decade later he admitted to Lord Byron that the ruins of Melrose abbey, not far from Abbotsford, would probably afford little interest 'to tempt one who has seen those of Athens'. One senses that Scott, in writing thus, was confessing to a certain feeling of incompleteness—then, and indeed most probably when he looked back to a missed opportunity at the time of the Peace of Amiens—at not having seen some at least of the lands that Byron had seen: 'I would rather cross-question your Lordship about the outside of Parnassus, than learn the nature of the contents of all the other mountains in the world.'[22]

After Scott's death, William Stewart Rose would write to John Gibson Lockhart of how 'picturesque wonders almost exclusively [had] engaged his [Scott's] attention', reminiscing of how the 'desire of seeing remarkable places & particularly such as awakened existing recollections' had been Scott's motivation in travelling. During these expeditions a 'spirit of feudal generosity' in tipping guides, custodians and the like had been evident.[23] These remarks alluded to domestic travel alone, and paid no heed to any possible wish on Scott's part to travel more widely. English scenery could be (as Scott himself put it) 'renderd classical' on account of its historical associations: domestic though his 'voyages & discoveries' might seem (and, of course, be) they were significant, nonetheless, because 'the scene is new to me'.[24] As was the case with many an English tourist before him—men of slender means and with professional ties, such as the antiquary William Stukeley—Britain, perforce, took the place of Italy in the traveller's imagination, and an inland English journey became, by literal definition, 'this our Mediterranean tour'.[25] Here 'Mediterranean', for Stukeley, meant not just the 'inner', 'inland' or 'midland' sea to the south of Europe, which those who could make the Grand Tour held in their imagination, but the inner England of Wiltshire, Warwickshire, Oxfordshire, Buckinghamshire, Northamptonshire and so on, where he and his friends in the Society of Roman Knights pursued the traces of an ancient past of Britain on the downland and among the hedgerows.

Walter Scott, similarly, might have viewed the Scottish Borders, or the Stirlingshire or Perthshire Highlands, as 'mediterranean' territory, substituting for more exotic Mediterranean lands. Even after he had been abroad, Scott never lost the sense of magic that Scotland and its scenery held for him: as

Lockhart recorded, the voyage down the Firth of Clyde 'is enough to make anybody happy: nowhere can the home tourist, at all events, behold, in the course of one day, such a succession and variety of beautiful, romantic and majestic scenery ...'[26]

Due to Scott's personal influence, and thanks to his writings, contemporaries came to view the landscapes of his verse (and later prose) as 'classical'. In *Peter's Letters to his Kinsfolk* (1819), J. G. Lockhart has the fictional Welsh visitor, Dr Peter Morris, report that Scott had told him he was 'treading on classical ground'; in other words, the landscape of the lore Scott had himself embodied in his *Minstrelsy of the Scottish Border*.

> The name of every hill and every valley all around is poetical, and I felt, as I heard them pointed out one by one, as if so many old friends had been introduced to my acquaintance after a long absence, in which I had thought of them all a thousand times.[27]

A country once (and always) 'romantic' was also 'now classical'.[28]

Scott hoped, by the force of his personality, the strength of his enthusiasm and the power of his writing, to make even real classicists see his domestic landscapes as classic ground. John Morritt and his wife came to stay at Scott's then home at Ashestiel, near Selkirk, in 1808. Scott reported triumphantly how

> some English visitors ... engaged me in my hobbyhorsical office of exhibiting the ruins of Melrose Abbey and some of the other wonders of our wilds, seasoned with many a tale of feuds and of legendary wonder.

He was unabashed by the parochiality, domesticity and tameness of what he had to show even a member of the Society of Dilettanti. Morritt might be 'deep in Grecian lore ... which led him some years ago to visit the very ground where Troy-town stood ...'. No matter: 'I shewed them all the remarkables in our neighbourhood & told them a story for every *cairn*.' It was as well for Scott that the erudition of the gentleman concerned, who had 'wanderd all over Greece and visited the Troad', should not have been 'of an overbearing kind: this was (as he admitted) 'lucky for me who am but a slender classical scholar.' [29]

In the south Midlands of England between London and Oxford—'tame and domestic', as Byron would have considered the landscape—and when Scott reckoned himself too old 'to rough it and scrub it' for economy's sake, time spent in travelling and domestic sightseeing allowed him to gain 'in health, in spirits, in a new stock of ideas, new combinations and new views'. Travel was good for 'scouring up one's mind a little'. Nevertheless, the joys of travel might pall: 'the eye becomes satiated with sights as the full soul loathes the honeycomb.' At one time his mind would have 'loved to dwell on all I had seen that was rich and rare ... or placing perhaps in order the various additions with which I had supplied my stock of information...'.[30]

The year 1808 saw the first stirrings of a wish to see the world beyond British shores, albeit in a way totally unconnected with the Grand Tour and its cultural and social aims. India—in the form of the potential riches and material success, coupled with social progress, that East India Company service (preferably at a high level) offered—tempted Scott, in theory. But the East remained a dream to which he paid lip-service, while encouraging kith and kin to make their fortunes there.[31]

In 1808, also, Scott had published *Marmion*. The fourth canto of the poem carries an affectionate introductory address to James Skene. In this, the difference between Skene's life of adventure abroad, and Scott's own world within the confines of Britain, is made abundantly clear, and with it a detectable pang of regret, moderated only by the thought that the two had at least served together in the yeomanry in the hour of their country's peril.

> Though thou o'er realms and seas hast ranged,
> Mark'd cities lost, and empires changed,
> While here, at home, my narrower ken
> Somewhat of manners saw, and men ...

Scott, Quartermaster of the Royal Edinburgh Volunteer Light Dragoons, was chafing at the bit. India would not do. He would emulate Skene: Europe would be the real scene for foreign adventure.

3

Ideas of Iberia

Scott's eye fell first upon the Iberian Peninsula. France had been at war with Portugal since 1807, and now in 1808 was also ranged against Spain, its erstwhile ally. Great Britain was in alliance with both countries, and what became known as the Peninsular War was in the initial stages of an extended campaign that would be long, brutal and bloody.

It is ironic that Scott's first projected European destination was one beyond and outwith the traditional 'Grand Tour' circuit. One might say that there was a 'standard', or 'core' Grand Tour, and many permutations of—and variables governing—this basic framework. Italy was, and had always been, the heartland of the Tour, with Rome the great and essential goal. Venice and Florence were regularly included, of course, but also sometimes cities like Turin or the towns of the Po valley: Bologna, Mantua, Ferrara. Naples was naturally a highlight, and was widely regarded as the southern turning-point in the regular itinerary. Some hardy travellers went on to Sicily, a handful to Dalmatia. A small minority extended their expedition to Greece; fewer still to Asia Minor and the Levant. The roads to Rome were generally via the Low Countries, Germany, Austria and so on towards the Venetian *terra ferma* and its historic cities: Verona, with its Shakespearean associations; Vicenza with its architectural connections to Palladio, whose delightful villas along the Brenta river and canal were so much admired and envied by the British, for whom Palladio assumed the status of a near divinity; Padua with its ancient university, so influential in medical teaching; and thus to Venice, *La Serenissima* herself. Alternatively, the traveller might make first for Paris, then take boat down the Rhône to Provence, thence along the coast road to Genoa and Livorno and so into Tuscany. A coasting sea voyage from the south of France might also take the traveller to these same regions of Italy. Or, from Lyon, one might go eastwards through Savoy and so over the Alps via the Mont Cenis pass to Piedmont and Lombardy. There were many routes, but all ultimately focused on the same essential destination: Rome.[1]

But Spain and Portugal were, together or separately, if not exactly beyond the pale then certainly very much less common as a destination for travellers. 'One who ventured to travel in Spain was rather an explorer than an ordinary tourist', wrote W. E. Mead, summing up the relationship of Iberia to the regular Grand Tour, and adding for good measure the ironic understatement that 'the tour in Spain was at best a very modified form of pleasure.'[2] The British, as one modern scholar has written, albeit with perhaps a measure of exaggeration, 'did not go anywhere near Spain if they could avoid it. The country was regarded as primitive and dangerous.' There was little or no 'tourist traffic'.[3] Prejudice against the country and its people was matched by profound ignorance of both. These facts make it all the more surprising that Burns should have chosen to include Madrid in his catalogue of 'Grand Tour' destinations in 'The Twa Dogs'; but maybe it was just that the city's name fitted his rhyme-scheme better than 'Venice', 'Florence', 'Rome' or 'Naples'—and that the place sounded exotic and 'foreign'. Scott himself, writing ten years after the notion of going there had first occurred to him, described Spain as 'lying also beyond the ordinary course of travellers and tourists', and admitted that it has 'little familiar to us as readers of history or as members of British society.'[4] Only when the Grand Tour proper—as a cultural and social institution with prescribed routes and required sites, sights and experiences, the whole being governed by an accepted code of aristocratic or elite behaviour—was well-nigh extinct, and as a new type of travel had become popular after 1814/15 and increasingly so as the nineteenth century progressed, did Iberia really become a 'niche market' for the British. As late as 1828 the painter David Wilkie could refer to southern Spain, with its cultural riches, as the 'wild, unpoached game-preserve of Europe'.[5]

'No country is less known to the rest of Europe', Samuel Johnson had declared of Spain to his friend Giuseppe Marc' Antonio Baretti.[6] Since neither Spain nor, for that matter, Greece, had been 'included in the Grand Tour'— so John Pemble reminds us—'they remained unsanctioned by habit and convention ...'.[7] Robert Southey had attracted literary attention by his time spent in Portugal and Spain in 1795-96 and again in 1799. In the intervals between his sojourns in Lisbon and Madrid he had published his *Letters Written During a Short Residence in Spain and Portugal* (1797), which Scott acquired in its third edition of 1808—a significant moment for him to have bought this book. Southey would gain increased celebrity in an Iberian context when he wrote his major history of the Peninsular War between 1823 and 1832. Scott also added to his library the less well known and less regarded works by Robert Semple: *Observations ... through Spain and Italy to Naples* (two volumes, 1807), and Semple's *Second Journey in Spain*, published in 1809.

Wherever he might go, the potential for book-writing was key to Scott's inclination. He will have seen the literary possibilities and realized how he might, perhaps, put something of the essence of Iberia on drawing-room sofas or library-tables at home at a time when the Peninsula was prominent in the public mind. This was a popular interest into which he might tap. Henry Fielding's *Journal of a Voyage to Lisbon* (1755) was a favourite of Scott's. Doubtless Fielding's justification for making a book out of an Iberian voyage will have struck a sympathetic note. 'The vanity of knowing more than other men', Fielding had confessed, is

> perhaps, besides hunger, the only inducement to writing, at least to publishing, at all. Why then should not the voyage-writer be inflamed with the glory of having seen what no other man ever did or will see but himself? This is the true sense of the wonderful in the discourse and writings, and sometimes, I believe, in the actions of men.[8]

* * * * *

Scott claimed that he had wanted to go to Spain with John Hookham Frere, the Foreign Office under-secretary and diplomat. Frere, who had already served in both Portugal and Spain between 1800 and 1804, was once again dispatched to Spain in 1808 as British Minister Plenipotentiary to the Central Junta at Aranjuez. Scott asserted that he would 'never pardon [himself] missing the opportunity'.[9] His possible role in Frere's suite went unexplained; but he was a little clearer about his more general motives when he wrote to Lady Abercorn in October 1808:

> ... I should greatly like to spend this winter in Spain. I am positive that in a nation so strangely agitated I might observe something both of the operation of human passions under the strongest possible impulse and of the external pomp and circumstance attending military events which could be turned to account in poetry.[10]

As if to assure himself, just as much as his noble correspondent, he went on to tell her that 'I learn languages easily & can without inconvenience suffer a little hardship as to food & lodging.'[11] The poet of *Marmion*, and the amateur soldier of the volunteer cavalry who drilled and charged on the sands of Portobello or Musselburgh and sabred turnips on sticks, would now see *real* war. He would also stock his mind with vivid images for future writing. He would visit the Peninsula not so much as a 'tourist' in the long-established way—even if his destination was out of the traditional 'Grand Tour' circuit—but almost as a war-reporter or war-correspondent, albeit that his 'reporting' was likely to take poetical form.

Almost in the same breath in which he confessed his Iberian ideas to Lady Abercrorn, he also betrayed that element of uncertainty and pusillanimity which early tinged his travelling thoughts and which came, indeed, to characterise his entire career as a would-be European tourist. Referring back to what he had just told her of his proposed winter in Spain, in proximity to whatever military action he might chance upon, he continued in a dispiriting tone: 'All this is of course an airy vision yet I cannot banish the wish from my mind though without any hope of gratifying it.' Right at the start, Scott appears to have damned his own plans as 'mere romance' and not allowed his dreams to assume reality.[12] Furthermore, one travelling notion was conceived rapidly after another, almost as if he was setting up skittles of good intent only so that he could knock them down with his ball of procrastination and excuse. In fact, precisely at the time he was telling friends of his proposed journey to Portugal and Spain, he was also juggling the prospect of a visit to Ireland. That, too, was an idea long postponed, but it was one finally achieved in 1825. The Irish jaunt is, in fact, by no means irrelevant in any consideration of Scott's wider, Continental travelling experience; it will be discussed in Chapter 6.

*   *   *   *   *

One of the distinguishing characteristics of traditional 'Grand Tour' travel was that it took men (and it was very largely men) who were thoroughly educated in Greek and Roman literature, philosophy, mythology and history, to the actual, physical scenes of a world with which they were familiar through the printed page and the school or college classroom. In the Iberian context, it struck Scott as strange that a land he knew so well in literature (in picaresque romance, for example *Don Quixote* and *Gil Blas*) should now be the scene of what he termed 'real and important events', namely the war in the Peninsula.[13] Miguel de Cervantes was an author revered by Scott to the end of his life: it is recorded by a friend that, in Rome in 1832, Scott expressed 'unbounded admiration' for Cervantes, and that he asserted it was the *novelas* of Cervantes that had first inspired him 'with the ambition of excelling in fiction'.[14] Scott accumulated seven editions of *Don Quixote* in Spanish and English, two modern English stage versions of the book, and at least five separate editions and collections of the *novelas*. Of Alain-René Le Sage, author of *Gil Blas de Santillane*, Scott himself wrote in the highest praise. The biographical sketch of Le Sage included by Scott in the fourth volume of *Ballantyne's Novelist's Library* (Edinburgh 1822) displays both admiration of and affection for the Frenchman's 'enchanting pen' and his almost uncanny understanding of a language and county not in fact his own. Cervantes and Le Sage has convinced Scott that Spain was a destination to be dreamed of. In writing of what had captivated Le Sage, Scott could well have been writing of himself:

The high romantic character of chivalry ... the vicinity of the Moors, who had imported with them the wild, imaginative, and splendid fictions of Araby the blessed—the fierceness of the Spanish passions of love and vengeance, their thirst of honour, their unsparing cruelty, placed all the material of romance under the very eye of the author who wished to use them... a country in which Castilians and Arragonese, Spaniards and Moors, Mussulmans and Christians, had been at war for so many ages, could furnish historians with real events, which might countenance the boldest flights of the romance.

Scott came to love the idea of Spain through the literature he read, and Le Sage was his guide. What he liked was the way his hero considered 'the human figures which he paints as his principal object', but 'fails not to relieve them by exquisite morsels of landscape...'.[15] It was through Cervantes and Le Sage that Scott had become familiar with Spanish customs, language, manners and habits. Now, those 'real events' of the first decade of the nineteenth century might, he felt, be his entrée to that world of mystery and magic.

Four years before he published his memoir of Le Sage, Scott had written, in another context, of how, for him at least, poetry and fiction 'as well as *reality* [my italics] can impress local associations of the most fascinating kind'. The implication was that this applied to other people of sensibility too. It was the discovery, during the Peninsular War, of a Spain previously only *imagined* that he was actually thinking of. But what Scott also said about the way he tended to have 'impressed associations upon so much scenery' has a wider application to his entire travelling aesthetic. He continued: '... but the authors of fiction had given associations to this country of the most interesting kind, to supply the deficiencies of the slender list afforded by history or conversation.' To paraphrase his other remarks in the article in question, Scott was essentially suggesting that the British had marched and fought through a landscape of literature.[16] In reading this, one can see how he would like to have been there alongside the army, almost as some sort of intelligence officer, interpreting the campaign by reference to the landscape of literary association.

Nevertheless, in 1808, thoughts of 'dipping my desperate pen in Castalian streams' had been put on hold 'for this long and many a day'.[17] A shame: for otherwise the 'soldier's lover' (as he once facetiously described himself)[18] might actually have come to know something of real, battle-front 'fear' in taking

a peep at Lord Wellington and his merry men ... but I found the idea gave Mrs Scott more distress than I am entitled to do for the mere gratification of my own curiosity ... Not that there could have been any great danger ... and I think I should have been overpaid for a little hardship and risk by the novelty of the scene ... I should have picked up some curious materials for battle scenery.[19]

Meanwhile, with his map and pins, Scott displayed an almost obsessional desire to follow the course of the campaign, and would customarily pore over the map even in his carriage between Edinburgh and Ashestiel.[20] His devotion to the cartography of the war echoes the emotional involvement of the mother, sister or wife imagined so effectively by Anna Laetitia Barbauld in her poem *Eighteen Hundred and Eleven* (1812): a woman who similarly 'the spread map with anxious eye explores' (line 35) so as to follow the movements—and, sadly, often the fate—of a son, brother or husband killed beside 'some stream obscure, some uncouth name', which 'By deeds of blood is lifted into fame' (lines 31-2).

Scott would have gone to the Peninsula in search of the 'picturesque' in war, which under his keen and observant eye—so vital in a traveller—would have been translated into narrative verse or perhaps, better, into excellent prose reportage. Boastfully, he told Miss Sarah Smith that he would have gathered 'poetic images… at the cannon mouth'.[21] More realistically, he confided to Lady Abercorn that, having described so many battles, he would, 'for a moderate degree of risk' like to see one in actuality; but admitted that the notion was 'rather a vision than a scheme.'[22] The actual *vision* that came out of Scott's unrealised Peninsular scheme was *The Vision of Don Roderick*, a narrative poem sold for the benefit of the 'suffering Portuguese', and a by-blow of 'the most picturesque region of old romance', the image of which Scott contrived entirely at second hand. But first he wanted to write of the war in prose, and did so in the form of an essay entitled 'Cursory Remarks upon the French Order of Battle, Particularly in the Campaigns of Buonaparte', which was published in Scott's own periodical venture, the unsuccessful *Edinburgh Annual Register*.[23] (The *Register* was always late, its nominal year of reference being out of synchronisation with its actual year of publication. In the end the essay in fact appeared a month after the poem had been published.)[24] This article displays some impressive military knowledge. The author alluded to it in a letter to John Morritt. 'I have been writing a sketch of Buonaparte's tactics for the Edinr. Register and some other trumpery of the same kind.' He went on to share with Morritt his other, more extensive plans for literary exploitation of the war.

> Particularly I meditate some wild stanzas referring to the Peninsula: if I can lick them into my shape I hope to get something handsome from the Booksellers for the Portugueze sufferers … My lyric[s] are calld the Vision of Don Roderic … Pray do not mention this for some one will snatch up the subject as I have been served before; and I have not written a line yet. I am going to Ashestiel for eight days to fish and rhyme.[25]

The Vision of Don Roderick—'Drum and Trumpet performance' though Scott considered it, rather dismissively[26]—did in fact help to bring Britain and

Spain closer together in the literary imagination. There were clear parallels between the resistance of the Gothic king Roderic (or Rodrigo) to Islamic conquest, and that of the Spanish *guerrillas* or 'freedom fighters' to the forces of Napoleonic France. The poem took its place along with a substantial body of other contemporary verse that emerged from the war, or which was inspired directly or indirectly by instances of Spanish valour and patriotism, and which opened up Iberia to British consciousness. In a reverse direction, Scott's narrative verse with a Scottish theme went (so to speak) to Portugal to do its bit for the war-effort: his old friend Adam Ferguson, an officer of the 58th Foot in Wellington's army, read Canto VI of *The Lady of the Lake* (1810) to his men when under French artillery fire in the Lines of Torres Vedras.[27] So Scott served and soldiered, as it were and in his way, vicariously in the Peninsula: 'my heart is a soldier's and always has been though my lameness rendered me unfit for the profession which old as I am I would rather follow than any other. But these are waking dreams in which I seldom indulge …'.[28] Looking, in 1844, at the formidable batteries and ramparts of the rock-fortress of Gibraltar, the whole a vast killing-machine in waiting, William Makepeace Thackeray—well named in this context—mused that 'It is best to read about wars comfortably in … Scott's novels, in which knights shout their war cries … without depriving you of any blessed rest.'[29]

More than any other writer, however, it was Byron who lodged Portugal and Spain in the collective mind of northern Europeans. Along with the equally exotic and 'foreign' Greece, Spain became 'salient in the geography of the Romantic imagination after the publication of the first two cantos of *Childe Harold's Pilgrimage* in 1812 …'.[30] But Byron did not go to Iberia until 1809, when he then rode across the Peninsula to Cadiz. Scott might, therefore, have beaten Byron to it by a year. Any narrative poetry of Scott's that might have resulted from direct personal encounter with Portugal and Spain could also have pipped *Childe Harold* at the post, and stolen (or at least muted) his thunder. However, Scott's intitial scheme of 1808 was shelved and, despite the repeatedly expressed desire for an expedition thence, Scott's acquaintance with Iberia was pursued remotely. One thinks of Scott's rather weak and fatuous later explanation for his abandonment of narrative verse in favour of prose fiction, when he laconically maintained that the change was because Byron had 'bet' [that is 'beaten'] him in the poetic genre.[31] Whole generations would come to see Spain, as they would Greece, through Byron's stanzas, not Scott's. Whereas Scott merely dreamed of travelling hither and thither, Byron actually went. The one wrote from secondary sources, and through the manipulation of the knowledge of others; the other from personal experience. Scott's *The Vision of Don Roderick* may have appeared first, but it was no match for Byron's passionate evocation of 'lovely Spain! renown'd, romantic land!'[32] Scott's failure to visit Portugal and Spain set a pattern for his future intercourse with Europe as a whole. He preferred the vicarious to the first-hand experience.

These tendencies to dreaming, to procrastination, and to willing dependence on a second-hand distillation rather than a direct acquaintanceship, were noted by his contemporaries and by his critics, and by Byron most of all. Although Byron's jibe was in fact directed elsewhere in the literary firmament, it is nevertheless difficult *not* to see Scott and his vision of Spain—as from the wrong end of a telescope—reflected in the lines found in a suppressed version of *Childe Harold*, Canto I.

> Ye! who would more of Spain and Spaniards know
> Sights, Saints, antiques, arts, anecdotes, and War,
> Go hie ye hence to Paternoster Row ...
> Then listen, readers, to the man of ink,
> Hear what he did, and sought, and wrote afar
> All these are cooped within one Quarto's brink ...[33]

*   *   *   *   *

Probably late in 1810 or early in 1811, Scott took up the unfinished narrative of his early life—what is known as the 'Memoirs' or the Ashestiel Fragment of autobiography, which he had begun in 1808. There he wrote concisely of his fondness for 'excursions', doing so at a moment when his first scheme to go abroad had come to nothing: 'I have all my life delighted in travelling though I have never enjoyed that pleasure upon a large scale.'[34] The truth of this statement is as incontrovertible as is its candour undeniable. Scott also recorded in the 'Memoirs' that his father, concerned by his early wanderings, suggested sarcastically that he was 'born to be a strolling pedlar'. This surely is the real-life origin of the remark that Scott, in *Redgauntlet*, puts into the mouth of Saunders Fairford (a character based on his own father) who remarks to Alan Fairford (a character based, in large part, on the young Scott himself) of Darsie Latimer (also displaying certain distinct elements of Scott's own nature) that Latimer should apply himself to the law rather than go 'scouring the country like a land-louper [a vagabond or adventurer] going he knows not where, to see he knows not what ...'.[35]

A decade after he had initially conceived the notion of going to the Peninsula, but had found reason or excuse for not actually doing so, an opportunity arose for Scott to visit Portugal and Spain in circumstances altogether different. Once again, a literary motive and a likely outcome in the form of a travel book—albeit one of an imprecisely defined kind—underpinned the project. The immediate purpose of the jaunt, however, was to spend some time with, and to offer companionship to, Charles, 4th Duke of Buccleuch. The Duke had decided to go to Lisbon for his health, taking with him the Peninsula veteran, Adam Ferguson, almost in the role of the old-fashioned 'bear-leader' of Grand Tour tradition: Buccleuch (with a nod to classical precedent) preferred 'mentor'—neither term, however, paying full regard to the relative ages of the protagonists, there being only two years between Ferguson and the Duke. Furthermore, both men were in their late forties, so hardly the archetypical young bucks of Grand Touring custom and legend. A plan was concocted whereby Scott, whose own age fell exactly between those of the others, might join them in 1819. The Peninsular destination was a variant of an even vaguer scheme Scott entertained of going elsewhere in Europe.[36]

'I have the desire', wrote Scott to Ferguson,

> like an old fool as I am *courir un peu de monde* … I care so little how or where I travel that I am not sure at all whether I shall not come to Lisbon and surprize you instead of going to Italy by Switzerland that is providing the state of Spain would allow me without any unreasonable danger of my throat [i.e. the possibility of having his throat cut by bandits] *passe pour un peu* to get from Lisbon to Madrid and thence Gibraltar. I am determined to roll a little about for I have lost much of my usual views of summer pleasure here.[37]

Scott was not a well man at this time. In 1819, indeed, there was a serious crisis in his health, so he did not rush to go south, writing instead to the Duke in terms surprisingly amusing in the circumstances of the two sick men involved:

> I conclude you will go to Mafra, Cintra, or some of these places, which Baretti describes so delightfully to avoid the great heats when the palace de las Necessidades [Palácio das Necessidades, dedicated to Our Lady of Needs] must become rather oppressive. By the bye though it were only for the credit of the name I am happy to learn it has that useful English comfort, a Water-closet … Your Grace sees the most secret passages respecting great men cannot be hidden from their friends.[38]

He sympathised with Ferguson on account of the likely heat, which 'must be a serious draw-back', but hoped that Ferguson would 'by & bye get away to Cintra or some of those sequestered retreats where there are shades & cascades to cool the air. I have an idea that the country there is eminently beautiful.'[39] Sadly, the Duke died just days later, compounding the fear that Scott himself always had of dying abroad.

On 7 November 1818 John Ballantyne had written to Archibald Constable from Abbotsford, telling him that a work, to be entitled 'New Travels on the Continent', had been contracted for from an author discreetly left unnamed. 'This work', Ballantyne told his fellow publisher, 'must have great success—for we certainly know little of the present state of the Continent—from such high authority, both political and literary.' A further letter of Ballantyne to Scott, written the same day, and from the latter's own house, expands in detail: this 'continuation of Paul's Letters'—in Chapter 4 we shall discuss in detail the book to which Ballantyne refers—was to 'contain your own further travels on the Continent next season', and was to be in three volumes with a print-run of 10,000 copies. All this before Scott had much idea of where and how he might go, and for what duration any such late-in-the-day 'Grand Tour' might be! However, an escape-clause allowed Scott to resile from the agreement on grounds of ill-health. The work was indeed abandoned. Archibald Constable's son later stated, with masterly vagueness, that this was on account of some 'circumstance of intervening difficulty.'[40] However, as we shall see, the idea— under varying *ad hoc* titles, or convenient shorthand descriptions such as 'Continental Travels', 'Travel Letters', etc.—was never entirely extinguished; and indeed it was later revived, although ultimately it was to remain as but a gleam in Scott's publishers' eyes.

In 1810 Scott had pleaded his wife's likely concern for his safety as a partial excuse for not yet having gone to Portugal and Spain. In 1819 he appears to have been worried, on his own behalf, about bandits. A consistent seam of worry and prudence had early emerged as fatal to Scott's best intentions as an adventurous traveller. He was certainly no Byron, but neither was he a Southey or many another Romantic with an insouciantly fearless penchant for exotic travel. As he grew older, the deaths abroad of both Henry Fielding and Tobias Smollett seemed to haunt him. In his life of Fielding, he alluded to that author's unfinished *Journey to Lisbon*, 'abridged by fate'. 'The hand of death was upon him and seized upon his prey...'. As ill-health and the effects of over-work took hold, Scott was, unquestionably, conscious of strong parallels between himself and his eighteenth-century predecessors. The similarities were compounded by infirmity and financial ill-fortune, coincidences brought into even greater relief when the subject of travel to southern Europe was added to the mix. Both Fielding and Smollett had died 'of the diseases incident to a sedentary life and to literary labour,—and both drew their last breath in a foreign land, to which they retreated under the adverse circumstances of a decayed constitution and an exhausted fortune.'[41]

In the year of Scott's own death, his friend Washington Irving published *The Alhambra*.[42] To read of Irving's positive delight in the hardship of Spanish travel is to realise how limited Scott himself had been as a traveller or even would-be traveller. Despite many protestations and some braggadocio to the contrary, anything further from a 'bold contrabandista, or hardy bandolero' than the Laird of Abbotsford can hardly be imagined. Irving, by contrast, positively relished that life, having laid in an ample stock of good-humour, and a genuine disposition to be pleased; determining to travel in true contrabandista style; taking things as we found them, rough or smooth, and mingling with all classes and conditions in a kind of vagabond companionship ... what a country it is for a traveller, where the most miserable inn is as full of adventure as an enchanted castle, and every meal is in itself an achievement! Let others repine at the lack of turn-pike roads and sumptuous hotels, and all the elaborate comforts of a country cultivated and civilised into tameness and commonplace; but give me the rude mountain scramble, the roving, hap-hazard, wayfaring; the half wild, yet frank and hospitable manners, which impart such a true game-flavour to dear old romantic Spain![43]

4

A Sudden Frisk to Paris

Napoleon's abdication in April 1814, and the ensuing Treaty of Paris, opened the Continent to British visitors once more. But, as with its predecessors, the peace of 1801 and the Treaty of Amiens of 1802, Scott was unable to take advantage of the peace to enjoy whatever travelling opportunities the times might offer.

Looking back a dozen years later, Mary Shelley caught the mood well:

> When peace came, after many long years of war, when our island prison was opened to us, and our watery exit from it was declared practicable, it was the paramount wish of every English heart, ever addicted to vagabondizing, to hasten to the continent, and to imitate our forefathers in their almost forgotten custom, of spending the greater part of their lives and fortunes in their carriages on the post roads of the continent.[1]

John Morritt told Scott how 'flesh and blood like mine could no longer resist the temptation and I set out for Paris ... there I have been enjoying a scene I believe unparalleled in the annals of history...'.[2] Scott himself, however, whom one might have expected to want to indulge in some modest 'vagabondizing', remained in Scotland. He confided thus to Morritt:

> I heartily wish I had been of your party for you have seen what I trust will not be seen again in a hurry since to enjoy the delight of a restoration [i.e. that of the Bourbon King Louis XVIII] there is a necessity for a previous boulversment [sic] of every thing that is valuable in morals and policy ...[3]

Although Scott had originally hoped that an excursion to Iberia might have its pay-off in some literary guise, now it was the demands of the literary activity besetting him at all quarters that made it impossible for him to go to Paris. There was the small matter of the completion of *Waverley*, published in July 1814, and with it Scott's remarkable transformation from an author of narrative poetry to a writer of prose fiction. Despite his new persona as a novelist, Scott was not tempted by the lure of France or the wider Europe beyond. Yet Mary Shelley was soon to describe the rage to make a jaunt to the Continent in 1814 as that 'new chapter in the romance of our travels', in which the traveller of feeling was 'acting a novel, being an incarnate romance'.[4] Later in the year he confessed to friends that he felt unable to escape either the persistent clutches of his muse, 'a Tyranness', or (more specifically) the 'tyrannical domination of a certain Lord of the Isles', that eponymous poem being his current 'literary tormentor'.[5] Then, even before that poem was published on 5 January 1815, he had begun to write his second novel, *Guy Mannering*. This he completed in the astonishingly short time of about seven weeks during in the winter of 1814-15: it was published on 24 February 1815.

So Scott was undeniably busy—exceptionally so—with verse and prose composition, not to mention the editorial labours on his nineteen-volume edition of the works of Jonathan Swift. But perhaps he could just have made time for a quick and spontaneous frisk to Paris that summer of 1814. After all, he did embark on a cruise with the Commissioners of Northern Lighthouses to the Orkneys, the Shetlands, and round the north of Scotland to the Hebrides and so to the west coast and finally, having just touched on the north-eastern tip of the island of Ireland, to the Clyde estuary. This voyage occupied more than five weeks from the end of July 1814. At the outset, Scott had told Morritt that he would have the opportunity of 'visiting all that is curious on continent and isle': by 'continent', Scott meant the land-mass of mainland Scotland. After the conclusion of the excursion, he informed this same correspondent that his 'principal employment this autumn will be reducing the knowledge I have acquired of the localities of the Islands into scenery and stage-room for the 'Lord of the Isles'.[6]

This telling phrase—'scenery and stage-room'—captures perfectly Scott's general motive in travel, whether in Scotland, in the wider realm of the United Kingdom, or ultimately on the Continent (that is the 'other', the European, Continent). To travel was to collect ideas, information and inspiration for current and future writing. Thus, when he told James Ballantyne that he had seen 'some of the greatest and most tremendous sea scenery in the world', this information would be fed into the word-processor of his mind for use, not just in the current narrative poem, but also ready to be dredged up again, when required, in the novel *The Pirate*, published in 1822.[7] In the 'Magnum Opus' edition of that novel, Scott's new introduction reprised his experiences of the summer of 1814, which he described as having been a voyage 'connected with the amusement of visiting the leading objects of a traveller's curiosity … the wild cape, or formidable shelve … the most magnificent scenery of rocks, caves and billows'.[8] Those experiences would furnish, also, the detail which he set down in the *periplous* that he compiled for the use of William Daniell when the artist was making his great *Voyage Round the Coasts of Great Britain*, specifically for the Scottish sections of that enterprise. Scott's notes informed Daniell's route, and his choice of subjects for illustration.[9] There is a parallel here (and indeed proximity in date) with the itinerary and suggestions for sightseeing that James Hakewill provided to J. M. W. Turner for his first visit to Italy in 1819.[110] Both are cases where travellers who had been over the ground—whether in Scotland or in the heartland of the Grand Tour—subsequently shared their knowledge with an artist bound for regions they had themselves explored.

There were those who were part-intrigued, part-puzzled and part-contemptuous that Scott should be seen to prefer this domestic excursion to a European tour, however unambitious or circumscribed. Byron had heard from James Hogg that Scott had departed on the 'lighthouse' voyage, and in weather (moreover) not to his taste. Scott had, in fact, merely told Ballantyne, in the letter quoted above, that he had experienced not much more inconvenience 'than *roughing* it a little in the rain and spray, and occasional sickness.' Hogg may have dined out on this, so to speak, and magnified the element of discomfort. Writing to Thomas Moore, Byron was sharp in his satire.

> Lord! Lord! If these home-keeping minstrels had crossed your Atlantic or my Mediterranean, and tasted a little open boating in a white squall—or a gale in 'the Gut' [of Gibraltar],—or the Bay of Biscay with no gale at all—how it would enliven and introduce them to a few of the sensations!—to say nothing of an illicit amour or two upon shore, in the way of Essay upon the Passions, beginning with simple adultery, and compounding it as they went along.[11]

Scott clearly got wind of Byron's slighting comments on his preference for the less exciting and exacting forms of travel and, bridling somewhat, wrote to Morritt in an attempt to set the record straight, not least in the matter of the length of his northern expedition. He parodied Byron's actual words.

> Lord help us!—this comes of going to the Levant and the Hellespont, and your Euxine and so forth. A poor devil who goes to Nova Zembla and Thule is treated as if he had been only walking to Barnard Castle or Cauldshields Loch.[12]

And yet Byron had a point, and he had scored a palpable hit. Scott *did* appear timid and risk-averse, always ready with an excuse for not going abroad. Mary Shelley may even had him in mind when she wrote amusingly of her compatriots' unfamiliarity with Italy, and of the 'unitalianized' who 'are endowed with Spurzheim's bump, denominated *stayathomeativeness* [my italics]'.[13] This sally had even more point given the interest displayed in Scott, as the possessor of a cranium of unusual form and dimensions, by the phrenologists and 'skullologists' of Edinburgh (those practitioners of 'turnipology', as Scott deridingly called the pseudoscience), and possibly even by Dr Johann Gaspar Spurzheim himself.[14] Scott had never, as we have noted, been to Portugal and Spain, like Southey or Byron himself; he had not yet been to France, like Wordsworth or Samuel Rogers, who had each been twice, or Maria Edgeworth, who visited Paris in 1802; he had not been to Germany, like Wordsworth, or Coleridge, or Matthew Gregory ('Monk') Lewis; and of course he had not undertaken more exotic travelling further afield as Byron, Coleridge and his own close friends Skene, Ellis and Morritt had. This caution remains one of the distinctive and puzzling features of Scott's life as a traveller.

*   *   *   *   *

Scott had, in fact, wanted—even more than in the summer of 1814—to go to the Continent the *previous* year, specifically in December 1813, to witness the events which (as it was hoped and supposed) would bring about the downfall of Napoleon.

> I had a strong temptation to go ... this Christmas and should certainly have done so had I been sure of getting from Amsterdam to Frankfort where as I knew Lord Aberdeen and Ld Cathcart I might expect to get a welcome. But not withstanding my earnest desire to see the allied armies cross the Rhine which I suppose must be one of the grandest military spectacles in the world, I should like to know that roads were tolerably secure and the means of getting forward attainable. In spring however if no unfortunate change takes place I trust to visit the camp of the Allies and see the power pomp and circumstance of war which I have so often imagined and sometimes attempted to embody in verse.[15]

As once theoretically in Spain, so now notionally on the borders of France, Scott would seek to gather ideas for fresh and original ways to portray military action in poetry—but in this case with the benefit of personal experience of campaigning, even if in a non-combatant role. Yet it should be noted that his habitual caution tempered the excesses of his enthusiasm, and his tendency to procrastinate (a postponed Christmas jaunt was to be replaced by a putative spring one, etc.) soon conquered any wild idea of rushing to the front if there might be the slightest personal danger.

The winter of 1813-14 and the spring of 1814 passed, however, with the Allies advancing on and into Paris, but with Scott tied to Scotland and his various literary undertakings. 'I intended to have been with the grand advance upon Paris', he told a correspondent, rather carried away from reality by the emotion of the times, 'but things came in the way, which I regret excessively, for such a scene the eyes of men will never again open upon.'[16] His plan had been to witness 'the great Entrée into Paris'. He assured a friend that 'few people submit with more indifference to want of accommodation', thus establishing his credentials (perhaps with greater bravado than the actual facts warrant) as a hardy would-be traveller in the mould of the more extreme Grand Tourists of old, or, in this instance, rather as a hardened war-reporter. And he gave vent to real if somewhat theatrical annoyance at missing the fall of Napoleon's empire: 'I was so angry at not seeing the grand crash ...'.[17]

The year turned. He remained desk-bound, and smarting still at the lost opportunity to see the Bourbons restored and the armies of occupation in Paris. In March 1815, however, Napoleon returned; the Hundred Days followed, culminating in the Waterloo Campaign of June, with the battles of Quatre Bras, Ligny, Wavre and the climactic contest of Waterloo itself. And so Scott's moment came again; this time he was not prepared to let anything stand in the way of his witnessing 'this grand finale'. But of course the risks, though still present to some degree, were now much moderated. Towns and small garrisons that still held out for the Emperor and had yet to be subdued, Valenciennes and Condé for example, could doubtless be avoided. Save, perhaps, for the occasional surly inn-keeper, the greatest danger on the roads to Paris was posed by *francs-tireurs*, disaffected Napoleonic loyalists or resentful soldiers of the *Grande Armée* still under arms and often drunk and dangerous. Scott's friend and fellow Edinburgh advocate, James Simpson, would shortly find that allied but ill-disciplined Prussian troops on the loose posed an even greater threat to travellers.[18] The Grand Tourists of tradition had always had to face the worry of brigands on the road from Naples to Rome, or in the lonely Campagna. Now a similar threat had moved north into a part of Europe previously considered very much more tame and secure. But in mid-July, and assuming a gung-ho stance, Scott told Daniel Terry he would cross the Channel, 'just to hear the Grenadiers March resounded from the Walls of Paris'.[19] Somewhat peremptorily, he asked his London legal friend John Richardson to get him a passport: 'Brussells [*sic*] is our first object next Paris—I write in haste having just taken this sudden frisk into my head'.[20]

An early letter describing the aftermath of Waterloo, written by a Scottish surgeon who had gone over to Brussels to help deal with the wounded, had come into Scott's hands. This had (as he said) set him 'on fire' with enthusiasm to see for himself both the field of battle and the occupied French capital.[21] His passion is evident in his correspondence: how he was possessed by 'the extreme desire to hear a British drum beat in the streets of Paris ... But the sight that is now in Paris is such as only occurs once in five hundred years ... I expect a great deal from this trip...'.[22] A great deal in terms of personal experience; a great deal, too, in material for literary exploitation. As Lockhart expressed the matter, the trip to Belgium was designed to give Scott the opportunity 'of seeing probably the last shadows of real warfare that his own age would afford...'.[23]

*   *   *   *   *

With Napoleon finally disposed of, travel to Europe entered a new phase. As had been the case with the temporary truces and peace-treaties of 1801-2 and 1814, so now in 1815 British tourists flooded the Continent once more. As the politician and diplomat, Constantine Henry Phipps, Viscount Normanby (later Earl of Mulgrave and, later still, 1st Marquess of Normanby) put it in his novel *The English in Italy* (1825), Europe was 'opened to our insular curiosity'. The British could not

> resign themselves at once to the dull and newsless state of peace, without seeking to supply the means of excitement which they had lost by some other as absorbing. Foreign travel alone appeared to supply this void, and all who could... rushed to enjoy it.'

Foreign travel became a substitute for 'the expired excitements of war'. The British, Normanby declared, were 'the veriest *roadsters* that ever put hoof to travel'. Obviously they looked first to France and the Low Countries and, using an analogy derived from that quarter of the Continent, Normanby explained that the mania for travel spread rapidly, with Italy becoming the great goal once more, just as it had been in the classic age of the Grand Tour: 'when the dyke of separation was taken away ... Englishmen inundated Italy.' With some charm, and deft use of metaphor, Normanby described the English sweeping down on Milan. 'The Gauls and Goths of ancient times did not make the descent more eagerly...', and now British tourists 'tumble down the Alps in living avalanches.'[24] On many occasions between 1816 and the later 1820s Scott imagined a time when he, too, might be among them. But, before any serious thought of Italy, he first had to see Paris and, on the way, the field of Waterloo. His account of this trip, his first personal encounter with Europe, was published pseudonymously in January 1816 as *Paul's Letters to his Kinsfolk*.

Paul's Letters was Scott's prose account of his European adventure. The book was written in tandem with his narrative poem *The Field of Waterloo*, which was altogether much less well received. As was the case with Scott's Peninsular enthusiasm, which had given rise both to a technical essay on Napoleonic tactics and a narrative poem, so now the excursion to Paris via Waterloo produced literary offerings of both kinds. The poem was, like *The*

Vision of Don Roderick, written with a charitable purpose in mind, namely the fund established to assist the bereaved and wounded of the campaign. Scott may have wished to aid the sufferers in this way; but the largely poor reception of his poem did his own literary reputation no favours, and the squibs written in response to it have generally been regarded as more memorable than the work itself. *Paul's Letters*, on the other hand, was a considerable success.

Paul's Letters was one of a number of near, or relatively nearly contemporaneous, British accounts of visits to Paris and to the Waterloo battlefield. All have their merits, as well as their similarities and differences. The structure of these individual narratives naturally varies in the emphasis and space they devote to Paris itself, to the roads leading to the city, and to descriptions of Brussels and Waterloo which form the high points en route. Philip Mansel has asserted that the torrent of cumulative description of all kinds devoted to Paris in this period (that is 1814-15) forms 'the richest portrait of one city ever drawn by writers of another nation.'[25] In an Edinburgh literary setting, this rash of publishing was remarked upon with precocious but characteristic acerbity by the young J. G. Lockhart, only recently arrived in Edinburgh to read for the Scottish Bar. He wrote to a friend thus:

> And as for travellers—good Jehova! I think I am safe in saying that there have appeared at least twenty different lucubrations that way concerning Paris alone... profound disquisitions on national character and Napoleon by another [tyro author] who never had seen the tenth milestone from Auld Reekie.[26]

It is in this context that Scott's travel book has to be considered. Certainly *Paul's Letters* is a lively and often amusing account, and one that is penetrating in its analysis of many topics. But it is constrained by its form. Scott's decision to structure his book as a series of ostensible 'letters'—clever and effective though this in some ways was—deprived his narrative of a single, personal view of places, scenes and events uninterrupted by the need to change gear, so to speak, as 'Paul' addressed different imaginary recipients. And admirable though the book is, one could object that, in any account of a jaunt to Waterloo and Paris, the reader wants to know the author's own opinions without the complication of the alias of his nominal letter-writer, and to know who that author actually is. Scott conceals himself behind a mask. It might have been better if he had simply allowed himself to speak in his own person, his unguarded opinions being delivered within the immediacy of the narrative of his own adventures. But to have done this would, very probably, have required his name on the title-page, thus compromising his evident desire for anonymity. He probably wished to avoid this because his poem *The Field of Waterloo* was to appear under his own name. Two books from the same author on closely-related themes might have been over-egging the Continental travel pudding.

In structuring *Paul's Letters* as he did, Scott played the traditional Grand Tourist in a way that even he might not fully have understood. The epistles from Belgium and France were addressed to five fictitious correspondents, and the broad subjects of the individual letters were designed to appeal to each recipient according to his or her interests: it was Scott's intention (in the persona of his alter ego, Paul) to 'send to each of them, from foreign parts, that species of information with which each is most gratified.'[27] Thus, for example, Paul's cousin 'the Major' received communications that were heavily military in content. This approach was not unlike that of an earlier, 'real' Grand Tourist from a Borders family, Roger Robertson, younger of Ladykirk, Berwickshire, whose letters to his family from Italy in the early 1750s were arranged on a basis that was rather similar.[28]

Scott himself (in the final letter of 'Paul' to his 'cousin Peter') was generous enough to pay tribute to a small handful of contemporary works by other authors which were similar in theme to his own, but somewhat different in approach.[29] First was *A Visit to Paris in 1814; Being a Review of the Moral, Political, Intellectual, and Social Condition of the French Capital* (London: Longman, 1815) by John Scott (no relation), editor of the London newspaper *The Champion* and later of *The London Magazine*. This was a book 'very spirited and acute' according to Walter Scott. It was soon to be supplemented by John Scott's even more interesting and immediate *Paris Revisited, in 1815, By Way of Brussels: Including a Walk over the Field of Battle at Waterloo*.[30] Second was the account of travels in France in 1814-15, 'the joint production of two young gentlemen, whose taste for literature is hereditary': these were Patrick Fraser Tytler and Archibald Alison.[31] Third was the book by James Simpson, already alluded to above.[32] When Walter Scott was writing *Paul's Letters*, Simpson's memoir was not yet published; but it would, in fact, appear before Scott's own book. Scott referred to the author as 'another ingenious friend, (Mr S—n of Edinburgh) whose extreme assiduity in collecting information cannot fail to render his journal interesting'. Scott later called him 'Waterloo Simpson', in a jesting way that conceals, perhaps, just a slight hint of a sentiment somewhere between amusement and envy.[33]

*   *   *   *   *

The history, especially the military history, of Flanders had, as Scott told Robert Southey, 'rendered the land classic'.[34] The works of Jean Froissart and 'Philip de Comines', historians of the country themselves, compounded this sense of special significance inherent in this part of Europe. (Scott would return to, and depend upon, the *Memoirs* of Philippe de Comines—or Commynes—when assembling his materials for *Quentin Durward* in 1823, and again in his *Anne of Geierstein* in 1828-29.) In using the phrase 'rendered the land classic', Scott was writing very much as a Grand Tourist, and moreover in the characteristic 'Grand Tour' vocabulary, even though the European travels he had completed thus far comprised no more than parts of Belgium and the road to Paris. But the classic ground of the Cockpit of Europe was for some, like Scott, arguably more significant and even more moving than the actual 'classic ground' of the Roman Campagna or the Phlegraean Fields near Naples. As a quasi-Grand Tourist, too, with money a-plenty, he stood in the tradition of the rich 'Milords Anglois' who had bestridden the Continent in the eighteenth-century heyday of such travel. His kinsman and travelling companion, John Scott of Gala, recalled their purchasing of souvenirs—some ghoulish, such as a French cuirass pierced by a musket ball—from the battlefield of Waterloo.

> The extraordinary love of relics shewn by the English was a subject of no less satisfaction to the cottagers who dwelt near the field, than ridicule to our military friends. One enthusiast had carried off a brick, another one of the doors of the house [of La Belle Alliance].[35]

Waterloo had been fought on 18 June 1815. Scott and his companions visited the field on 9 August. There they behaved exactly like traditional Grand Tourists at some Italian archaeological site, where they might have purchased from a local peasant, or picked up for themselves, an arrow-head from the site of Cannae or a spear-point from Lake Trasimene, as evocative mementoes of their experience and their encounter with Antiquity. The only difference is that Scott's were souvenirs of a terrible modern battle fought just weeks earlier, collected from the field while the stench of death still hung in the air.

Scott and his travelling party from Scotland were by no means alone or even very unusual in being visitors to the battlefield, nor were they the first. Collectively, these visitors really invented what today would be called 'battlefield tourism'. Scott and his contemporaries were actually developing a sub-genre of the more general, wider and more strictly culturally-focused Grand Tour. Their early battlefield visiting represents an aspect of the shift in tourist priorities from the 'Classical' and historic towards the 'Romantic', the sentimental and the present or very recent past.

The story of Charlotte Waldie—she who later (as Mrs Eaton: see Chapter 1) would attempt to solicit Scott's acceptance of the dedication of her *Continental Adventures*—is fascinating. More adventurous by some measure than Walter Scott, she and her brother and sister had gone to Belgium on 10 June 1815. Napoleon and the *Grande Armée* were marching the other way, towards them. Her narrative of the Waldies' doings over the next month or so is noteworthy.[36] The account was not published until 1817, so Scott (and others) achieved priority, even if they did not quite match the immediacy of her narrative. Scott must have been impressed. Charlotte Waldie was suitably deferential to what she described as the 'abler pens' of the other writers 'of talent and genius' who had visited the location of these epic events in world history, and who had described the scenes; Scott will, of course, have been uppermost in her mind. Nevertheless, she could not refrain from observing that she had actually *been* in Brussels and Antwerp while momentous events were taking place.[37]

Charlotte Waldie's reportage is fully worthy of Scott in its melodramatic description. By15 July she was able to visit the field of Waterloo, admittedly nearly four weeks after the action but almost a month before Scott made it there. She was rewarded with more gruesome spectacles, and a heavier smell of putrefaction. Even greater quantities of 'relics' were to be picked up, or to be found for sale. She came away with ashes from the pyres where the dead of the fighting in and around the farm of Hougoumont (a critical battlefield location) had been burned; the broken sword of a British infantry officer; and a French cuirass from La Belle Alliance which she had to lug about during the hot day. Scott could not beat her grisly report of the skeletal human hand she saw sticking out of the ground near Hougoumont, 'as if it had raised itself from the grave. My blood ran cold with horror, and for some moments I stood rooted to the spot, unable to take my eyes from this dreadful object, or to move away ...'.[38] This episode has been described as 'a gothic intrusion built into the psychic economy of the picturesque', and Miss Waldie's reaction to it as one leading to 'a feeling of inarticulacy in the face of the sublime.'[39]

John Scott, the journalist, must have visited the field some time after mid-July. Of the mass graves he wrote: 'On these the eye instantly fell,—and the heart, having but a slight call made upon it from without, pronounced with more solemnity to itself, the dreadful thing that lay below, scarcely covered with a sprinkling of mould.' John Scott asserted that quantities of French corpses stll lay on a part of the field they had occupied as living, fighting men. Unforgettable is the following description of

> the complete impression of a man's body on the ground, as distinctly marked as if he had fallen on the snow... and the hole, which had taken the shape of his head, was full of a corrupted fluid, that one shuddered to look at.[40]

A couple of generations later, post-Grand Tour visitors or Cook's tourists visiting Pompeii and Herculaneum would marvel at Giuseppe Fiorelli's plaster casts of victims of the eruption, and would be both moved and morbidly fascinated by a similar sort of immediate contact with the corporeal and material evidence of past tragedy.

Walter Scott's poetic version of the same sort of sentiment as that of
Charlotte Waldie and John Scott—that of the encounter between an author
with the awful actuality of the aftermath of slaughter on a massive scale—
which (as a recent critic has put it) 'only a man who had stood close to a fresh,
thinly covered mass grave in the heat of summer could have written', ran thus:

> And feel'st thou not the tainted steam,
> That reeks against the sultry beam,
> > From yonder trenched mound?
> The pestilential fumes declare
> That Carnage has replenish'd there
> > Her garner-house profound.[41]

It has recently been asserted that Walter Scott appears to suggest in *Paul's
Letters*—or rather to let it be assumed from what he writes—that he had
visited the battlefield much earlier than in fact he had done: that at one point
he describes how mangled corpses exhibited terrible wounds.[42] So, no doubt,
they did; but Scott could not possibly have seen such shocking sights, and
in fact he says no such thing. He was writing from a combination of reports
gleaned from his military friends and from his own perfervid imagination. In
Paul's Letters he makes it quite clear that when he himself visited the battlefield
'All ghastly remains of the carnage had either been burned or buried, and
the reliques of the fray which yet remained were not in themselves of a very
imposing kind.'[43] On this (now disputed) point, Philip Shaw has commented:

> The incongruous relationship between fact and fiction, history and myth, seems
> to reach a point of crisis in this image [of bodies with skulls cleft open by sword
> strokes], as if the writer were less concerned with the poet's desire for romance
> than the novelist's appetite for the corporeal and the contingent.[44]

One suspects that Scott was actually rather disappointed *not* to have seen
more 'ghastly remains of the carnage': heads cleft to the chin, bodies cut in
two by cannon shot. He should really have got to Waterloo long before he
did. As things were, perhaps the most affecting sight was the great mass of
paper of all descriptions which littered the ground: he commented on this in
Paul's Letters.[45] As befitted another Edinburgh advocate of literary tastes and
inclinations, James Simpson was also struck by this feature of the field: the
leaves of books, the letters (like one he found opening 'My dear Husband …')
defaced by rain and mud, the whole resembling 'the rubbish of a stationer's
shop'.[46]

But, in a way, Scott *did* make it to the battlefield earlier than 9 August.
During his own visit on 31 July, James Simpson and his friends rested for a

while at the inn of La Belle Alliance. There they took out and read a newspaper which happened to contain an account of the recent Edinburgh meeting for the Waterloo Subscription, in aid of the wounded and bereaved, at which Scott had spoken. Not content with reading out Scott's speech, they went further in insinuating Scott into their battlefield visit. On a whitewashed wall of the inn they added another graffito to the rest: lines from *The Vision of Don Roderick*. 'We quoted the following lines ... on the very spot of Napoleon's final defeat and ruin, on his first trial of strength with "the Wellington"'—a passage Scott had written after Massena's defeat at Fuentes De Oñoro. As Simpson has it

> Tell him thy conqueror was Wellington,
> And if he chafe, be his *own* fortune tied,
> God and our cause, to aid, the venture we'll abide.[47]

To revert to Scott's own visit to the field of Waterloo, it has been perceptively noted that this was effectively a valedictory occasion: Scott was actually 'saying goodbye to the imaginary conflict that had sustained him since the beginning of his career' as a narrative poet, strong on the depiction of war and battle.[48]

*   *   *   *   *

As many a Grand Tourist before him, Scott had much to say about the peculiar methods of conveyance *en route*, and particularly of the infamous stage-coach or *diligence*:

> We travel in a long black queer looking hearse of a thing open on all sides but with curtains to draw if it rains which holds us very conveniently. It is drawn by three horses with a driver who shrieks at them like a highland drover pushing on his bullocks.[49]

Like Scottish Grand Tourists of tradition, he drew parallels between the sights, sounds and local people seen, heard and observed abroad, and those of his native land. The interest Scott had begun to display, in his first two novels, in the lives, manners and speech of the Scottish peasantry, was also evident in Flanders and Paris. Particularly affecting was the sight of soldiers of Scottish regiments of the army of occupation as he watched them in the bivouacs, streets, churches and even the museums: 'It was something to hear the bagpipes playing before the Thuilleries [*sic*] & to see the highlanders broiling on the cuirasses of the French Imperial guards their rations of beef & mutton.'[50] Scott, as indeed was the case with other contemporary travel writers, endows the Scottish troops of the British army of occupation in Paris and northern France with an almost Roman nobility of manner and bearing, totally in contrast to the French caricatures of the day. Carle Vernet, artist of caricature portraits of 'the English in Paris', and his *confrères*, did not flatter their occupiers. But the Highlanders whom Scott describes could well be descended from the 'Classical', heroic, almost superhuman figures that Benjamin West had designed for the decorative elements of Highland Society of London diplomas and the like.

Scott's remarks on the first Parisian museum he chose to mention have been little commented upon. Of this establishment he wrote in *Paul's Letters*:

> The antiquary who visits Paris must be deeply interested by a visit to the Museum des Monumens Français, assembled by Mons. Le Noir [*sic*] in the church, convent and gardens of Les petits Augustins. This collection proved a sort of asylum for such monuments of art as could be saved from popular fury during the first revolutionary fever, comprehending the tombs of princes, legislators, and heroes. When the churches were sacked and pillaged ... Mons Le Noir had the courage to attempt to save from impending ruin objects invaluable for the history of the arts and for that of the nation, and he had the address to devise a probable mode of succeeding in a plan, which, in those furious days, might have been represented as savouring of aristocracy and *incivisme*.

While giving Alexandre Lenoir full credit for his efforts, and admitting that by his actions much had been saved that might otherwise have been destroyed, Scott the antiquary nevertheless did not conceal his preference for keeping monuments *in situ* in the actual locations for which they had been designed and made, and not, as he put it, 'torn from the graves which they were designed to mark out and to protect, and divided from all those associations arising from the neighbourhood of the mighty dead.'[51] Huddled together like bric-à-brac in their makeshift quarters, the importance of individual pieces was lost, and their effect diminished by the mass. These were significant views on the principles underlying the museology of the period, and indeed that of future times: one imagines that Scott was thus prepared for what he might one day see, on some more extended cultural tour, in the great collections of Europe.

Scott was a man more concerned with family history, genealogy and mediaeval antiquities than he was with either ancient history and classical archaeology, or indeed with paintings and fine art. Hence his giving priority to Lenoir's museum in his survey of the cultural riches of the city. But, in the realm of traditional connoisseurship, he was also able to share in something of the standard 'Grand Tour' experience which, a generation or so before, the *milordi* would have had to go to Italy, or through much of Northern and Central Europe, to enjoy. But the French had looted and purloined the art of Italy (and that of Flanders, and of many German and Austrian princely or

Imperial collections), with Napoleon acting 'less like a soldier than a brigand or common highwayman, whose immediate object is to rifle the passenger whom he has subdued by violence or intimidation.' Thus did Scott piquantly express the matter, using a metaphor taken from the world of contemporary travel and, as such, one that would be immediately comprehensible to all who had made or might make a Grand Tour.[52] John Pemble has well described the story of the enforced removal of art to the Louvre—or rather to what became the Museé Centrale des Arts, and later the Museé Napoléon—as 'one of the most audacious projects ever perpetrated in the long history of cultural rapine.' Sculptures and paintings previously held in Milan, Modena, Parma, Piacenza, Bologna, Perugia, Mantua, Verona, Venice and Florence, and in the Vatican and other Roman palaces, were now displayed all together in Paris. The Neapolitan collections alone were spared from becoming war booty.[53]

In 1802 Scott had written a 'War-Song of the Royal Edinburgh Light Dragoons' which had contained the line 'Their ravish'd toys though Romans mourn', alluding to the removal to Paris of the treasures of the Vatican and elsewhere.[54] The word 'toys'—in contemporary usage meaning things of little or no intrinsic value, trumpery prized merely as ornaments or curiosities—hardly shows great respect for the art of Antiquity, and its use in the jingle was insouciantly laddish. Quite possibly Scott never imagined he would actually see such classical masterpieces. In the event, he was just able to catch them in the halls of the Louvre before the great process of restitution began in earnest, or at any rate before it had progressed too far. So, in a manner, the core 'Grand Tour' experience had come to Scott, rather than it being a case of him having to go to Italy in order to tick off what—to paraphrase Samuel Johnson again—it had long been expected that an educated man should see. But Scott was also quite clear on a point that he had already alluded to in his discussion of Lenoir's museum of French monuments. The Napoleonic ransacking of Italy had removed art from its context. In Paris now were sculptures and paintings 'whose very names had become associated with classical situations, from which a true admirer of the arts would have deemed it sacrilege to have torn them.'[55]

In the Louvre, Scott was fascinated to see two Highlanders—private soldiers, at that—with their wives, admiring the Venus de' Medici and 'criticizing the works of Titian & Raphael'.[56] The Grand Tour was an inherently 'gentlemanly', elite institution; yet here were enforced 'Grand Tourists' of another class, playing their 'betters' at the same game of connoisseurship, and perhaps even gaining more. John Scott, the London newspaper editor, but a Scotsman nonetheless, was similarly stuck by the spectacle of Scottish troops sightseeing. He watched them looking at the print stalls in the rue Faubourg St Denis, where they and their like were caricatured by the Parisian print-makers. It is a pleasing conceit to think of Highlanders chuckling at the images they saw of themselves: too-short kilts, lasciviously curious Frenchwomen stealing a look at what might (or might not) be underneath, and so on. And like Walter Scott he observed the troops touring the Louvre: a Highlander with his wife 'walking steadily along ... both drinking in, with inflexible gravity, the sights around them'; or soldiers looking at sculpture and paintings, some with printed catalogues in hand, spelling out the titles 'syllable by syllable'.[57] One is reminded, in a more modern context, of the splendid drawing by Edward Ardizzone of 'Jocks in the Museum at Leptis Magna', Tripolitania, in 1943: the squaddies with their rifles gawping among the nudities, while their officer leans sagely on his crook, thinking the thoughts of a gentleman when confronted by classical statuary.[58] And, conversely, in an authentic Italian Grand Tour milieu, it is salutary to recall how John Morritt described the attitude of a culture-weary fellow *milord* who asked him whether there were any fine pictures in a particular Roman palazzo. 'No', Morritt had replied; 'God be thanked', his friend had said in relief, 'nobody will plague me to look about me.'[59] Some eighteen months after Scott was in Paris admiring the culture-conscious Highland soldiers, Stendhal had been half-amused, half-astonished to be overtaken at the gallop on the road back to Naples by three British naval officers returning from Portici. They had entered the Royal museum there, just as he was leaving, to see paintings from Pompeii and Herculaneum. Everything on display there was 'admirable', they declared, 'and some of the most curious things in the universe'; but Stendhal reckoned that they could have spent only three or four minutes in total in the twenty-two rooms of the museum.[60]

The experience of the Louvre, replete with the Napoleonic loot of a once-conquered Italy, must have allowed Scott to feel that he had, at last, encountered the art of the ancient world, and the canvasses of the Renaissance, Mannerist and Baroque masters, as surely as if he had been to the great museums of the Popes, and the cabinets of the princes of Italy. 'But the finest of all sites', he wrote to Margaret Maclean Clephane, recently married to Lord Compton,

> required no charm being constantly accessible to people of all classes ... the famous Louvre which no one will ever see again in the same state of perfection. The coup d'oeuil was the most magnificent in the world for the gallery is near a quarter of a mile in length and was then crowded with paintings all of the very first order. But I think on the whole the dispersion of this celebrated collection will be favourable to the arts. You saw too many chefs d'oeuvres at once and became like the glutted epicure who could only endure a bit out of the sunny side of a peach. All the pictures could not hang in the best lights and if that had been possible all could not be regarded with the attention to which they were entitled. So that in point of taste alone I think the separation of their masterpieces fortunate for the art and its admirers. In a much more important respect it is

a most useful measure for in the first place it gave the French through a very sensitive point, their national vanity namely, a lesson of retributive justice and besides the depriving that immoral and vainglorious people of the reputation of possessing the finest collection of the arts possible. There are so many of the unthinking that would be glad of so good an apology to make their headquarters at Paris the most worthless and dissolute city in the universe that even at a great loss to the fine arts (and it is impossible but what they must be gainers) I should have rejoiced at the toasted cheese being forcibly withdrawn from the mouse trap.[61]

Some of this very phrasing recurs in *Paul's Letters to his Kinsfolk*, where the account of the Louvre reinforces the idea that to have seen the art there assembled was to have enjoyed a kind of Italian Grand Tour *in absentia*.[62]

From *Paul's Letters* we get a hint of Scott's own ideas of connoisseurship, and can approach in some way to an understanding of how he would have reacted to the pabulum of ancient sculpture, and Renaissance and Baroque painting, that the Grand Tourist was supposed to digest. The Apollo Belvedere apart, Scott seems to have preferred the show of paintings in the galleries of the Louvre to the display of sculpture. But Scott's un-academic taste is revealed by the remark that he would have preferred to own a Rubens hunting-piece, or a painting of a group of Flemish peasants going to market, than all the history pictures in the Luxembourg Palace.[63] Teniers was more to his taste than Titian. We do not, however, know precisely what Scott himself thought of a superb and eclectic private collection such as the personal museum of Baron Vivant Denon, to which admission had presumably been arranged by Jean Baptiste Le Chevalier. Archaeologist, librarian and astronomer, Le Chevalier (also known as 'Constantin Koliades') was noted, inter alia, for his scholarly topographical work on the site of Troy. He was able to insinuate Scott and his friends into such places which otherwise they might not have found it possible to visit, or to visit as profitably. Le Chevalier was evidently as pleased to act as *cicerone* for Scott in Paris as Scott himself was for visitors to Border abbeys, castles and places of lore and legend. He had spent six months in Edinburgh, and had read a paper before the Royal Society, of which he had been elected a Fellow. No doubt he was repaying a debt both of hospitality and of scholarly regard. He had been praised, while in Edinburgh, for 'the variety of his knowledge, the vivacity of his conversation, and the agreeableness of his manners.' Scott was fortunate to have his learned company. The relationship is an example of the best of that theoretical Grand Tour interaction between men of science, learning and letters which was one of the ideals of pan-European travel.[64]

Writing to James Ballantyne, Scott described how, the previous day in the Louvre (of which Denon had been Napoleon's Director-General), he had noticed

that they had begun to loosen with wedges the Venus de Medicis & the Dying
Gladiator which I suppose is symptomatic of their removal. They have also begun
to work on the celebrated Bronze horses which were brought from Venice but this
excited such a mob that they were forced to turn out the guards. The scaffolding
remains around the arch [the arc de triomphe du Carrousel] on which these horses
are place[d] & I have no doubt that they will descend one of these fine mornings.[65]

The Parisians were bereft. Their sense of value in their looted works of art
appeared to rise

> as the hour of parting with them approaches. They talk to them, weep to them,
> kneel to them, and bid adieu to them, as if they were indeed restored to the rank
> of idols. But Baal boweth down, Nebo stoopeth—the hammer and wedge have
> given awful note of preparation: the Venus, the Dying Gladiator, and many other
> statues, have been loosened from their pedestals, and stand prompt for returning
> to their native and appropriate abode. Many a lowering eye and frowning brow
> marks the progress of these preparations…[66]

With language such as this, one feels that Scott might easily have been tempted
to venture into verse to describe this epic tale of restitution and repatriation,
and its effects on the erstwhile despoilers, the despoiled and soon to be
re-possessed, and (perhaps) even on the *spolia* themselves. But he was not so
tempted; though the next year he was able to add to his library the poem by
Felicia Hemans on just this subject, *The Restoration of the Works of Art to
Italy*. But then Scott found Mrs Hemans (as he would later say) 'somewhat
too poetical for [his] taste—too many flowers I mean and too little fruit but
that may be the cynical criticism of an elderly gentleman … I am hastening to
think prose a better thing than verse…'.[67]

There was huge resentment on the part of the Parisians at early suggestions that
their looted art be restored to its legal owners, sentiments that were compounded
when the occupying forces began the actual physical process of removal and
restitution. The Louvre had become a focus of national pride.[68] James Simpson
wrote memorably of the effects resulting from the stripping of the Louvre: he
described the Apollo Belvedere, packed and padded securely for ultimate return
to the Vatican, lying crated in his 'coffin' and the artists of Paris weeping over
the statue: 'they pressed his hand to their lips and bad him a last adieu … Every
spectator who leaves them [that is, the looted sculptures] seems to go away to
die.'[69] John Scott actually wondered whether the European Powers might not just,
through indifference, let the looted treasures remain where they were and thus
'leave to Paris the darling boast of being the capital of the world as to Fine Art.'
When he saw the paintings being prepared for return to Italy, the Netherlands,
Prussia and elsewhere, lying on the floors of the Louvre, he thought the scene

reminiscent of 'a large auction room after a day's sale ... It seemed as if a nation had become ruined through improvidence, and was selling off.'[70]

Unlike John Scott of the *Champion* newspaper and *Paris Revisited*, Walter Scott of *Paul's Letters* does not seem to have been able or willing to ascend to the top of the Arc du Carrousel, or (if he did) to write about it. John Scott was present when the ancient horses of San Marco were disentangled from their grandiloquent Napoleonic triumphal chariot, loosened from their fixings, lowered to the ground, and taken away in carts for return to a Venice now under Austrian control.[71] The process of restitution of art from Paris might 'lower her pride and mortify her vanity'. In future the young artist would lack the boon of seeing and studying all the masterpieces of less-readily accessible parts of Europe gathered in one convenient place. John Scott makes this very point: art was more easily and conveniently to be seen and studied in Paris than in Rome. However, he also admitted that in Paris the works of art looted from all over Europe 'were but feeble auxiliaries to the Champaign of Beauvilliers [the famous restaurateur], and the profligacies of the Palais Royal' as additional 'amusements' of this 'gross city'.[72] But, on the other hand, this would confer benefit to the aspiring student in terms of the wider horizons experienced through the necessary travel, even as it would deprive him of the conveniently 'packaged' study possible at present. In discussing this same matter in *Paul's Letters*, Walter Scott in fact writes in praise of the old 'Grand Tour' spirit, where one had to go in diligent and sometimes difficult or even dangerous search of the treasures of Italy. The student of art—as, equally, the gentleman-traveller—might, in future, have to extend his journeys in pursuit of 'those excellencies which are now to be seen collected in the Louvre'. But, in so doing, he

> will have greater benefit from the experience which has cost him some toil; and if he must traverse Switzerland and Italy, to view the sculptures of ancient Greece, and the paintings of modern Rome, he will have the double advantage of taking lessons on his route from Nature herself, in the solitary grandeur of the one and the profuse luxuriance of the other.[73]

Scott, who had never yet made the conventional Grand Tour—but who had seen in Paris the collected wealth of art from the Italian heartland of that Tour—was here not just recommending the traditional course of a travelling education in Italy, but appears also to be looking with a romantic eye upon the scenery of the Alps. This was a commentator, after all, who had gazed with wonder and awe on those Perthshire mountains of his boyhood. Dramatic Alpine scenery was coming to be appreciated, more fully than it had been before, by those possessed of a new aesthetic sensibility.

*   *   *   *   *

There were strong words of condemnation of the licentiousness of Paris, as exemplified by the purlieus of the infamous Palais Royal, of which 'Paul' wrote in rather prissy disgust to his supposed clergyman friend, 'Minister of the Gospel at—', who was among the five recipients of the *Letters*. These might almost be the words of a real, if strait-laced, Grand Tourist shocked by what he encountered in Venice, widely regarded as 'the brothel of Europe'. Scott gave free range to all his characteristic British feelings of disgust and outrage at the classic example of European moral laxity and excess that the Palais Royal constituted. In these 'unhallowed precincts' was 'Vice with her fairest vizard ... a Vanity-fair of shops for jewels, trinkets, and baubles, that bashfulness may not lack a decent pretext for adventuring into the haunts of infamy.' Enticed in by luxury goods, the visitor would find more scandalous scenes in the inner recesses of a notorious city within a city, one 'in whose saloons and porticos Vice has established a public and open school for gambling and licentiousness': prostitution and all manner of 'the most hideous and unheard-of debaucheries'. Scott's writing seems a perfect literary counterpart to visual images such as Louis-Léopold Boilly's of the demi-monde inhabiting the Galleries of the Palais Royal. Just as one did not need to go to Rome to see the art of Antiquity because so much of it was in Paris, so one did not need to visit Venice since all that rendered the latter city notorious among Grand Tour destinations was replicated, and probably far exceeded, by the 'central pit of Acheron' that was the Palais Royal. 'Paul' fulminated to his minister friend that it should all be 'levelled to the ground, with all its accursed brothels and gambling houses'.[74]

Everyone wrote about the Palais Royal. Walter Scott described it well, and memorably. But several of his contemporaries did too, so his comments in *Paul's Letters* were not exactly unique, even if they were rich in terms of expression and (as we have just seen) feigned outrage. Edward Planta, to cite but one example, made similar observations on it as a haunt of vice and ruin.[75] John Scott described the 'living stream of all nations, ages, ranks, costumes, and physiognomies'—he was writing of the Allied armies of occupation, from rough Cossacks and Prussian *Junkers* and white-uniformed Austrians, to red-cheeked and red-coated British Guards officers—'driven, as if by some insatiable impulse, towards its fatal vortex.' They provided the place, John Scott observed, 'with a glut of prey'.[76] The young men of Europe, many of whom would in earlier times have sown their wild oats in the cities on the old Grand Tour circuit, were all clustered together on a 'petit'-Grand Tour of Palais Royal gewgaw shops, cafés, brothels and gambling dens. Patrick Fraser Tytler and Archibald Alison, two young Edinburgh advocates, must have been extremely unusual in claiming that in the Palais Royal at 'no hour of the night do you witness scenes of gross indecency or riot.'[77] Unusual, or else very innocent or, yet again, very sarcastic. James Simpson, if hesitating to call it 'a world in itself', satisfied himself with suggesting that it was 'at least a city'. Like Scott's alter ego, Paul, Simpson looked forward to a time when 'this immense gangrene' might be 'cauterised'.[78] Modern scholars describe the Palais Royal admirably. Gregor Dallas points out that the 'corruption was organised vertically'. The higher one climbed in its notorious Galleries, the more vice one encountered.[79] In a way, this may have struck Scott as in some small measure akin to the tenements of the Old Town of Edinburgh where fading gentility petered out as one ascended the common stair. Philip Mansel describes the Palais Royal as a centre of all pleasures, and as an island of light—literally, because of its brilliant illumination.[80]

In *Paul's Letters*, Scott fails to discuss one of the most famous establishments within the curtilage of the Palais Royal, nor does he mention it in any of his correspondence: this was the Café des Milles Colonnes. The café was celebrated not just for its beautiful columns but for its still beautiful, long-presiding deity, *la belle limonadière* as she was widely known, an exotic creature whose somewhat vulgar yet elegant figure insinuates itself into so many verbal and visual records of the place. She sat, bejewelled and blowsy, on what was called 'the throne'. James Simpson recorded Scott's presence there, and published his remarks long after Scott's death.

> To my great amusement I saw sitting at the right hand of 'the throne', eating ice [cream], and now and then conversing with the lady, Mr Walter Scott ... I was delighted to hear Mr Scott's remarks on the truly French scene in which we sat, and his commentaries on the singular personage who solemnly, brilliantly, and correctly presided, sparkling with diamonds, multiplied, front, back, and profile, in mirrors, and intrenched in arrondisments [*sic*] of sugar, peaches, and nosegays ...[81]

Our knowledge of Walter Scott's presence in the Café adds a subtle nuance to John Scott's urbane commentary—the publisher referred to it pompously as 'the Literary Department'—on the relevant plate in *Picturesque Views of the City of Paris*, where he describes how 'the bucks commence the labours of the day by paying their devoirs to the jolie limonadière ...'.[82] One thinks, too, of the superb illustration by George Cruikshank of the two friends, Dick Wildfire and Captain O'Shuffleton, heroes of David Carey's splendidly satirical *Life in Paris; Comprising the Rambles, Sprees, and Amours, of Dick Wildfire ... and his Bang-up Companion, Squire Jenkins, and Captain O'Shuffleton ...* (1822), rendering 'hommage' to 'la belle limonadière', with an ice-eater taking his place in the scene.[83]

Scott did write to his wife Charlotte from Paris about some of what he got up to. But, perhaps wisely, the 'beautiful matron' of the Café des Mille Colonnes went unremarked. He told her, however, how he was playing

'Cavaliere servante' [*sic*] to two English ladies of his acquaintance now in the city; an element—albeit one entirely innocent in its execution—of the traditional role of *cicisbeo* assumed by the more adventurous of Grand Tourists in the *palazzi* and *conversazioni* of sophisticated but morally relaxed Italian society was here imagined to be descending on the unlikely shoulders of the Laird of Abbotsford.[84]

The prose portrait in *Paul's Letters* apart, nothing else Scott wrote in and of Paris perhaps quite conveys the charm of his verses on Saint-Cloud, just to the west of the city. These captured not only the magic that a northerner felt in the 'southern summer night' with its 'veil of darksome blue', but also the profound sense of *sic transit* experienced at the ruin of a splendid palace and its famous cascade wrecked by revolution and war. Scott may not yet have seen Roman ruins such as those of the Forum (which had become through time merely the Campo Vaccino, or 'field of cows'), or of Hadrian's vast villa at Tivoli, or of the baths of Caracalla, so stupendous in their decay; but in this poem he came close to the sensibility that pervaded the world of the Grand Tour. With added piquancy, romantic reverie was thrown into relief by the sounds of varied national music emanating from the camps of the Allied armies of occupation. Scott long remembered this experience as one of the most delightful of his life.[85]

It was in Paris that, traditionally, many British tourists first began to adopt 'foreign' ways, manners and dress. Scott, of course, at this time had been no further; but he was nonetheless affected by this very different world.

> I am quite a Frenchman in eating & drinking & turn up my nose at roast beef and port-wine—fricasses & champagne are much better ... After all it is a delicious country if the people would be quiet which I fear they never will.[86]

Surely he cannot have forgotten that his wife Charlotte was of French birth!

Throughout his time in Paris, northern France and Belgium, Scott had been motivated primarily by an interest in humanity: a curiosity about how human beings operated and interacted was of greater concern to him than buildings, ruins, pictures, or works of art. In this he showed himself to be a characteristic exponent of the new ethos in post-Napoleonic War travel. 'Romantic' experiences, things, people, were preferred to the traditional diet of the old Grand Tour, with its circumscribed itineraries and its preferred canon of art, architecture and set-piece sites and sights. In October 1815 he reported thus to Lady Compton:

> My journey to France was ... however most highly interesting. If I saw no old castle and little Romantic scenery I beheld the ocean of humanity in a most glorious storm of confusion—towns just reeking from storm and

bombardment—fields of battle where the slain were hardly buried—Immense armies crossing each other in every direction—villages plundered a la mode de Prusse—soldiers of all kindred and nations and tongues—Emperors kings princes dukes and generals without end—and our Scotch highlanders mounting guard within musket shot of the Tulleries [*sic*].

> Who is't mount guard at Versailles and at Marli
> Who but the lads wi' the bannocks o' barley.

In short you saw everything and anybody at Paris excepting Frenchmen and Frenchwomen who to say truth shewed a feeling of modesty under their disasters and made themselves scarce.[87]

*   *   *   *   *

Scott's rapid composition of *Paul's Letters* was noteworthy. The first two of the ostensible epistles were in fact despatched to James Ballantyne from Paris before 30 August 1815: the first portions of the book were actually in the press in Edinburgh before the author had even left the French capital. But that was how Scott and his printers worked. Moreover, *The Field of Waterloo; a Poem* had been advertised in the *Caledonian Mercury* as 'In the Press' and 'speedily [to] be published', not just before a line had been committed to paper, but even before its would-be author had left Britain for the Continent.[88] It was not for nothing that Thomas Moore introduced, into one of the verse letters which form his enjoyable *The Fudge Family in Paris* (1818), a droll remark alluding to Scott's speed of composition and publication. Bob Fudge is the dandified writer of some of the humorous epistles: the other letters are by his father, sister and their Irish tutor. In Letter VIII, Bob writes to a friend at home on the pleasures of eating in Paris. He explains that sometimes he lunches—on waffles—'with the Gauffrier Hollandais' in the Palais Royal,

> That popular artist, who brings out, like SC-TT,
> His delightful productions so quick, hot and hot; ...[89]

Writing six years later, John Hughes cited Scott's travelogue with approbation. He thought it sufficient to refer to it simply as 'Paul's admirable letters', giving no author or other details, and praised it as work which afforded the reader 'everything about Paris': one needed little more.[90] This, of course, was a biased and clearly over-enthusiastic judgement, for books such as John Scott's were in fact superior in many ways, and (as we have seen) the literature of the British in Paris in 1815 is as extensive as it is profuse in variety and excitement. Nevertheless, Walter Scott had put into the mouth of

the eponymous Paul an excellent summary of what Paris must have meant
to visitors from Britain. There was so much to admire, so much to dislike.
Real taste and genius were mixed with much frippery and affectation; the
sublime mingled with the ridiculous; the pleasing with the fantastical and
the whimsical. He could hardly determine which train of ideas the city had
planted most firmly in his mind. But it was certain that Paris displayed the
greatest range of objects of curiosity imaginable, all easily accessible. Scott's
alter ego epitomised everything with a few lines that are double-edged if they
are anything: that 'of all capitals in the world, Paris must afford the most
delightful residence to a mere literary lounger'; and that the city might be
'safely pronounced one of the most entertaining places of residence which can
be chosen by an idle man.'[91]

*   *   *   *   *

Observations on contemporary French life, manners, opinions—and, not least,
of the French table—resurfaced in Scott's amusing and whimsical Introduction
to his novel with a late-mediaeval French setting, *Quentin Durward* (1823).
In this Introduction, too, Scott made a wittily tart allusion to a reason for
foreign travel, and for temporary residence abroad, reflecting an attitude and
a motive far from the 'integer vitae scelerisque purus' ethos of the ideal of
the Grand Tourist as a type, free from all sin except acquisitiveness in art
and some affectation in manners. That other reason for going abroad, and
remaining abroad for a longer or shorter time, was 'impecuniosity'. A man so
afflicted by need, and thus bound for a southern clime and a 'very merry land',
might well say, with Scott's narrator, that 'I sought it, and it did not seek me.'[92]
In other words, the warm south might call to some for superior reasons of
cultural education, self-improvement (and perhaps just a bit of lotus-eating);
but, equally, France and Italy might well claim others for reasons far from the
elevated and intellectual. Life in the sun was cheap, and creditors might be left
a long way behind in cold, foggy Britain.

As has been indicated above, Scott's recollections of aspects of French
life came to his mind as *Quentin Durward* emerged after a long gestation.
Lockhart remarked that, in this novel, Scott was breaking new ground,
in terms of scenery and history, by the 'bolder experiment of a continental
excursion.' James Skene had recently been to France and had furnished Scott
not only with a journal of his travels, but also with a series of drawings
recording landscapes and buildings of a kind which (as Lockhart put it)
'would have been most sure to interest Scott had he been the companion of
his [Skene's] wanderings.'[93] This was vicarious touring on Scott's part, and the
instance stands as an example of how the records of others, both verbal and
visual, supplied his own deficiencies, and supplemented both his own extensive

reading and his active imagination. Lockhart went on to offer a personal anecdote: how he himself recalled Scott at work in the Advocates' Library in Edinburgh, 'poring over maps and gazetteers with care and anxiety'.[94] Scott wrote to Archibald Constable about a tiresome and ineffectual geographical search for a small French town which had (as a result of Scott's unrequited efforts) become 'a vile place ... that can bafle [sic] both you and me.' Maps had failed him; books yet to be located and consulted might still help. 'In the meantime', Scott wrote optimistically and ebulliently, 'I am getting on and instead of description holding the place of sense I must try to make such sense as I can find hold the place of description.'[95]

*   *   *   *   *

Reminiscing to Joanna Baillie some nine months after his return from France, Scott—having listed other Continental destinations he might like to visit— quite openly stated that Paris was not a place he was 'anxious to see again'. His assessment in 1816 was that 'There is more of good and bad in it than anywhere else in the world. I do not mean *moral* good of which there is rather a paucity but worldly grandeur and display.' An epithet he had previously applied to a discrete but most significant and striking part of the city, namely the Palais Royal, he now applied to the metropolis as a whole. Paris was 'quite a Vanity-fair'.[96] However, ten years later he was to return. The second Paris visit that Scott made, in 1826, was motivated ostensibly by the needs of his current research (partly pursued in London) for his monumental *Life of Napoleon Buonaparte*, published in nine volumes in 1827. Compared to the visit of 1815, it was in many respects anti-climactic. He did not really want to go. This second visit was not even to be dismissed as a frisk or a frolic. He told his lawyer, John Gibson, that he was going to 'make a run over there'; it was to be, effectively, a business trip. 'Neither the time nor expense are agreeable circumstances but I must not oeconomize upon either to the prejudice of literary reputation.'[97] Lord Melville was informed that he was going over to France 'with very great unwillingness'.[98] But he made the best of the jaunt and large elements of it assumed, in the end, the character of a cultural and social progress rather than a mere working visit.

The Louvre was, of course, divested of the looted treasures of Italy which he had seen there previously, and the 'great French daubs' that replaced the Italian masterpieces disappointed even a man who actually had little visual sense.[99] The salons of the British Embassy seemed inhabited by the ghosts of the great men he had hob-nobbed with in the summer of Waterloo. He could not do other than look back to that astonishing time when he 'had often seen and conversd familiarly with many of the great and powerful who had won the world by its [sic] sword and divided it by their council.' When he wrote in his journal that a second visit he paid to Saint-Cloud on this present occasion was 'rich in remembrances', it is probable that it was not just images of Revolutionary and Napoleonic events that started to his mind, but his own happy discovery of the delights of the place eleven years before.[100]

When Scott made his second Paris visit, he found himself by far the most popular novelist of the day, the idol of the reading-rooms and lending-libraries known as *cabinets de lecture*.[101] Perhaps the oddest moment for him was going to see an operatic version of *Ivanhoe*: 'it was strange to hear anything like the words which I ... dictated to William Laidlaw at Abbotsford now recited in a foreign tongue and for the amusement of a strange people.' Memories of home were stirred, too, by the sight of 'a whole covey of princesses of Russia arrayed in tartan', whom Scott encountered at a soirée of Princess Gallitzin. This Russian general's wife had sought out Scott as a curiosity and a trophy: she wished to see him 'in the heroic vein', which (though 'precious tomfoolery') he considered was probably better than to be 'neglected like a fallen sky-rocket'.[102] Princess Gallitzin had gushed that she would 'traverser les mers' to see him. Scott, one suspects, would not have reciprocated. He crossed the seas so infrequently that the prospect of a season of Parisian 'lion-hunting'—as celebrity-seeking was known: the celebrities hunted were themselves the 'lions'—would have been unlikely to have changed the reluctant travelling habits of a lifetime. In Paris, Scott recorded meeting 'one lioness walking at large in the jardin [the Jardin des Plantes, also, by amusing coincidence, the seat of the Paris zoo]': this was the celebrated Madame de Souza Botelho, novelist, *salonnière*, adventuress and mother of Napoleon's *aide de camp*, the Comte de Flahaut.[103]

In Paris, Scott met his fellow novelist, James Fenimore Cooper. Recognition of a shared talent and a common interest in the mechanics of publishing drew them together, and they appeared at the Gallitzin reception in literary double-harness as what Scott termed 'the Scotch and American lion[s]' who jointly 'took the field'.[104] Cooper's wife described how her husband was made 'quite a Lion of in Paris', and how they met Scott repeatedly. Susan Augusta Cooper told her sister that the older writer treated James like a 'son or younger Brother in the same vocation ... He is a Giant in form as He is one in Literature.' She ventured the opinion, too, that 'craniologists' would be interested in his head, which was high and narrow, with very grey hair. His complexion was fine and florid; his appearance healthy and 'quite rustic'. This put Mrs Cooper in mind of one of their New England 'Presbyterian Pastors'. In conclusion, she thought, 'He looks like a Man of powerful mind—kind and amiable, as if He liked fun—and withal very countrified.'[105] The covey of Russian princesses probably preferred to overlook the rustic manner of the homely Laird of Abbotsford for that of the 'Olympian' one of the Monarch of Parnassus.

An odd 'souvenir' of the 1826 Paris visit survives, little recognised, in a strange series of 'Scènes historiques et chroniques de France'. These are the work of the Parisian *littérateur* Paul Lacroix (born 1806), whose pseudonym was P. L. Jacob. Three years after Scott's visit, Lacroix issued the first of what became a two-volume collection of tales and romances purporting to be those told by Scott during his Paris evenings in the fashionable *bureaux d'esprit* of cultural high society. *Soirées de Walter Scott à Paris* (subsequently published with the second volume of similar stories *en suite*, but with much altered and expanded front-matter) is a complete fiction: no such tales, however 'impregné de gothique' they may be, were ever told by Scott either in French, English or what 'Jacob', terms a 'langage barbare et inintelligible' – presumably the Scots speech of some of the Waverley Novel characters. In actual fact, Scott returned from Paris to 'son château d'Abooswod' [*sic*] without having left any legacy of French mediaeval tales behind him. But the idea that he might have done so was appealing, and Lacroix exploited the opportunity to write what he fancied Scott – whom he addresses as 'Maître – could (and, in Lacroix's opinion, perhaps should) have done, given Scott's known admiration for Froissart and his ilk.[106] Unknown to Lacroix, Scott's genuine moment for telling stories from the history of France would indeed come, in 1830, with the Fourth Series of his *Tales of a Grandfather*, three volumes of them.

Throughout the Paris visit Scott was fêted, and 'almost eaten up with kindness'; '… if honied words from pretty lips could surfeit I had enough of them. One can swallow a great deal of whipd cream to be sure and it does not hurt an old stomach.' Yet it was all too much: 'there are so many compliments. I wish for a little of the old Scotch cau[s]ticity.' On his return to Britain, he wished only for 'a sheep's head and whisky-toddy against all the french cookery and Champagne in the world.'[107] Surely few tourists had met with more 'great folks' in a mere eight days in a European capital city. Yet, though in the end grand, this second brief Paris visit can hardly be called a 'Grand Tour', or anything approaching it, even in the changed realm of Continental travel in the world after the Napoleonic Wars.

5

'To Roll a Little About'

In 1814 Scott had been derided as a 'home-keeping minstrel'. Though this was indeed true when the remark was made, he had by the end of 1815 at least been to Paris, and had seen something of northern France and Belgium. But his correspondence over the next few years gives a very confused picture of what he did or did not want to do by way of further European travelling. On the one hand, he confessed (in 1819) to caring little about how or where to travel; on the other, he asserted his determination to 'roll a little about', and a number of possible destinations were mentioned in a rather cavalier way but, one suspects, without any great conviction.[1]

At one point in *Paul's Letters*, Switzerland and the 'solitary grandeur' of 'Nature' had been introduced by Scott into his notional artist's ideal journey towards the fountainhead of art in Italy. Switzerland had, for some reason or reasons, embedded itself in his consciousness. That country, and the Tyrol, may have had a special resonance for Scott as regions which had resisted Napoleonic tyranny.[2] As a European travelling destination, Switzerland had certainly become popular among the British of the age of Romanticism. Byron and Wordsworth had been there. Many others were, and would increasingly be, attracted to its Alpine scenery as indeed they were to the refined life of its cities.[3] The Swiss mountains seemed to Henry Cockburn to betoken a 'land of promise', and the views around Zurich afforded a spectacle more magnificent than anything witnessed before: he 'panted to be on the tops' of the Alps.[4] From Paris, Scott had written to his wife of his hopes that they might perhaps next year 'take a frisk together as far as Switzerland which would be delightful.'[5] But he added that he felt no inclination at present to go further. So, although artists would have to go to Italy, Scott himself betrayed no pressing need nor entertained any real desire to do so. Or so he said. But, in January 1816, it was once again James Skene's example that appeared to influence his own wishes.

Scott was keen that Skene should publish his travel journals, which could be illustrated with prints after his own drawings. A 'tour through Sicily and

Malta' struck Scott as the best start to a potential series of travelogues. He assured Skene that he would be happy to mould the text into publishable form, an offer that would make him (Scott) a vicarious Grand Tourist through the medium of the printed page—arguably his most comfortable position. [6]

Yet again, one has the strong impression that Scott was happier to form his views of European sights in this secondary way than he was to experience those same sights for himself. It is as if reality might blur or tarnish his imagined landscapes. His library-based knowledge of the world might possibly be upset by what he might find in the realities of France, or Spain, or Germany, or Italy. Thus the products of his *imagination* were the sights and sounds which he transferred, first into his narrative poetry and then, most notably, into his fiction. To have seen or heard the real thing might almost have hobbled his imagination and so curtailed his literary output. This, indeed, may well be the reason for his undoubted reluctance to travel as widely as most certainly he should, and possibly could, have done. It was only at the end of his life, when his literary career was all but extinguished and his creative powers were effectively spent, that he consented to go abroad for an encounter at the last with the reality of the Mediterranean. Only then, when there was little left in the store of his imagination, and he was himself a man worn out, both physically and mentally, did he accede to the worn-out status of the Grand Tourist.

Nevertheless, travel did have had its own undeniable appeal, at least in the realm of the theoretical, however little it was truly attractive to him in actuality. And so Scott kept telling his friends how much he wanted to see this and that country—but only if and when the time was right, other matters in abeyance, and the mood upon him. Thus Scott wrote to Skene in January 1816:

> I hope you will have no objection to take a scamper to the Continent one of these days. I think of it seriously either this year or the year after, for as my children are getting up and my household can go on as well in my absence as presence, I would willingly, while I have some stamina left, take a view of the Rhine and Switzerland and as far as Italy as I could, returning by Spain and the South of France. Should you think of this seriously we will go together, for you, like me, are I know of opinion with the old song:
>
> > A light heart and a thin pair of breeches
> > Go through the wide world, brave boys
>
> and we are not therefore disposed, when out of England, to bother ourselves for want of English comforts. [7]

But the projected trip or trips to the Continent did not happen. Again, there was always one good reason or another for postponement. A scamper to the study, or a frisk round the library shelves, always produced the inspiration Scott needed in his creative world; and the country life at Abbotsford supplied his needs in terms of restorative relaxation in a way that no European frisk or scamper could ever do. Skene noted, in retrospect, that a 'journey to the continent continued for some time to be a favourite subject in [Scott's] contemplation.'[8] So indeed was the case. But mostly it was just 'contemplation'. Scott's ideas for European travel were pursued with a rather unsettling frequency, and they oscillated between commitment and procrastination.

Of course he cannot have been entirely immune to the allure of Italy, or to that 'idealization of the Italian peninsula, which dazzled and exhausted the imagination of admiring travel writers' of his day. The fact that much of the appeal of Italy lay in how it was *imagined* rather than actually experienced in reality, and the way that many British contemporaries chose to blend the two and to 'add a bit of the imaginary to the real', must surely have appealed to a man whose mind worked as Scott's did.[9] An acquaintance with the Italian countryside and with the Italian peasantry would have offered rich pickings for a novelist who had such a facility for describing the life, manners, conduct, customs, pursuits and dwellings of the common people just as surely he could portray the world of castle, palace and manor house. Mary Shelley, indeed, recommended the observation of the Italian countryside and the country people, about which and whom she herself wrote so well. In fact, these aspects of the Italian scene were often preferable, as she suggested, to those so familiar—*too* familiar—to the Grand Tourists of tradition, who were merely 'connoisseurs in paintings, and frequenters of drawing rooms'.[10]

When the summer of 1816 came, Scott suggested to Joanna Baillie that he and she might meet the following year (1817) in Switzerland or Italy. He proposed that 'nothing gives such a fillip to the imagination' as 'going abroad'; had he health and strength 'for such frolics', he was minded 'to take a little frisk as far as Rome and Naples—perhaps as far as Athens'.[11] His ideas were certainly developing, and broadening significantly. But of an expedition to these wider shores no more is heard, other than in the kind of remarks made in passing (though with some regularity, indeed almost as a matter of rote and without a great deal of either serious intention or overwhelming enthusiasm) until a time when health and strength—vital travelling assets—were sadly lacking in a man by then infirm and prematurely ageing.

Joanna Baillie had, in fact, actually been to the Continent in the summer of 1816. She had joined a small family party for her niece's wedding tour. 'I have had,' she told Scott, 'a kind of passion all my life for the mountains of Switzerland; but it was a love cherished without hope, for I never expected to see them.' Her niece's new husband, an officer of dragoons wounded at

Waterloo, was, Joanna Baillie said, 'scantily provided with book learning'. But that deficiency would be remedied on the European tour, when he would be set to reading Scott's verse. This literary knowledge, freshly acquired, might be combined happily with the dragoon's innate ability to 'observe accurately & well the face of nature.' All might coalesce in the paradise of the Swiss Alps.[12]

Scott was, as he generously conceded, 'truly glad you are going abroad'. He wanted her to write when on her travels. So she did. Switzerland had not disappointed. She enthused of Lake Lucerne: 'The beautiful, desirable & sublime are there most happily combined; and if I were to fix my abode in Switzerland it would be on the shores of that lake.' She liked the Swiss peasantry in their costumes and with their 'frank, cheerful, honest familiarity', though she was surprised and disturbed by the prevalence of begging. On the way from Lucerne to Geneva she had visited Voltaire's former house at Ferney. Mont Blanc had been

> ungracious to us while we were on his skirts & at his feet humbly & wistfully looking up for one sight of the lofty summit, but he has in some degree made us amends for this by unveiling his lordly head when we were at a distance and shewing himself in all his superior dignity amongst the loftiest peaks of the snowy Alps.

This letter, mostly written earlier on the road, was posted to Scott in the course of her return journey when the party had been forced to stop at Fontainebleau with a broken carriage axle: it was fortunate that this mishap should occur (as she philosophically put it) at a place where there were things to see, such as Napoleon's desk.[13]

Scott's reply, on Joanna Baillie's return, is fascinating. It tells us a great deal about his attitude to foreign travel and about his views on the Continent. But, even more, it demonstrates that his preference was for Scotland and (within Scotland) for his own broad acres. For he blithely counters all that Joanna Baillie had to tell him of Switzerland and the Alps, and of Ferney and Fontainebleau, with a hymn of praise to Abbotsford:

> Wellcome my dear friend to the country which you honour and the friends who love you. The act of travelling [is] in itself delightful as affording so many new grounds of reflection and exciting so many new ideas that it almost gives advanced life the vivacity of youth. Yet after all to Britons its greatest charm is the return home and the power of comparing social life as it exists among us with the precarious state in which it is found on the continent. The grinding power of the military system[,] the want of respect paid to the civil power[,] the total carelessness and corruption which attends the administration of justice[,] the want of religion in its true state of influence upon the moral feelings and

habits of the people[, all] reconcile us wonderfully to our changeful climate and stormy politics. All I ever longd for on the continent was their light wines which you dont care about and their fine climate which we should both value equally. And to say truth I never saw scene or palace which shook my allegiance to Tweedside and Abbotsford though so inferior in every respect and though the hills or rather Braes are just high enough 'to lift us to the storms' when the storms are not so condescending as to sweep both crest and base—which to do them justice is seldom the case. What have I got to send you in return for the sublime description of the Alps—alas nothing but the history of petty employments and a calendar of unceasing bad weather...

So he told her of the recent visit to Abbotsford of the now-widowed John Morritt; and he wrote at length on the poetry, and more particularly the psychological state, of Byron—'the flight of such a Balloon as Lord B'— with (in the context of 'Romantic' tourism) an amusingly sarcastic aside about Byron's 'recommending to others to catch cold by visiting old Abbies [sic] by moonlight which he never happed to see under the chaste moonbeam himself.' But very soon he reverted to his 'own petty affairs':

I have some thought of enlarging Abbotsford this year and I have got a very pretty plan which may be ex[ec]uted at moderate expence having the local advantage of plenty of stones on the property. I have always had a private dislike to a regular shape of a house although no doubt it would be wrong headed to set about building an irregular one from the beginning. But when the cottage enlarges itself and grows out of circumstances ... the outs and inns [sic]afford without [i.e., on the exterior] so much variety and depth of shade and within give such an odd variety of snugg accommodation that they far exceed in my estimation the cut-lugged bandbox with four rooms on a floor and two stories [sic] rising regularly above each other. From this you will be disposed to augur something rather whimsical and I believe you will be perfectly right.

What price the regularity—albeit the comparative rural simplicity and provincial classicism—of Voltaire's elegant and regular Ferney? Scott was to have a small conservatory and 'a little Boudoir [French terminology was acceptable!] for my fine bust of Shakespeare, a good eatingroom and a small den for myself in particular'. Antiquarianism would govern all. And the spirit of antiquarianism commonly experienced abroad on a Grand Tour might just as satisfactorily be enjoyed and exploited at home. Whereas others might bring home from the Mediterranean and Aegean ancient marbles, Scott was content to scavenge the rubbish-heaps of muncipal development where Progress was depositing the outmoded and unfashionable mediaeval past of Edinburgh.

He would rather have some architectural mouldings from 'the Heart of Mid-Lothian' (the Old Tolbooth) than a metope from the Parthenon.

> The front [of Abbotsford] I intend shall have some resemblance to one of the old-fashioned English halls which your gentlemen of 500 a year lived comfortably in in former days. To augment the resemblance I have contrived to bespeak certain canopies which at present adorn that ancient and venerated mansion the tolbooth in Edinburgh so if my building does not give me a niche in the present at least I will get one out of it. They are finely carved being intended for the reception of Saints and having held them I suppose till John Knox knockd them down. This curious old building the Bastille of Edinburgh and formerly the place where the parliament met came down this year and the Magistrates have very politely promised me any part of [the] ornaments which may suit my purpose and it will be hard if I cannot find a purpose for all that is worth carrying thirty miles. My plantations have grown this year like any mad ... these are encouragements to an improver like me to ruin myself in carrying on all my hobby horsical plans ...[14]

Scott must have been delighted to read the passage in Letter XLIII of young J. G. Lockhart's *Peter's Letters to his Kinsfolk* where the latest topographical publications on display in an Edinburgh bookshop are described. Dr Peter Morris writes of the 'books of Voyages and Travels, and innumerable books of scenery—those beautiful books which transport one's eyes in a moment into the heart of Savoy or Italy...'. But this remark is followed by another paean, this time to

> that still more beautiful [book], which presents us with exquisite representations of the old castles and romantic skies of Scotland, over whose forms and hues of native majesty, a new atmosphere of magical interest has just been diffused by the poetical pencil of Turner—Thomson—or Williams.[15]

This is nothing less than a description—albeit unstated as such— of the first parts of Scott's own *The Provincial Antiquities and Picturesque Scenery of Scotland* (first issued in 1819 and continued until 1826), with engraved plates after oil and watercolour paintings by, among other artists, J. M. W. Turner, John Thomson of Duddingston and by Hugh William Williams (one view only by this last).[16] The notion that Scott's own country could more than hold its own against the landscapes and architectural set-pieces of the Continent is powerfully supported.

*   *   *   *   *

However much we may speculate about Scott's invention of excuses not to go abroad, we do have to remember that, when not being 'The Author of Waverley', he actually worked for a living. He played his not-insignificant part in the administrative structure of the Court of Session at Parliament House in Edinburgh, and in the dispensation of local justice in the Scottish Borders. He sat on boards, committees and commissions, and at various times held offices of some importance. He was not free just to drop things and go off to the Continent on a whim. In 1818 the illness of colleagues kept him in particularly close attendance on his legal duties in the Court of Session. Furthermore, the developing Abbotsford house and estate were voracious consumers of his time and trouble. He pleaded this excuse to Maria Edgeworth in May 1818:

> My rustic employments are so numerous and require so much of my own eye that I have no thoughts this season of quitting Scotland. If I can get away in winter I should much like to see Italy, but I fear I cannot do this very conveniently. Ireland I trust I will one day visit, but I must first get my dominions here put into some sort of order. I have been of late rather an extensive planter and incloser in proportion to the extent of my property, and these operations require a good deal of personal superintendence.[17]

Ideally, he would have liked to take his elder son Walter to the Continent in 1819 in preparation for his prospective military career (Walter would be commissioned into the 18th Hussars in June 1819). Father and son might then spend the winter in Italy, returning via the German principalities so as to give Walter 'some knowledge of the world and firmness of character so very necessary in his profession.' In a way, the elder Scott hints at a sort of reduced 'Grand Tour' for his son—a 'Petit Tour', as a more compressed version of the old, extensive, stately, traditional progress round Europe was sometimes known—with himself playing the role of the travelling governor.[18] However, ill-health—this time, his own—and the demands of literary labour, as well as that of official duty, supervened: the putative trip was postponed till 1820. Until then, the young cavalry officer should 'look after [his] French and German', in the expectation that the languages would be needed. Almost immediately, the tentative plans were enlarged in scope. Scott might now take his younger son, Charles, to a Swiss academy, where he might remain for two or three years. And it seems that a fuller family Continental expedition was in prospect too. If Walter *fils* were to come along on such an occasion he might return via Paris, escorting his mother and sisters, and leaving Scott *père* to proceed alone to Italy.[19]

James Skene, having been educated from the age of sixteen at Hanau (in Hesse), had shared an interest in German literature with Scott when they were young men in Edinburgh. This was at the time when Scott was first emerging on the literary scene as a translator of German verse. Skene had travelled in Germany again in 1802. Lockhart, whom Scott first encountered in 1818, had been to Germany the previous year, and indeed had met Goethe in Weimar. Scott himself had thoughts (as we have just seen) of visiting Germany in 1819: it does seem strange that he had not sought to travel in Germany rather earlier. One wonders whether this omission is not symptomatic of his general reluctance to commit himself to the rigours, and disruption to domestic life, that even a limited encounter with the Continent might have involved. Scott might have been 'German-mad' (as he described himself) in a safely bookish way; but he was not mad enough actually to travel in Germany.[20]

After one period of serious illness, he entertained the notion of a recuperative trip to Carlsbad (Karlovy Vary) in Bohemia. He told John Morritt that he liked the idea of Bohemia and its 'seven castles'. Safely abroad, he might escape 'the confounded lion-hunters who haunt English Spaws [spas].'[21] In 1822 he confided to the Shakespearean translator, Johann Heinrich Voss, of Heidelberg, that he had been 'now for a great many years a sincere admirer of the German literature which has something in it so similar to our own'. And he continued:

> I have long wishd to visit Germany but my knowledge of the language is superficial & so totally confined to books that I fear I should lose what I should much regret[,]the opportunity of holding easy and familiar intercourse with its inhabitants. Still however under every disadvantage I must see if possible a country of which I have read and thought so much and Heidelberg will now have greater temptations for me than its beautiful & celebrated vicinity and its great Ton [the famous Tun, or immense wine-cask in the castle cellars] when at the fullest could have afforded.[22]

In 1822 also, Walter, now promoted and transferred to the 15th (The King's) Hussars, went to Berlin as part of his extended military education. Scott the elder was able to partake of this European experience at one remove through the younger Walter's letters, but also through the medium of the advice he himself gave—very much in the way that any father of a young traveller on the Continent might have delivered himself of similar opinions and warnings. Thus we find the elder Scott writing almost in the manner of Lord Chesterfield (whose famous *Letters to his Son on the Art of Becoming a Man of the World and a Gentleman* long remained bywords of guidance in matters of conduct and comportment), and as if he had indeed personal experience to share.

> With the advantage of good introductions to foreigners of distinction I hope you will not follow the establishd English fashion of herding with your countrymen

and neglecting the opportunity of extending your acquaintance with the language and society. There is I own a great temptation to this in a strange country but it is destructive of all the purposes for which the expense and trouble of foreign travel are incurd ... Labour particularly at the german as the french can be acquird elsewhere ... I pray you do not lose time in dawdling ...[23]

What parent of any British Grand Tourist had ever, at some moment, written otherwise? But, perhaps, in the younger Walter's case, the elder Scott had misunderstood the possibilities for conversation, and profitable interaction with the locals on a cultural level. From iron Berlin, Walter wrote rather despondently that 'there is nothing but military in this town'.[24] Father urged son to labour at his German, but within five years he himself would admit that his own German had become shaky.[25]

There was a further brief thought that Scott might go to Germany in 1823 to 'fetch Walter home'. Together they might then 'take a peep at Italy' and return either by the Tyrol, Switzerland and the Rhine, or alternatively through France (Scott was surprisingly fond of the rather coy expression 'peep' in the context of European travel and tourism). 'I would have the advantage of your protection and you would not be the worse accueilli [*sic*] that you had the old gentleman with you.'[26] As well he knew, the courts of Germany offered good art, excellent music, military displays, hunting and mountain scenery. It was always possible to extend such a trip, a veritable *Kavaliersreise*, to include Vienna, and to go on from there to northern Italy.[27] There was the added attraction that Scott might meet Lord Byron again, if he were still to be in those same parts, and so Scott wrote thus to Byron:

> My son is at Berlin studying the great homicidal art of Mars and shooting wild boars. I intend to go over in spring and having him with me shall be tempted to take a ramble on the continent.[28]

However, as so often, his own health (and now also that of his wife), together with the needs of an ever-expanding Abbotsford, the constant claim of literary labour, and the other customary matters which diverted him and claimed priority, all conspired against Scott's project.

Then, in 1825, Scott clearly felt he must give travel advice to Charles, his younger son. His comments are particularly significant in one specific matter: Italy does not figure in the European tour which was mapped out for the young man. Paradoxically, the analogy Scott chose was actually one that was Italian-inspired. It matters little that the Shakespearean allusion—to *The Two Gentlemen of Verona*, Act I, Scene 1, line 2—should actually read 'Home-keeping youth ...'. But it was this same line that Byron had appropriated, in part, in his jibe against Scott as 'a home-keeping minstrel'.

Shakespeare says that homebred youths have ever homely wits and besides as
you think of something diplomatic the sooner you have a glimpse of foreign
parts [the better]. Now suppose you had any intelligent friend Mr Surtees for
example [probably Matthew Surtees, sometime Fellow of University College,
Oxford] willing to take such a tour with you I should have no objections to your
going over to Paris[,] running as far as the verge of Switzerland then descending
the Rhine and returning by Brussells [*sic*] & Holland.

But there was, however, an alternative at that particular juncture. Scott was
planning an Irish jaunt—the one that actually came to fruition, and which is
discussed below—and Charles might well join in that. On the other hand, he
might take the opportunity of making a northern Scottish tour and thus 'see
something of [his] own country'. So the choices might be either 'to scour the
Highlands or to storm Walter in his camp at Dublin'. Scott conveys the distinct
impression that a man should not travel abroad until he knew properly his
native land. 'Perhaps this may do as well as the foreign trip & next year you
will have studied the french & german a little in order that you may make
your journey conveniently & usefully.'[29]

Scott, who himself had never been near Germany, also played the would-be
elder statesman of travel when corresponding with Lord Montagu (guardian
to the young 5th Duke of Buccleuch) about *that* young man's European
excursion.

I rejoice to hear that the Duke has made a successful debut. Nothing encourages
youth so much as the sense that they can succeed and I know my young friend will
feel the delight of acquiring for himself those accomplishments over which fortune
has no power but which must be won by industry & intelligence and may then be
worn as honorable trophies … If he had diverted to Weimar I should have wished
to give him a letter to Goethe one of the most extraordinary men of his age …[30]

When Charles Scott was actually travelling in Europe in 1828 with a scheme
to 'see well Holland, the Rhine up to Heidelberg, and Belgium', Sir Walter had
played the part, to the letter, of a disapproving parent of a European tourist:
funds were denied the young man to go any further, or for any longer a time,
and cynicism was directed in full measure at his plans. Why, it was almost as
if the elder Scott actually had personal experience of such matters and such
territories! In fact, of course, he was dependent upon mere reading. He relied
upon works such that by Charles Tennant, with its evocative narrative of a
magical, autumnal progress up the Rhine, followed by a freezing winter's
active scrambling among the Alps.[31]

But sometimes so limited was Scott's interest in the 'foreign' that he did
not even trouble to acquire books which one might imagine to have held

some appeal. For instance, James Robinson Planché—antiquary, historical costume authority, herald, playwright and theatrical producer—published a handsome volume of his own poetic compositions entitled *Lays and Legends of the Rhine*. Illustrated with views 'from sketches made on the spot in 1825' lithographed by the great Louis Haghe, and with accompanying musical scores by Jeremy R. Bishop, the book was published in or after 1827, and it was actually dedicated to Scott. Certainly, Planché seems to have neglected to present a copy to the dedicatee; but the dedicatee did not then make good the omission by purchasing in support of the author.[32]

This was the advice and instruction Charles Scott received from his father:

> Going over less space and seeing better what you do so is the better plan & for languages you will get little good french and worse German on the road. As for the Swiss German it is the worst possible and the Alps which are legitimate objects of curiosity will be found where they now are when you have leisure to go to seek them. The love of travelling far is very natural and proper but the power of travelling to any useful purpose is dependent on the degree in which you possess the language.

Lockhart, with his own experience of Germany to support his view, reckoned that the more limited plan constituted as extensive a tour as his young brother-in-law should make with the 'time & purse' available, and that it would be sufficient to 'convey him through to advantage.'[33]

6

Irish Interlude:
a 'Grand Tour' in Microcosm

Walter Scott had long hoped to visit Ireland. As mentioned briefly above (Chapter 3), he first conjured up the notion in 1808. This was just when he was also musing about going to Portugal and Spain; and for a while, indeed, he surrendered to a sort of double-dreaming. To indulge himself thus, in mind and on paper, and at one and the same time, about both Iberia and Ireland, allowed him also the easy option of taking *neither* travelling course. That was exactly what he did.

To have visited Ireland in 1808 would not exactly have been going 'abroad'. 'Overseas', perhaps; but still across a narrow sea within the territorial limits of the relatively new United Kingdom of Great Britain and Ireland. Nevertheless, Scott's actual Irish visit of 1825 has direct relevance to his wider 'foreign' travelling notions, aspirations and ideals.

In the course of a period of ten years from 1808 Scott had frequently touted the prospect of a visit to what he regularly called 'Green Erin'. As he confided to Lady Abercorn and Lady Louisa Stuart, and as he confirmed also to John Morritt, his motivation was to give topographical substance to a literary quest.[1] He wanted to visit localities associated with Jonathan Swift, sometime Dean of St Patrick's, Dublin, and to immerse himself in the intellectual world of Ireland in which Swift had worked. In a way, this wish was akin to that of so many scholarly or sensitive Grand Tourists: men who, in Italy, sought out evocative landscapes of literary association in order to put topographical flesh on the bones of literature previously studied in the classroom or library. The countryside of Horace or Virgil, the townscapes of Martial or Juvenal, the villa-world of Pliny the Younger—all as revealed in actual or imagined locations—were visited, and then described in travel journals, letters home, or retrospective memoirs. In Act V, Scene I of *A Midsummer Night's Dream*, Theseus surely spoke for all to whom the literary association of the past remained vivid:

> ... the poet's pen
> Turns them to shapes and gives to airy nothing
> A local habitation and a name.

Scott, however, demonstrated his ambivalence about travelling to Ireland just as he had to Iberia. Within weeks of his conceiving the idea, the likely Irish visit was aborted. Postponement was the predominant tendency in nearly all Scott's peregrinatory planning. Lady Abercorn was the recipient of the tell-tale words 'next year', albeit modified by Scott's assurance that he had 'very serious thoughts' of making the trip—some day.[2] To a clerical correspondent in Leixlip, County Kildare, Scott also expressed the hope that 'if it please God to give me life and health next year I hope to profit by personal solicitation [of the Irish literati on Swiftian matters]'.[3] To the actress Sarah Smith, herself of Irish parentage, he confessed, a year later still, that he would indeed like 'one day' to visit Killarney; but it would be research on Swift that would be his main motivation for crossing the Irish Sea.[4] An even greater note of doubt and vacillation had set in by the time Scott wrote to Richard Lovell Edgeworth at his seat in County Longford: '... should I ever visit Ireland ...', was the refrain in the summer of 1811, whereas other correspondents in Ireland had been led to believe that they might see him in the spring of 1812.[5] Maria Edgeworth was told in February 1815 that he might come that summer.[6] She would be disappointed; and indeed she would have to wait another decade after that before his carriage, at long last, rolled up to the gates of Edgeworthstown.

The notion of an Irish visit was rekindled in 1825, and the journey was actually made that summer. This trip is of significant interest in any consideration of Walter Scott's 'Grand Touring' propensities. So much of his thirty-six days in Ireland encompasses, in microcosm, the sensation of 'foreign' travel that had customarily been enjoyed by British participants in the traditional Grand Tour. Paradoxical as it may at first seem, this 'home' journey finds its place in the wider story of Scott's travelling. The visit to Ireland in 1825 was a sort of hybrid. It afforded Scott an experience at once both 'domestic' and 'foreign', a reduction of the traditional Grand Tour and a rehearsal, on a miniature stage, of the more recognisably authentic and properly 'Continental' adventure perhaps yet to come.

Swiftian studies apart, the principal motive was to visit his recently-married son Walter, then a captain in garrison at Dublin. As such, it was to be an informal expedition for a few members of the family: Scott's younger daughter Anne and his son-in-law John Lockhart made up the party that left Scotland. (It was to be augmented by Walter, and by others from time to time, when actually on tour in Ireland.) Lockhart, Scott unashamedly confessed, was to be on hand to 'save me all the plagues incident to travelling by acting as what gentlemen call *Boots*'.[7] By this Scott meant, jocularly, a servant at an hotel who, literally, cleaned the boots; but he was also, in all probability, thinking of the contemporary term for the youngest officer in a regiment, or for a junior member of a club, and so on. Lockhart was, in fact, to act as *cicerone*, or *valet de place*, for his father-in-law on the Irish jaunt.

At one time Scott had hoped to attract to the expedition that highly experienced European traveller John Morritt, to whom Scott had written: 'Why should you not toss up your hat for a trip to Dublin … you like travelling and never saw Patt [Patrick, or Paddy] in his own green island. Pray think of this…'.[8] But family purposes were linked also with those of straightforward tourism and sight-seeing. To take a 'peep at Killarney', and as many other sights as possible, was always the intention.

And, Scott being who he was, there was inevitably likely to be a major element of public exposure. Indeed the jaunt assumed the character of a quasi-royal progress, as Scott was honoured and fêted wherever he went. The element of 'lion-hunting' was strong. This is made abundantly and amusingly clear in letters to particular friends. There is much humour shown on the subject of lions and 'lion-lovers' in a letter to Maria Edgeworth, in which Scott describes himself and his temperament in 'leonine' terms.[9] Similarly, writing to Lady Louisa Stuart about the forthcoming trip, he categorised himself as 'an often-hunted and experienced lion' on the point of venturing to Dublin, where, he was told, 'the lion-hunters are already preparing stake and net.'[10]

Letters written prior to the visit carry the suggestion that the forthcoming jaunt might in some sense stand in for the longer Continental European journey that Scott had so often contemplated, but from which he had always shied away. Maybe he sensed, inwardly, that he was now unlikely ever to be able to make a serious European journey: age and ill-health were increasing, and the grip of literary work closed ever more tightly upon him. The experiences and sensations Scott might have had in Europe at large, or more specifically in Italy, might in some measure be replicated in Dublin, and in the Irish countryside. Indeed, in surprisingly large measure, this was very much the case: hence the value of considering here the Irish tour of 1825. Two letters to his two great aristocratic female confidantes are especially redolent of a wider meaning in his decision to go to Ireland, and his wish to make as much as possible of the opportunity afforded by travelling there. To Lady Abercorn he mused thus of how he would like to see the scenery of County Wicklow, and the lakes of Killarney:

Time has been that I should have had other & yet more interesting objects to visit but Time steals friends & objects of interest & we must be thankful that it leaves friendships worth enjoying & power of taking the part in them which they deserve.[11]

And to Lady Louisa Stuart he confessed:

> ... but I am not now as I was forty years since convinced that in changing
> countries I shall find much that is new—I neither expect to kill myself laughing
> at Pats jests and blunders nor to be beat on the head with Pats Shilella nor to
> jump out of the boat and drown myself with sheer delight as my road book says
> folks are apt to do at the Lake of Killarney.[12]

There speaks the voice of a world-weary man, for whom travelling—once to
be regarded as a blessing—might now have become more of an expected duty,
and an only partly-profitable pleasure.

Unlike his previous 'lighthouse voyage' in 1814 and his crossing to north-
west Europe in 1815, the journey to Ireland in 1825 was accomplished by
steamship. This new method of locomotion was by then well established;
and although he might jocosely call the vessels 'steam kettles', Scott had been
smitten with a form of transport that was going to dominate the very last stage
of the Grand Tour tradition.[13] Writing from Edinburgh to Lord Montagu in
1821, with a visit to London in mind—the occasion was nothing less than the
coronation of George IV—he explained:

> I have been on board the Steam Ship and am so delighted with it that I think I
> shall put myself aboard for the coronation. It runs at nine knots an hour (me ipso
> teste) against wind and tide, with a deck as long as a frigates to walk upon and to
> sleep on also if you like as I have always preferd a cloak and a mattress to these
> crouded cabbins. This reconciles the speed & certainty of the mail coach with
> the ease & convenience of being on Shipboard. So I really think I will run up to
> see the grandee show & run down again. I scorn to mention oeconomy, though
> the expence is not one-fifth & that is something in hard times especially to me
> who to chuse would always rather travel in a public conveyance than with my
> domestics [i.e. his servant's] good Company in a po-chay.[14]

Although he might write to an intimate somewhat dismissively and
patronisingly of being now 'in Pat-land', the 'Grand Touring' spirit equally,
and concurrently, began to hold him in thrall. 'Dublin is splendid beyond my
utmost expectations. I can go round its walls and number its palaces until
I am grilled almost into a fever'.[15] He might have been writing of a visit to
Rome. Even the heat that July was Mediterranean. As he told Morritt, he had
been 'sweltering under the hottest weather I ever experienced for the sake of
seeing sights [is] of itself as you know the most feverish occupation in the
world.'[16] Throughout the duration of the Irish visit, and for weeks afterwards,
the letters of Scott and Lockhart give a picture of an episode uncannily
akin to that of a southern European tour. So many vignettes of the Scott

party's adventures reflect elements of that wider and more exotic travelling experience.

There were 'obstinate postilions and impudent beggars', just as these categories of humanity were to be encountered on the roads of the Grand Tour. Those dusty roads left them (as Scott termed it) 'pie-poudreux'. There was the occasional frisson of danger as they passed through localities notorious for a disaffected populace, mail-coach robbery, and the occasional cut-throat murder. Everywhere they noticed heavily-armed paramilitary mounted police: these characters put Scott in mind of French 'Gensdarmerie' [*sic*], both in their weaponry and their omnipresence in the landscape. In the occasional scares of possible violence against them, Scott and his party found it necessary to travel well-armed and prepared to show their pistols: 'once or twice par precaution we slept outside the ladies rooms as the stags lie always on the outside of the herd of doe.'[17] Lockhart wrote, rather contemptuously, of the local peasantry, and of the beggars so frequently in attendance on their coach, as 'swarms of vermin'.[18] 'Pat' was thus made to seem well-nigh Neapolitan; the visiting traveller's disapproval, and his suspicion of an almost alien race, was indeed similar.

Fine natural scenery was encountered, giving Scott almost as much pleasure as he derived from the landscape of Scotland. He scrambled up a sheer rock face overhanging the lake, and in peril of a drop of many feet to the water, in order to gain access to the cave called the Bed of St Kevin at Glendalough, County Wicklow. There he 'perched like a solan goose'. Lockhart maintained that his father-in-law, who crawled along the precipice to reach his goal, was 'the first lame man that ever tried it.' He was not deterred from such schoolboy feats even by the knowledge that the historian Henry Hallam had recently broken his thigh in similar scrambling circumstances at Killarney. As young Grand Tourists had long done, so the ageing Scott took risks in order to see sights, or for the sheer exhilaration of danger. The party escaped with their lives when a road-blasting operation was disgracefully and dangerously mis-timed, and they and their carriage were very nearly caught in the detonation of the explosive charge.[19]

Many are the records of British travellers on tour in Italy—or indeed British soldiers serving in the Peninsula—looking in ways half-pitying and half-lascivious at nubile novices and pretty nuns confined behind convent grilles. Patrick Brydone had captured the dichotomy when he wrote of 'the soft melancholy' on the countenances of girls otherwise 'extremely handsome' and characterised by 'sprightliness', and noted that nothing could 'produce half so strong an effect, as the modest and simple attire of a pretty young nun, placed behind a double iron grate', adding cryptically that to go again to this convent in Messina 'might prove dangerous'.[20] Thomas Rowlandson's 'Pastime in Portugal: visit to the Nunnerys' (1811) catches the idea well in terms of visual satire. In Ireland the Scott party saw nuns in strict seclusion, and Sir Walter noted how they read their breviaries with one eye and looked at the lookers-on with the other. The returned gaze of the tourist was, in Scott and Lockhart, certainly confined to the curiosity and pity of the spectacle, although Captain Walter Scott, who before and after his marriage had an eye for the ladies, may perhaps have inclined to the salacious. All witnessed at first hand the 'bigotry of the Catholic religion', just as any traveller in southern Europe did.[21] But the physical remains of Catholicism afforded Scott, the antiquary, infinite pleasure in exploring the ruins of churches and abbeys. One evening, at Cashel, County Tipperary, he was so entranced by the ecclesiastical buildings in their splendid setting that he requested dinner not to be on the table until 'after dusk should have rendered it useless to linger longer among the ruins.'[22] He was concerned that the ruins of the seven churches in Glendalough would 'not stand long unless measures are taken to preserve them.'[23] So might any antiquary be moved by the plight of neglected and abused ancient ruins in Italy or Greece.

Scott spent lavishly on books in Dublin and Cork, largely works on Irish history and antiquities. There were visits to the private collection of antiquities assembled by Dr Tuke, and Scott showed special interest in ancient Irish armour and weapons in the museum of the Royal Dublin Society.[24] Grand Tourists would have pursued similar antiquarian activities in the course of French or Italian travels, buying books as records of what they had seen in museums and cabinets of curiosities, or in many a *wunderkammer* in a German *schloss*. Secular buildings were just as appealing, if not more so, than ecclesiastical ruins. As Francis Mahony, the Irish humourist and stalwart of *Fraser's Magazine* (who used the pseudonym of 'Father Prout') wrote retrospectively of Scott's visit to Blarney Castle, 'No token of ancient days escapes his eagle glance, no venerable memorial of former times his observant scrutiny … He shall fix his antiquarian eye and rivet his wondering gaze …'. And so indeed Scott did, and was drawn doing so by the young Daniel Maclise.[25]

A rather different visual record of Scott's visit survives in a splendid and very rare cartoon published in July 1825. Drawn by Isaac Robert Cruikshank, elder brother of the greater and better-known George Cruikshank, this is entitled 'The Great Unknown Lately Discovered in Ireland'. Scott had chosen to conceal his identity as author of *Waverley* and its many successors; but the fact that he was the writer was an open secret. Only in 1827 did he publicly admit authorship of the novels. Until then, Scott had employed a series of aliases, leading to his being regarded as 'The Great Unknown'. In this caricature, his kilted figure, standing before the buildings of Trinity College, Dublin, mocks the tartan extravaganza he himself had orchestrated for the visit of King George IV to Edinburgh in 1822. The pile of his own books on his blue-bonneted head makes it clear that he is anything but Unknown. His elder son, the Hussar officer, holds his father's right hand, while, to his left, Irish locals look up at the wonder come among them. The 'speech bubbles' are worth transcribing.

Walter the younger: Our Colonel says you should have made a <u>poet</u> of me instead of a souldier[,] father

Scott: Ner mind what they say bearn [*sic*: i.e. 'bairn' or 'child']. Come along Watty and let us speer [see] a the curiosities o the auld celtic Island. I'll make a poem on it to a certainty.

Irish urchin: Who is dat[,] daddy[?]

Irishwoman: And sure Paddy is this the man they call the <u>great unknown</u>? What a power of books he has, but it would be decent if he put on a pair of breeches.

Paddy the peasant: Don't touch him Judy for the life of you, he's a great man from Scotland.

Irishman of a slightly better and more sophisticated stratum of society: Och botheration.

Some recalled the moment of Scott's jaunt ever after. For them he was the Great Remembered. Thomas Babington Macaulay, on a visit to Killarney in August 1849, recorded a whimsical episode in his diary. Having ridden a pony twelve miles to the head of the Upper Lake, he

> met the boat which had been sent forward with four rowers. One of the boatmen gloried in having rowed Sir Walter Scott and Miss Edgeworth, twenty-four years ago. It was, he said, some compensation to him for having missed a hanging which took place that very day.[26]

Narrating this phase of Scott's life, Lockhart resorted to the idiom of the Grand Tour. The Scott party had visited the 'classical resorts' of County Wicklow; and 'in the course of our movements we saw many castles, churches, and ruins of all sorts—with more than enough of mountain, wood, lake, and river, to have made any similar progress in any other part of Europe, truly delightful in all respects.' Only the extreme contrast between the poverty of the peasantry and the plenty of the gentry 'would have been sufficient to poison those landscapes, had nature dressed them out in the verdure of Arcadia, and art embellished them with all the temples and palaces of Old Rome and Athens.'[27]

7

Painting Scenery in Words; or, Travels in the Library

There were moments in the fifteen years between 1816 and 1831 when it seemed possible that Scott might still venture on a substantial European tour. James Skene recalled how his old friend 'had long wanted to make a Continental tour of some length, in which I had engaged to accompany him—but circumstances prevented its accomplishment at this time.'[1] For this failure Skene advanced two telling and interconnected reasons: first, Scott's commitment to literature; and, second, his commitment to the development of Abbotsford—the latter being (as I have observed elsewhere) dependent upon the success of the first.[2] Scott himself, if pressed on the point, would doubtless have failed to advance any better excuses for his on-off relationship with foreign travel. Skene expanded on these reasons by explaining that it had been Scott's wish to earn as much by his pen as he could, for the benefit of his family.[3] It is understandable that, in these circumstances to which Skene alluded, the claims of travel abroad lost out to other priorities. Nobody actually demanded that Scott travel abroad. Everyone *did* demand that he kept writing books that they wanted to read. Scott, for his part, needed to keep working on those books to make the money he required to fund his compulsion to buy more land and to enlarge Abbotsford and, later, also to raise money to pay the debt that overshadowed his life after 1825.

In 1820 Skene went to France once more, to Aix-en-Provence, largely but not exclusively on account of his wife's health. 'It is a sad thing', Scott wrote in commiseration,

> that you are obliged to begin your rambles again, but prevention is easier than
> cure ... I must comfort myself by thinking that you are amused both of you ...
> If I take the Continent, which I should wish greatly, I will not fail to direct my
> course so as to insure our meeting, for you will scarce choose a nook in the
> Continent where I will not poke you out.'[4]

But there would be no European excursion for Scott that year, or for the next half-decade.

Archibald Constable had just given him a copy of the newly published *Travels in Italy, Greece and the Ionian Islands* by Hugh William Williams.[5] Williams was one of the few artists whom Scott admired, and his book was a good one. There was a hope that Scott would review it, but he does not appear to have done so. This may suggest a lack of compelling interest in the subject. But if so, it is worth mentioning that in the decade after 1820 Scott acquired a number of significant works on European travel. An early one was James Hakewill's influential *A Picturesque Tour in Italy*, published by John Murray that year, and comprising a series of fine illustrations by leading artists accompanied by supporting letterpress description of the scenes. Scott was thus in a position to know what contemporaries wanted to see, especially in Italy; and when he himself did at last pursue parts at least of the old Grand Tour itinerary he was aware of what he was likely to encounter and what to expect in, for example, the urban chaos of Naples.

This said, however, it should also be pointed out that Scott lacked many basic works relating to Grand Tour travel: for example, he owned neither Richard Lassels's classic *Voyage of Italy* (1670) nor Maximilien Misson's long-standard *New Voyage to Italy* (1695); neither did he have Addison's *Remarks on Several Parts of Italy* (1705) nor Thomas Nugent's *The Grand Tour* (first edition 1749). These, of course, were works that had informed the taste, judgement and itineraries of a 'classical' generation of travellers. The 'romantic' tourist had other priorities. Certainly he owned Smollett's *Travels in France and Italy* (in a collected edition of Smollett's miscellaneous works), which would have given him a rather unflattering picture of the Grand Tour *loci classici* and of the character, habits and outlook of those British travellers who frequented these scenes, for Smollett had (as a modern critic suggests) undermined much of the status and ethos of the Grand Tour.[6] *A Tour through Sicily and Malta* (1773) by Scott's fellow-Borderer Patrick Brydone was in his library and would be an inspiration to him in 1831. (In London before his departure for the Mediterranean, and looking for a book to read again in advance of his trip, he talked of 'old Brydone—still as good a companion as any'.)[7] But it is surprising to find that he did not possess Dr John Moore's much-admired *View of Society and Manners in Italy* (1781) or John Chetwode Eustace's *A Classical Tour through Italy* (revised, four-volume edition, 1817) which was perhaps the most heavily relied-upon, 'standard' guide for Scott's generation of post-Napoleonic War travellers, and which was one of the small handful or works which established 'a bedrock of continuity with the eighteenth century' in terms of experience and aesthetics.[8]

Byron's *Childe Harold's Pilgrimage. Canto IV*, with its powerful evocation of Italy, made its mark upon Scott just as it did on all readers of his generation.

Scott also reviewed it (as he had done the Third Canto) in *The Quarterly Review*. Through Byron's lines—which he quoted liberally—he came to 'know' what he he called a 'land of existing beauty and heroic memory'. Modern Rome, a city cruelly tossed by the tides of recent history and now adrift in the new post-Napoleonic Europe, was described by Scott as

> first empress of the bodies, then the souls, of all the civilised world, now owing its political and, perhaps, even its religious existence to the half contemptuous pity of those nations whom she formerly held in thraldom.

Most interestingly, in his *Quarterly Review* article, Scott openly declared his wish to see a united Italy. Such a political move would not, however, change the essence of a land decribed by Byron thus, and quoted admiringly by Scott:

> Thou art the garden of the world in which
> Thy very weeds are beautiful, thy waste
> More rich than other climes' fertility;
> Thy wreck a glory, and thy ruin graced
> With an immaculate charm, which can not be defaced.[9]

Mention will be made below of another highly influential poetical evocation, namely Samuel Rogers's *Italy*. To these works by Byron and Rogers, Maura O'Connor has added a third: Germaine de Staël's novel *Corinne; or, Italy*. 'All three became key Romantic lenses through which English travelers, travel writers, and artists, as well as their audience back home, came to see and understand Italy…'.[10] In Scott's case, however, Madame de Staël can be left out of account, even though the male hero of the novel is a Scottish aristocrat; also regardless of the fact that Oswald, Lord Nelvil, was said to have gone to Italy to escape 'some cruel attending circumstances' at home—very much as Scott himself would ultimately do. In 1813 Scott told Joanna Baillie that he had tired of some of Madame de Staël's works and imagined that he might also well tire of her, if and when she came to Edinburgh, where she was soon expected to appear. Writing to John Morritt he referred to her, playfully, as 'Corinne'.[11]

In June 1821, travellers to the Continent with a penchant for Scott's works might have been both satisfied and amused to take cross-Channel passage in the new paddle steamer *Rob Roy*, which actually provided the first official means of crossing from Dover to Calais.[12] Some travellers from Britain saw parts of Europe through Scott's eyes, or at least through his novels. Maria Graham (née Dundas), for example, brought *Waverley* to mind when seeking a comparison for the *banditti* of the Apennines in her own day: 'it is scarcely "sixty years since," [that is the subtitle of the novel] the Caterans of the

of Sir W. Scott's Novels.'[22] This island is by no means commonly mentioned in the travel literature. Jane Waldie (later Watts), sister of Charlotte, did actually refer to it in her *Sketches Descriptive of Italy*, and did so as the 'little rocky island of Revigliano [sic], crowned with a tower'; but despite her family's acquaintance with Scott, his name and his genius for topographical evocation appears not to have occurred to her.[23] Henry Matthews confided to readers of his *Diary of an Invalid* that one had to tour the Colosseum by the light of the moon, as most visitors to Rome indeed did, just as the artists sketched it in those conditions. But Matthews went further, suggesting that 'To see it aright, as the Poet of the North tells us of the fair Melrose, one must "Go visit it by the pale moonlight"'. Matthews then deflates the amateur of Scott, however, by admitting that only Byron could capture fully the awful grandeur and 'the scene of romantic sublimity.'[24] Byron had beaten Scott yet again.

Something of Scott's standing would be restored in his admirers' eyes if they noted the comment of Lord Normanby in his *The English in Italy* on the great sculptor Canova. Normanby specifically drew a parallel with Scott when referring to Canova's simplicity of soul and to his amiability.[25] No wonder Scott rated Normanby's work (as he put it) 'a clever book', and something to cheer and stimulate him at a moment on 9 February 1826 when otherwise he had felt lazy and unable to write, and had surrendered to a rather languorous Italian mood of '*far niente*'.[26]

A fascinating and unusual conspectus of the Grand Tour or, more accurately, of the idea of travel in general, both foreign and domestic, was offered for Scott's pleasure and edification in 1822. The draughtsman and engraver George Tytler presented him with a set of his 'historiated' initial letters: the complete alphabet formed a series of scenes of more or less celebrated 'tourist' locations. Looking over this engraved sheet, Scott will have encountered a few scenes of Scotland and England with which he was, perhaps, familiar either from personal knowledge or (in his accustomed way) from secondary verbal or visual sources. Similarly, he will have found in Tytler's little alphabet-card vignettes—these being later revised with a rather different variety of images when reissued in lithographed form—a delightful and appetising 'taster' for European destinations he was yet to see. Tytler's alphabet includes several miniature views of specific buildings and locations in Rome and elsewhere in Italy and in Switzerland, but also generic views of characteristic 'Grand Tour' scenes and situations, and images emblematic in one way or another of the experience of travel in Europe. No more intriguing or appealing epitome of the varied delights of the Continental tour can be imagined.[27]

Walter Scott himself had no personal talent in the graphic arts. Apart from a certain appreciation of portraiture, he displayed comparatively little enjoyment of painting and drawing beyond the admiration of a few contemporary landscape artists such as Hugh William ('Grecian') Williams

Highlands of Scotland might have emulated the brigands of Sonnino.'[13] It was Scott's new novel *The Monastery* (1820) that Byron wanted to read in Ravenna, not the latest effusions of John Keats: he was annoyed with John Murray for omitting to send it.[14] In the Ionian Islands three years later it was the Waverley Novels that Byron and his party chose to discuss in their boat when crossing from Ithaca to Cephalonia.[15] John Hughes, son of Scott's friends the Revd Thomas and Mrs Mary Hughes of Uffington, thought that the huge castle of Tarascon, perched on a rocky bluff beside the wide River Rhône in Provence, was like the tower of Westburnflat in *The Black Dwarf*—however improbably so, due to a vast difference in both size and setting.[16] In the Savoy Alps, William Hazlitt thought of Napoleon crossing the mountains and called him 'the Rob Roy of the scene', who alone 'seemed a match for the elements' and able to overcome the forbidding topography.[17] Richard Monckton Milnes found Scott novels being read aloud at meals in the refectory of the reconstituted English College in Rome in 1832.[18]

Reading *Anne of Geierstein* in Italy in 1829, Marianne Talbot (the middle-aged daughter of an English baronet, who spent long periods on the Continent) drew parallels between characters in that novel—and in other Scott novels—and the manners, conversation and circumstances of British people she knew either in Naples or at home. One woman she observed, for example, whose dark and weather-beaten complexion indicated that she had seen rather too much of the southern sun, struck her as just like the gypsy Meg Merrilies in *Guy Mannering*.[19] In an attempt to convey his impressions of Scott's person and manners, Owen Blayney Cole, who both observed and met him repeatedly in Italy in 1832, peppered his narrative of these occasions with quotations from the Waverley novels describing various scenes and characters which he thought reflected the actuality of Sir Walter as a living man of his day. Cole clearly had recourse to these passages in an attempt to arrive at a kind of amalgam of the essence of Scott.[20]

As antidote to the prevailing veneration of Scott by the British in Europe, or indeed by the Europeans whom they encountered, it is worth noting an observation made on Scott's great friend Mrs Marianne Maclean Clephane. (She was the mother of Margaret, Lady Compton—who herself was, by the date in question, Marchioness of Northampton.) Writing of time spent in her company at Villa Muti at Frascati, the Hon. Henry Edward Fox wryly remarked: 'Scotland, Mull, Walter Scott are the only topics upon which Mrs Clephane can bear to speak, and then only to be *narrative*, for on such sacred subjects not only criticism but observation is forbidden.'[21]

Marianne Talbot seems to have regarded Scott as a standard by which to judge other writers as literary depicters of landscape. In 1830 she gave it as her opinion that the tiny islet of Rovigliano, off Torre Annunziata on the Bay of Naples, was, with its miniature castle, 'just like something described in one

Sir Walter Scott in his study at 39 North Castle Street, Edinburgh. The portrait is both posthumous and idealised. It was painted by Sir John Watson Gordon, probably at least ten years after the subject's death. This engraving after the painting, by Robert C. Bell, was published for the Scott centenary in 1871. Scott is portrayed at his desk. His cat, Hinse of Hinsefeldt, and his dog, Camp, lie to either side of their master. On the wall is a targe (shield) with crossed basket-hilted broadswords behind: the traditional weapons of the Highland clansman, and as such redolent of history and heavy with Jacobite symbolism. The suit of armour to Scott's right is emblematic of Scott's interest in the warlike later mediaeval or early-modern past. The map on the wall shows northern Scotland, and it symbolises Scott's obsession with Scottish history and landscape. Indeed, the map seems almost a nimbus round Scott's head: Scott *is* Scotland. There is nothing in the room suggestive of an interest in anything other than Scotland, and certainly nothing alluding to a world beyond its shores. *Author's collection*

A passage in a letter of Walter Scott to Maria Edgeworth, 15 October 1824. Here, in the context of citing the behaviour and attitudes of ignorant British tourists in Italy, he uses the phrase 'Such are the frolics we play in the face of Europe'. *National Library of Scotland (MS 23130, f. 41)*

Opposite above: In this rare etching by Henry William Bunbury, illustrated here in a 'before letters' proof, a traveller is pictured in a chaise or *calèche* drawn by two horses. The leading, near-side horse is ridden by the postillion. These notoriously rough characters acquired almost legendary status in the age of the Grand Tour. French postillions in particular were instantly recognisable by their huge, stiff leather jack-boots, worn to protect the legs. *Author's collection*

Opposite below: Map of the Iberian Peninsula, from John T. Jones, *Account of the War in Spain, Portugal and the South of France from 1808 to 1814 Inclusive* (London, 1821). The map, dated 1813, shows places familiar to Scott in the course of a military campaign which he followed keenly with his own maps and by reading contemporary accounts—even if an early wish actually to visit the seat of the war remained merely a fantasy. *National Library of Scotland*

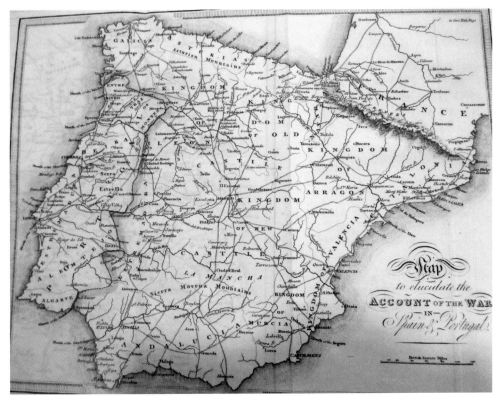

The inn of La Belle Alliance near the battlefield of Waterloo, where Wellington and Blücher were said to have met after the action. (The name of the place was too conveniently appropriate for history *not* to say that the two great allied commanders had greeted each other there.) There also James Simpson and his friends inscribed some lines from Scott's *Vision of Don Roderick* on a wall during their visit some nine days before Scott himself made it to the field. This view by James Rouse was published, along with other views of the field and of the aftermath of battle, in William Mudford's *An Historical Account of the Campaign in the Netherlands in 1815* ... (London, 1817). *Author's collection*

Opposite: Les Anglais à Paris by Carle Vernet, one of many contemporary prints satirising British 'types' whom French caricaturists observed in the streets, cafés, restaurants, museums and shops of Paris after Waterloo. This was the period of Walter Scott's first visit to the city. The couple on the left are representative of the new breed of British tourists in Europe: the sort of characters easily mocked as 'John Bull' and the female of his species. The same male figure, indeed, appears in other Vernet etchings of the period. The effete British Army officer is ridiculed in a way which shows French contempt for the nation which had defeated the invincible *Grande Armée* on 18 June 1815. This image demonstrates the Parisian way of coming to terms with a new order. *Author's collection*

The Grand Gallery of the Louvre, Paris, drawn by Frederick Nash and engraved by J. Mitan and Edward Goodall as one of an attractive series of topographical plates produced for *Picturesque Views of Paris and its Environs* (London, 1820). One detail shows a group of women artists copying paintings and, beyond, further up the gallery, a male painter at his easel being watched by a visitor; the other detail shows an artist on a high stool in front of a very large easel. Visitors to the Louvre, at the time when Scott saw its rooms, were overwhelmed by this vast room in which much of the art of Europe looted by Napoleon was on display. By the time this image was drawn, however, many of the confiscated paintings had been returned, leaving what Scott—no art critic—called 'great French daubs'. *National Library of Scotland*

The Arc du Carrousel, a plate of unattributed workmanship included in *Picturesque Views of Paris*. Upon this triumphal arch, of evidently Roman inspiration, the famous ancient Greek gilt-bronze horses looted from San Marco, Venice, had been set up and harnessed to a grandiloquent gilt chariot symbolic of Napoleonic victory. Some commentators around the time of Scott's visit saw this *quadriga* being removed. *National Library of Scotland*

The gardens of the Palais Royal, Paris, a green and well-watered oasis of calm at the centre of what many described as 'a city within a city'. The original drawing was by Frederick Nash and the engraving was published in *Picturesque Views of Paris*.

The southern façade of the Palais Royal, facing the Louvre, from *Picturesque Views of Paris*. This elegant entrance indicated that beyond might lie architectural splendours, but gave little indication of what Walter Scott called the 'central pit of Acheron' actually concealed within. *National Library of Scotland*

The infamous arcades of the Palais Royal, drawn by Frederick Nash with figures by James Stephanoff for *Picturesque Views*. Both the place and its people look far more respectable and innocent by day than the same location and those who frequented it probably appeared by night. The crowd is demure and well-mannered. The denizens of a later hour were not always so. The names of celebrated shops, cafés and restaurants are inscribed on the roof beams supporting the gallery above. That of the Café des Milles Colonnes is prominent. *National Library of Scotland*

A very different picture of the Galleries of the Palais Royal is offered in this splendid aquatint engraving by George Cruikshank—two details are reproduced here—published to illustrate David Carey's *Life in Paris* (London, 1822). Here the hero, Dick Wildfire, and his friend Squire Jenkins, sample—less or more reluctantly—the delights of the arcades, inhabited as they are by *filles de joie*, sharpers and other characters of the *demi-monde*. The caption explains that the English visitors are seeing 'real life'. *National Library of Scotland*

Details of George Cruikshank's plate of the famous Café des Milles Colonnes in the Palais Royal. Dick Wildfire and Captain O'Shuffleton 'pay their respects' to *La Belle Limonadière*. The portrayal of the man eating an ice brings to mind the passage in James Simpson's reminiscences, published in his *Paris After Waterloo* (1853), where he recalls how he had watched Walter Scott doing the same thing here in 1815. *National Library of Scotland*

Painted by G.S. Newton, R.A.

Engraved by W. Finden.

Very truly yours
Walter Scott

Abbotsford
3 Sept.
1824

FROM THE ORIGINAL PICTURE IN THE POSSESSION OF Mr MURRAY.
PAINTED 1824.

London, Published 1833, by J. Murray, & Sold by C. Tilt, 86, Fleet Street.

Sir Walter Scott was painted at Abbotsford in 1824 by Gilbert Stuart Newton, nephew of the American portrait painter Gilbert Stuart. The best version of the painting is the one commissioned the same year by the London publisher John Murray, who in 1833 issued this engraving after it by William Finden. The print was made more desirable for the public by the addition of a facsimile signature and other details linking it personally to the sitter and to Abbotsford. In the original oil portraits, Scott is portrayed not only as man of letters, with pen and inkwell beside him and books in the background (still evident in this engraving), but also as countryman: Lockhart observed that the belt passing across his chest was for 'carrying the forester's axe round the shoulders'. Scott's obsessive interest in the development of Abbotsford and its woodlands would prevent him from undertaking the wider European travel that he might otherwise, perhaps, have made. *Author's collection*

Also dating from 1824 is this portrait of Scott by Charles Robert Leslie, an artist (like Newton) of American origin. The picture was commissioned by George Ticknor, a man of letters in Boston, Mass. Above the corbel on the wall is a representation of Scott's arms, with the inescutcheon of a baronet of the United Kingdom, and his motto 'Watch Weel'. Though Scott liked Leslie personally, and admired his art, he did not enjoy sitting for this portrait any more than he relished sitting to any artist. A reduced replica of this picture was painted for Archibald Constable, the Edinburgh publisher, who had proposed Leslie as the artist of Ticknor's prime original, and it was this second version that was engraved in the print of 1829 by M. I. Danforth reproduced here. Like many contemporaries, J. G. Lockhart considered this image of his father-in-law 'the best domestic portrait ever done.' *Author's collection*

Above: John Gibson Lockhart, editor of *The Quarterly Review,* captured in a moment of domestic but still literary ease in London by Daniel Maclise for his portrait series 'A Gallery of Illustrious Literary Characters' published in *Fraser's Magazine* in the 1830s. Scott himself was portrayed early in this same series. *Author's collection*

Right: John Gibson Lockhart: an engraved portrait by H. W. Smith after the original painting by Henry William Pickersgill. Lockhart was noted for what Scott termed his 'reserve and a sort of Hidalgo air.' This, and what his father-in law also called his 'handsome exterior and face', may be perceived in this image. *Author's collection*

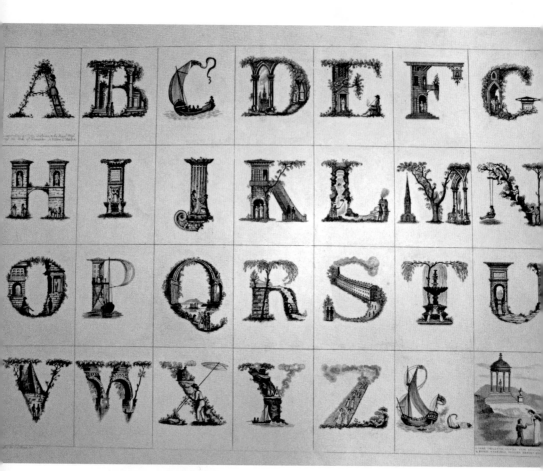

This is the engraved form of the historiated, or illustrated, 'Grand Tour' alphabet by George Tytler, signed and dated 'Romæ 1822'. It is the actual copy which the artist presented to Scott. A slightly later lithographed version is also known, though both are very rare. In this series of alphabet cards, Tytler offered a sort of conspectus or epitome of the world of the Grand Tour, but he also included some images relating to domestic British travel, with both English and Scottish scenes represented.

Opposite page: The letter 'J' represents two Grand Tourists looking at a map against a column shaft which has, perversely, a Doric capital and an inverted Ionic capital as its base! The form of 'V' neatly encloses a vignette of the Pyramid of Caius Cestius adjoining the Protestant Cemetery in Rome. These two come from engraved sets of the letters, though the titles, which vouchsafe that the tourists are (for some unexplained reason) in Spoleto, are featured only in the lithographed set. And from the lithographed set, too, comes the letter 'S'. It illustrates the Bay of Naples: the letter-form starts with smoke from Vesuvius, moves down though shipping in the harbour, and terminates in the *molo* with its lighthouse. *Faculty of Advocates Abbotsford Collection Trust; Author's collection*

Bay of Naples.

Scott's visit to Ireland in 1825, a kind of Grand Tour in microcosm, is mocked in this cartoon by Isaac Robert Cruikshank, elder brother of George Cruikshank. Even though Scott had chosen to conceal his identity as author of *Waverley* and its many successors, the fact that he was the writer was actually an open secret. Only in 1827 did he publicly admit authorship of the novels. Before that time a series of aliases had been employed, leading to Scott being regarded as 'The Great Unknown'. In this caricature, his kilted figure mocks the tartan extravaganza he had orchestrated for the visit of King George IV to Edinburgh in 1822. The pile of his own books on his blue-bonneted head makes it clear that he is anything but Unknown. His elder son, a cavalry officer then serving in Dublin, holds his father's right hand while, to Scott's left, Irish peasants look up at the wonder come among them. *British Museum*

Hotham Island, the volcanic phenomenon which suddenly arose from the Mediterranean in 1831. It had been renamed Graham Island by the time that Sir Walter Scott was taken ashore there on 20 November, and it is by this name that it is better remembered. In his journal, Scott referred to it as the 'Burning island' but noted, perhaps with some regret, that it did not make its 'terrors visible'. It later disappeared beneath the waves. *National Library of Scotland*

These are India proofs of four vignettes by J. M. W. Turner engraved for the splendid 1830 edition of Samuel Rogers's poem *Italy*. Rogers presented a copy to Scott, who called it 'in every respect a bijou'. When Rogers's gift arrived, Scott—whose health was deteriorating—must have thought that leafing through its fine plates would be the nearest he would ever get to actually visiting Italy. One view is a romanticised scene of Hannibal in the Alps, a topic that

had interested some of Scott's old friends and acquaintances, and a landscape that Scott himself had long expressed the desire to see. The other three are: a particularly effective vignette of the Roman Forum, seen through the Arch of Titus and looking towards the back of the Palazzo Senatorio on the Capitol); the Duomo of Florence, seen from Fiesole; and Venice seen across the Bacino, with the Doge's Palace, the Piazzetta, the Campanile and the Basilica of San Marco. *Dr Murray Simpson*

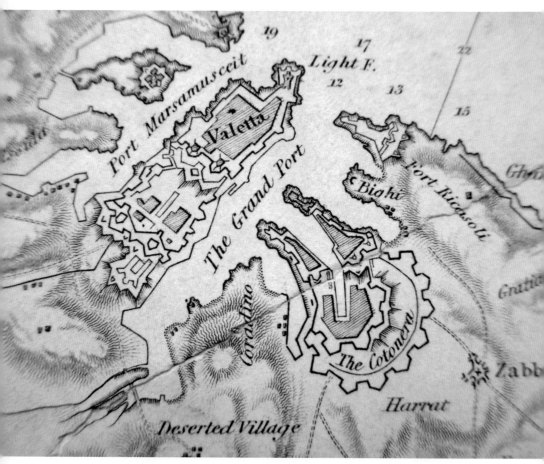

Valletta, the Grand Harbour and environs, a detail from a plan of the Maltese Islands by Captain W. H. Smyth RN, 1823. Scott described Valletta in his journal as 'a splendid town: the sea penetrates it in several places with Creeks formd into harbours surrounded by buildings and these again coverd with fortifications.' After being released from quarantine in Fort Manoel (located on the island north-west of the Valletta peninsula, and shown above it in this image), Scott enjoyed his near three weeks there. *Author's collection*

A plate from James Hakewill's *A Picturesque Tour in Italy* (1820), one of the works that gave Scott a vicarious view of a region that had always been the heartland of the Grand Tour. Drawn by Hakewill himself, and engraved by George Cooke, this image shows Naples from the west, looking from Posillipo down to Mergellina and along the Riviera di Chiaja towards the Castel dell' Ovo, with Vesuvius forming the dramatic backdrop to the scene. Scott took lodgings in Palazzo Caramanico, located in Chiatamone, below the hill of Pizzofalcone, at the centre of this image just to the right of the pole supporting the vine. The general mood of this view, and specifically the luxuriant, sun-ripened fruit so much in evidence, makes one think of Scott's sending greetings from 'the land of mist and snow' to his friend Lady Compton in 'the land of the vine and olive' (*Letters*, V: 90, 26 Feb. 1818). *Author's collection*

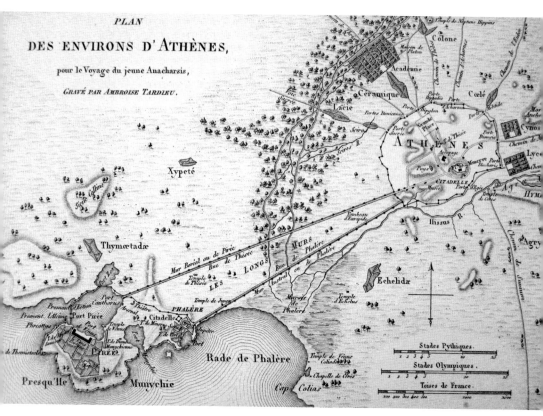

PLAN

DES ENVIRONS D'ATHÈNES,

pour le Voyage du jeune Anacharsis,

GRAVÉ PAR AMBROISE TARDIEU.

While in Naples, Scott toyed with the idea of going on to Greece. Though by no means a classicist, he had shown interest in the remarkable *Voyage du Jeune Anarcharsis en Grèce* by Jean-Jacques Barthélemy: this map of the site of ancient Athens comes from Barthélemy's book. It may have held added significance for Scott due to the contemporary idea of a parallel, both topographical and intellectual, between ancient Athens and modern Edinburgh, 'the Athens of the North'. The similarity of general layout—the ancient Long Walls connecting Athens with its port of Piraeus, even as Leith Walk connected Edinburgh with Leith—will not have been lost on anyone who considered the similarities, physical and cerebral, of the two cities. *Author's collection*

Opposite page: Three plates from Sir William Gell and John Peter Gandy's *Pompeiana: The Topography, Edifices and Ornaments of Pompeii* (1819), and the later *Pompeiana* volume (1832) which allowed Gell's discussion of the site to be expanded by reference to 'the Result of Excavations Since 1819'. Gell was Scott's companion and *cicerone* in Naples and its environs. The views are the Street of Tombs, which provided Scott with his first sight of Pompeii and which so moved him; the Forum; and a general prospect of the site looking back to Mount Vesuvius. The Forum was where Scott and his party lunched al fresco amid the ruins. *Dr Murray Simpson*

During his time in Naples and Rome, Scott was sketched a number of times by local artists. This drawing by Vincenzo Morani is perhaps the best and most true to life. It was made during Scott's visit to the monastery of La Trinità della Cava on 11 March 1832. In the library there Scott was shown some manuscripts and, while he was absorbed in looking at them, he was sketched unaware that his likeness was being drawn. Sir William Gell, who was with Scott that day, considered this sketch superior to another portrait made by the same artist during a later, more formal sitting in Naples. In his memoir, Gell recorded that this first drawing 'represented Sir Walter in his best moment and most natural position, not constrained... he being in fact at that time quite unconscious of the painter's presence.' *The Abbotsford Trust*

Rome had always been the climax of the traditional Grand Tour and even Scott, who disarmingly described himself as 'not being very Classical', was not wholly immune to its spell, saying that he wanted to see it before he died. This view by William Brockedon, a topographical artist whose work Scott admired, is taken from Piazza del Quirinale, in front of the Pope's palace, and it looks across the city to St Peter's and Monte Mario. The obelisk from the Mausoleum of Augustus is flanked by the ancient statues of the so-called 'horse tamers', or 'Castor and Pollux': the actual identity of the sculptural groups has long been disputed. The Quirinal area acquired the name of Monte Cavallo on account of the statues, and Scott, a life-long horseman, may have been attracted to the idea. The *Punchinello* booth at the right reminds us that Rome was inhabited not just by ancient statues but by modern people who liked to be simply entertained. *Author's collection*

Three examples of typical prints of Rome and its monuments produced for the market among late participants in the Grand Tour. The views are drawn and engraved by Antonio Aquaroni, who was active at the time of Scott's visit and whose output was generally of good quality and rather superior to that of some of his contemporaries. One shows the Colosseum and the Arch of Constantine, with the remains of the conical fountain of Meta Sudans visible through the left-hand small arch. Another features the Arch of Titus and the Colosseum from a different viewpoint. The third shows the Pantheon with Piazza della Rotonda in front, which served as the fish market of Rome. The Pantheon still bears the twin bell-towers added by Bernini and called the 'asses ears'; they were removed later in the nineteenth century. The fountain, in the form given to it by Pope Clement XI Albani (who had altered an earlier monument) is one of Rome's most delightful. *Author's collection*

Also working at precisely the time of Scott's visit was Deodato Minelli, who etched, printed and sold his own views of Rome. This one shows the Roman Forum with the surviving columns of the temples of Vespasian, of Saturn and of Castor and Pollux, as well as the isolated Column of Phocas. In the centre background appear the pavilions of the Farnese Gardens on the Palatine Hill, among which Sir William Gell had his little villa where he entertained Scott. *Author's collection*

This attractive lithograph by Godefroy Engelmann, from the series of large plates of Rome published in Paris by Alaux et Lesueur, 1826-28, shows a jolly group of young men, very probably artists, enjoying an *al fresco* drinking party in the Farnese Gardens on the Palatine Hill, close to Sir William's Gell's villa. The huge vaults in the background are those of the Basilica of Maxentius. *Author's collection*

S. P. Q. R.

L'ANNO MDCCCXXXII
VLTIMO DI SVA VITA
QVESTA CASA ABITÓ
L'ILLVSTRE ROMANZIERE SCOZZESE
WALTER SCOTT
DA EDIMBVRGO
MDCCCLXXXII

Commemorative tablet on the wall of Casa Bernini in Via della Mercede, recording Scott's residence in April and May 1832. It was placed there in 1882, fifty years on from his visit. *Photo: Dr Patricia Andrew*

Opposite page: Detail from an uncommon map of Rome by Angelo Uggeri, drawn 1822 and engraved 1826 and thus available at the time of Scott's visit. The heart of the Rome of the Grand Tour is shown. Casa Bernini in Via Mercede, where Scott stayed, is almost exactly at the centre point of this detail; above it are the long opposed but interconnecting triangles of Piazza di Spagna and Piazza Mignanelli, to the right of which, at the top of the distinctive rococo curves of the *scalinata*, is the church of Trinità dei Monti. Four streets north of Via della Mercede is Via Condotti, with the Caffè Greco, long frequented by foreign artists and men of letters. The large building at the right-hand end of Scott's street is the Propaganda Fide; S. Andrea della Fratte is at the opposite right-hand corner. Directly below is the Fontana di Trevi. The long stripe of the Corso is at the left-hand side of the image, with Piazza Colonna clearly visible. Monte Cavallo, and the Quirinal Palace, is at the extreme bottom right. *Author's collection*

The monument to the Stuarts in St Peter's Basilica, by Antonio Canova. It features portrait busts of (left) James Francis Edward Stuart, the 'Old Pretender', or (to the Jacobites) 'James III'; (right) Charles Edward Stuart, Bonnie Prince Charlie, or the 'Young Pretender'; and (centre) his younger brother and last of the line, Cardinal Henry Benedict Stuart, titular Duke of York and ultimately, in Jacobite eyes, 'Henry IX of Great Britain'. Their actual tombs are in the grottos below. *Photo: Dr Patricia Andrew*

Commemorative tablet on the wall of Casa Bernini in Via della Mercede, recording Scott's residence in April and May 1832. It was placed there in 1882, fifty years on from his visit. *Photo: Dr Patricia Andrew*

Opposite page: Detail from an uncommon map of Rome by Angelo Uggeri, drawn 1822 and engraved 1826 and thus available at the time of Scott's visit. The heart of the Rome of the Grand Tour is shown. Casa Bernini in Via Mercede, where Scott stayed, is almost exactly at the centre point of this detail; above it are the long opposed but interconnecting triangles of Piazza di Spagna and Piazza Mignanelli, to the right of which, at the top of the distinctive rococo curves of the *scalinata*, is the church of Trinità dei Monti. Four streets north of Via della Mercede is Via Condotti, with the Caffè Greco, long frequented by foreign artists and men of letters. The large building at the right-hand end of Scott's street is the Propaganda Fide; S. Andrea della Fratte is at the opposite right-hand corner. Directly below is the Fontana di Trevi. The long stripe of the Corso is at the left-hand side of the image, with Piazza Colonna clearly visible. Monte Cavallo, and the Quirinal Palace, is at the extreme bottom right. *Author's collection*

The monument to the Stuarts in St Peter's Basilica, by Antonio Canova. It features portrait busts of (left) James Francis Edward Stuart, the 'Old Pretender', or (to the Jacobites) 'James III'; (right) Charles Edward Stuart, Bonnie Prince Charlie, or the 'Young Pretender'; and (centre) his younger brother and last of the line, Cardinal Henry Benedict Stuart, titular Duke of York and ultimately, in Jacobite eyes, 'Henry IX of Great Britain'. Their actual tombs are in the grottos below. *Photo: Dr Patricia Andrew*

Archibald Philip, 5th Earl of Rosebery, sometime Liberal Prime Minister and eminent man of letters, acquired this manuscript in Naples in 1906. He annotated an envelope to the effect that this 'pathetic relic of Walter Scott' had belonged to Edward Cheney, who himself had known Scott in Rome in 1832. Apart from two short letters, the lines inscribed on this paper are very probably the last Scott ever wrote. The text on the left refers to John Murdo, a mason at Melrose Abbey, for whom there is a commemorative inscription which Scott is recalling. The lines on the right are also connected to Melrose. Thus, as his life neared its end, Scott's thoughts were on a ruined building close to his home at Abbotsford, parts of the decoration of which Melrose had inspired. *The Earl of Rosebery*

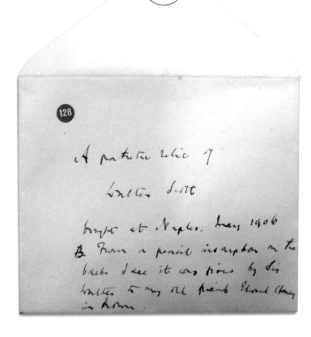

Despite his long interest in German literature and German culture, Walter Scott never succeeded in making a dedicated tour of Germany. His journey home from Italy through parts of Germany and down the Rhine was made hastily, lest ill-health should catch up with him—as indeed it did. Scott's reputation stood high in Germany. One of the finest minor memorials to Scott is this Berlin iron statuette, made as a commemorative piece shortly after his death. This is derived from several *ad vivum* images by British artists, and combines elements from them to form an effective and attractive memorial in its own right. Only a very few of these statuettes are known. *Author's collection*

and John Thomson of Duddingston, both of whom he knew personally as
practitioners in that genre. He also admired the work of a few gentlemen
amateur painters he knew, such as William Scrope, an Englishman who had
come to live near Abbotsford and whose views of Italy—of Tivoli, for instance,
or in Calabria—he remarked upon, and which must have afforded him a
further pleasing interpretation of Italian landscape.[28] Such visual 'translations'
fed back into Scott's writings. It is possible that a picture such as Scrope's of
Tivoli survived in his memory to inform a 'painting in words' of the kind that
occurs in a passage in *Count Robert of Paris*, where a tree-shrouded waterfall
is likened to the numinous spot that was the Sibyl's temple at Tivoli.[29] Scott
was fully aware of the value and attraction of the visual records of travel as
adjuncts to the manuscript or printed records of European voyages by friends
and acquaintances. From Naples in 1832 he would write to his kinswoman
Mrs Scott of Harden of how he had 'envied your management of the pencil
when in Malta, as frequently elsewhere; it is quite a place to be illustrated
…'.[30] In 1816 he had expressed a wish (as noted above) to see publication of
James Skene's illustrated journals.[31] He renewed this plea in 1820 on Skene's
departure for Provence, saying that he hoped Skene would add drawings 'of
whatever memorable may occur in your travels.' Skene's drawings of Aix
would later furnish visual source-material for Scott when working on *Anne
of Geierstein*.[32]

When John Hughes began to issue etchings of Provençal views after his
own sketches, Scott wrote to the artist's mother in terms so complimentary
that an element of personal friendship must be deemed to have swayed Scott's
artistic judgement (just as Hughes himself praised Scott's *Paul's Letters* as an
invaluable guide to Paris). 'It is really a charming quality', Scott effused to Mrs
Hughes, 'to be able to steal a country's beauties in this way for the amusement
of another.' Scott reckoned Hughes's draughtsmanship fully equal to his
powers of literary description.[33] Those verbal, and perhaps visual talents too,
might be turned to Scotland. 'We cannot certainly compare to Switzerland',
wrote Scott in making this proposal, 'yet I have heard people of taste say that
the Scots scenery from being brought nearer to the eye was in some places
fully as imposing though not in fact on the same enormous scale.'[34] In these
words lurks the suggestion that, despite his constant and oft-repeated desire
to see more of the Continent for himself, however sincere and practicable (or
otherwise) this may actually have been, Scotland held much to stir the senses
of writers and artists alike. Caledonia might still provide a passable alternative
to a European tour.

Scott's third-last novel, *Anne of Geierstein* (1829), would have an initial
Swiss setting: the rugged landscape of the Cantons and of the upper Rhine
would be described with an imaginative ease derived from extensive reading
and which belied the author's total lack of personal familiarity with his subject

matter. In July 1828 he was gathering material for the novel, which he began to write the following month. It was published in May 1829. A glimpse of his method is afforded by his reference to his reading of *Switzerland; or a Journal of a Tour and Residence in that Country* by Louis Simond:

> Solitude's a fine thing for work but then you must lie bye like a spider till you collect materials to continue your web. Began Simond's *Switzerland*—clever and intelligent but rather conceited in the manner of an American Frenchman. I hope to knock something out of him though.[35]

By this time Scott had also 'seen' Switzerland in the pages of *Swiss Scenery from Drawings* (1820) by Major James Pattison Cockburn of the Royal Artillery, and had read further of its dramatic topography in Charles Tennant's travelogue, with its vivid narrative of his adventures among 'the Stupendous Scenery of the Alps in the Depth of Winter'.[36] He had also read of Alpine scenery in Charlotte's Eaton's *Continental Adventures*. Here it had been well described topographically, and used imaginatively as a setting for physical and emotional excitement in ways well worthy of his own writing. In the major portion of Eaton's novel devoted to Switzerland and the Alps, a character suffers so many mishaps and perils among the mountains that (as Mary Shelley wittily, if waspishly, observed) a real woman would have grown prematurely grey had she had to cope with all that Mrs Eaton inflicted on her heroine.[37]

William Brockedon's *Illustrations of the Passes of the Alps by which Italy Communicates with France, Switzerland, and Germany* was published too late for Scott to have drawn information and inspiration for *Anne of Geierstein*. Brockedon was a topographical artist of some distinction. To say he had a particular interest in Alpine scenery would be an understatement: he is believed to have crossed the Alps nearly sixty times by some thirty different routes. He presented a copy of his profusely illustrated two-volume work to Scott (this remains at Abbotsford).[38] The recipient declared himself delighted with the view it afforded of the area. Brockedon's plates conveyed 'a distinct picture of so interesting a country as Switzerland, so peculiar in its habits, and its history', which had added 'a valuable chapter to the history of Europe, in which the Alpine regions make so distinguished a figure.'[39] It is significant that Scott had clearly come to regard Switzerland as a destination in itself, due to the inherent interest which the country and its landscape had assumed in his thinking. But he approached it, both physically and metaphorically, as a traveller from the *north*. The title of Brockedon's book, however, really reflects the view of an artist who had trained and worked in Italy, where he had become a member of the Academies of both Rome and Florence: to him the Alpine passes connected *Italy* with northern Europe. Scott, one senses, would have been more comfortable travelling *south* to the Alps, or to their north. He did not have an essentially Italian-centred view of European tourism.

Scott was also fortunate to be able to draw on the first-hand knowledge of others who had travelled in parts of Europe which, though they were germane to his novel-writing, were beyond his personal ken. Thus James Skene supplied topographical details for later parts of *Anne of Geierstein* by making available a journal he had kept while in Provence. In being able to quarry the memories, and harvest the visual records of his friends, Scott was indeed fortunate; and those friends responded generously for a cause they recognised as transcending that of friendship, and almost more as one of wider service to international culture. Skene's precociously early experience of European travel allowed him to retail 'matter of entertainment' to his friend; and Scott found that (in Skene's words) 'The peculiarities of foreign countries, the habits of the people, the striking features of scenery, and, above all, traditions, songs of the people, and legendary tales always supplied an ample and agreeable theme...'. Skene later recalled further that

> I never met with a stronger instance of the uncommon versatility of Sir Walter's genius than he displayed in the facility with which he took up the spirit of a narrative altogether new to him and the characteristics of a country which he had never seen. He had never been either to Switzerland or those parts of ancient Burgundy where the remainder of the scenery of that work [*Anne of Geierstein*] is placed, but he availed himself of the drawings which my collections afforded him, and the knowledge of the country that I was able to give him.[40]

Scott had praised Mrs Radcliffe for the way that her verbal description of scenery had a graphic quality: one series of imagined Italian scenes of highest melodrama he categorised as constituting 'the strongest painting which had been under Mrs Radcliffe's pencil, and are well fitted to be actually embodied on canvas by some great master.'[41] Walter Scott himself was widely acknowledged as what might be described as a 'painter in words'. The artist Charles Robert Leslie maintained that he 'talked of scenery as he wrote of it—like a painter.'[42] Scott's friend George Ellis, in an anonymous review of *The Lady of the Lake*, wrote of Scott's seeing everything 'with a painter's eye ... Whatever he represents is drawn with an accuracy and minuteness of discrimination which we are not accustomed to expect from verbal description...'. His paintings in words were not 'the imperfect sketches of a hurried traveller, but the finished studies of a resident artist.'[43] And Scott himself propounded to the amateur artist Sir James Stuart of Allanbank (who had been born in Rome) his notions of the association between painting and literature:

> To be able to produce either in writing or by pencil an accurate resemblance
> of nature in its grander features ... is a great gift. It is in fact the power of
> translating a chapter of the great book of nature for the benefit of those who
> will not or cannot read the original; sure it is strange to see that thousands enjoy
> the representation of scenes which had they witnessed them with their own eyes
> would neither have excited interest or pleasure.[44]

Scott's criticism of Ann Radcliffe is doubly resonant, for in the eighteenth
century 'pencil' habitually meant 'brush'. By the time Scott wrote these words,
his own novels were already being published in opulent illustrated editions
enhanced by high-quality topographical engravings of the scenery. Countless
artists would in future draw, engrave or paint works interpreting characters
from, and episodes in, his narrative poems and his novels.[45]

Nine years after Scott's death, the intrepid Frances Trollope rode out
from Florence to Vallombrosa, in the remote Tuscan Apennines, inspired to
make her visit by Milton's famous lines—in *Paradise Lost*—on the Abbey's
landscape. Milton, it was generally believed, had been there. (Modern
scholarship has now cast doubt on this. It would certainly have been a most
unusual Grand Tourist's divergence from any standard route in any century.)[46]
Almost certainly Milton composed his verses on Vallombrosa entirely from
his imagination. But Mrs Trollope assumed that he wrote from first-hand
experience. She then cited, as an instance of the power of a writer to capture
natural scenery in words, the shining example of Scott: 'Not even Walter
Scott himself, who to my feeling had the most singular faculty that man ever
possessed of painting scenery in words, could in truth have done it better.'[47]
Frances Trollope's comment may serve to support the notion that Scott's
way of blending historical narration with an appreciation and evocation of
landscape formed part of the more general process by which tourism became
an industry in the Europe of the nineteenth century—in the age after the
Grand Tour and its characteristic aesthetic had worn away to be overtaken
by other priorities in travel. The impulse to go touring was fed first by Scott's
writing. An initial urge to see the Trossachs and the scenery of his poems and,
later, his novels, influenced a more generalised vogue for visiting the Rhine,
the Alps and other picturesque and romantic regions of the Continent.[48]

8

'Methinks
I Will Not Die Quite Happy…'

The notion of going to Italy seems first to have occurred to Scott, as a semi-serious possibility, in 1816. With this proposition, he was at last moving towards acceptance that he, too, should embrace the one essential feature of the traditional, or standard, Grand Tour experience. If matters could be arranged satisfactorily regarding additions being made to the Abbotsford estate, he told Matthew Weld Hartstonge, 'I have serious thought while I have still strong health and active spirits to visit the classical scenes of Italy and perhaps of Greece.'[1]

Similar words were used in sharing his travelling intentions with Joanna Baillie. Abbotsford, however, which always seemed to control Scott as if it had a personality of its own, was making ever more demands on his time and his money. It was not for nothing that he called the place his 'Dalilah'. He could not think of going abroad while he was needed (so he protested to Hartstonge, himself about to go to the Continent) 'to make some arrangements about my little purchases of land … I wish to drain and plant and so forth to put my new territories… into some order…'.[2] An excuse *not* to go aboard? Quite possibly so. He had competent men on hand who knew as well if not better than he how to drain and plant. However, pushing the date forward, March to November of 1817 was the period suggested for the proposed excursion.

To Hartstonge (now returned from Europe) he wrote again:

I am glad your tour turned out interesting and amusing; to see foreign parts gives I think more the feelings of youth to those of an advanced age than anything they can engage [in]. You are too young to use travelling as a stimulus, but my journeyings like Sir Wilful Witwould's have begun on the wrong side of forty and therefore I am more sensible of it …[3]

Scott's cryptic reference was to the character in William Congreve's *The Way of the World*, a man 'minded to see foreign parts', though 'above forty'. Of him, another character (Fainall) says: 'No matter for that; 'tis for the honour of England, that all Europe should know we have blockheads of all ages.'[4] For his part, Scott continued: 'I sometimes think seriously of going to Rome next season—and yet I do not quite like to be so long absent from my own Family...'.[5] So if Scott the landowner, improver and forester could not go, neither could Scott the husband, nor Scott the father.

Were he to go, however, it was most probable that he would do so alone, without his wife—as of course he had done when he went to Paris in 1815: this despite Charlotte's French origins, and the likelihood that she might have been more at home on the Continent than many other British wives. Scott's correspondence in the years 1816, 1817 and 1818 is peppered with a series of proposals for tours which are in turn matched by postponements, for one reason after another, of plans just made. Then there was the idea that he might take his son Walter with him for a jaunt that was tantalisingly ill-defined but might have taken place in 1818. This was after he had told Joanna Baillie in the summer of 1817 that the target of his Continental adventure would be France and Italy, 'if I can make out a long projected tour in those countries. Methinks I will not die quite happy without having seen something of that Rome of which I have read so much.'[6] –

Ladies other than Mrs Scott were quite happy to travel in Europe, and frequently did so with ease and confidence. Scott, by contrast, appears diffident, irresolute and timorous. A recurring feature was his worry about safety, feelings apparently compounded by his incredulity that women might actually be travellers in their own right. Yet he had read the work of Charlotte Waldie (Eaton) on Waterloo, and thus was aware how competent and assured she was; later perusal of her book on Rome only confirmed this fact. But it still seemed strange to him that unescorted women might contemplate travelling at all, let alone in regions where he himself had not set a timid foot. After his own modest 'scamper to the Continent' in 1815 he sometimes liked to pose as an authority on the dangers and difficulties of travel, and of the mechanics of the process. In telling Miss Anna Jane Clephane of Carslogie and Torloisk how dangerous parts of the Continent were, and how she must take care of herself and preferably have male escorts to hand, he was perhaps saying more about his own worries than displaying real concern for the fragile women of his acquaintance.

> ... when I was on the continent I found more than once that a pair of loaded pistols in my pocket were necessary to secure both respect and security. It may doubtless be better now; but the English are always unpopular on the continent, and the innkeepers extremely encroaching and insolent when they see occasion and the speedy legal redress of the next Justice of the Peace altogether out of the question.—And I believe the banditti are very troublesome just now in Italy

although it applies rather to the road between Rome and Naples… Do ponder all this well. If you were men in your persons as you are in your sense and spirit I would wish you to go by all means. As it is, I sincerely hope you will have some proper male companion.[7]

In the Preface to her *Sketches Descriptive of Italy*, Jane (the younger of the two feisty Waldie sisters) made light of travel.[8] It was now perfectly easy, she asserted, to get to Rome. The journey there presented few problems. Was she perhaps making a slight dig at Scott, and his cautious kind, when she wrote of how, once the Continent was open again to the British, 'our idlers, artists, and men of letters contented themselves with a visit to Paris'—as Scott, of course, had done? But then they wanted to see more, and further—as Scott was constantly talking of doing. Her sister Charlotte, not content with putting the superannuated old Roman *ciceroni* in their place, also quite clearly wanted to give old Rome itself a good clean. The Pantheon was pre-eminently wonderful. 'Its beauty is of that sort, which, while the fabric stands, time has no power to destroy … Who does not feel an elevation of soul in this ancient temple of the gods?' But its setting and surroundings were unspeakably disgusting and squalid. 'Nothing resembling such a hole as this could exist in England.' Its splendour 'is as honourable to the ancient Romans as its filth is disgraceful to the moderns.' The Protestant Miss Waldie mused on how satisfactory it would be if she 'might be allowed to come in with a heretical mop'—the converted structure, originally dedicated to all the ancient gods, was, of course (as still it remains), a consecrated Catholic church—'I would have a pleasure in scouring it at my own expense, and almost with my own hands…'.[9]

The Waldie sisters stood for a type of formidable, no-nonsense 'Englishwoman' in Italy. So, in a different way, Margaret Maclean Clephane, Lady Compton, represented that kind of traveller who was respectful of, and completely acceptable to, local society. (Local society, of course, recognised little difference between visitors who were in fact Scots by birth or ancestry, and those who were English. 'Englishman' or 'Englishwoman' was a simple and serviceable linguistic term.) Walter Scott understood that Lady Compton was known as

one of the few English ladies now in Italy whose acquirements, conduct, and mode of managing her time induced that part of foreign society whose approbation is valuable to consider with high respect and esteem. This, I think, is very likely, for whatever folks say of foreigners, those of good education and high rank have a most supreme contempt for the frivolous, dissipated, empty, gad-about manners of many of our modern belles …[10]

Scott's reading in the 1820s would have told him of some very different British people abroad, whose company he might not have relished when he did actually venture to Rome. Henry Matthews, the professional invalid, lamented the fact that 'The English swarm everywhere'. Rome had become like a fashionable 'watering-place'. English ladies used St Peter's as a promenade or 'favourite lounge', where they 'jostle[d] the Catholics out of their own chapel.'[11] Anna Jameson went further, writing thus of the English on the loose in the basilica:

> ... every Sunday [they] convert St Peter's into a kind of Hyde Park, where they promenade arm in arm, shew off their finery, laugh, and talk aloud ... I was struck with a feeling of disgust; and shocked to see this most glorious temple of the Deity metamorphosed into a mere theatre ... This is not the first time that the behaviour of the English has created offence, in spite of ... the allowances which are made for our national character.[12]

Comments such as these must have made Scott more wary than ever of the disadvantages of 'herding with his country-men', and may well have gone a substantial way to confirming his preferences for the domestic tourism of the 'home-keeping minstrel'.

*   *   *   *   *

What did Scott know, or think, of Rome and the world of Roman antiquity? As a sickly child, he had spent a year (1775-1776) in Bath, the ancient Aquae Sulis, to take the waters and bathe in the hot springs of the Romans. There he will have first come face-to-face with Roman architecture and the remains of the classical past of Britain. At the High School of Edinburgh, he had been a pupil of Dr Alexander Adam, the distinguished classical scholar and author of the celebrated *Roman Antiquities*. A great influence at Edinburgh University had been Professor Adam Ferguson, an historian of the Roman republic and himself a traveller to Italy only in old age.

Another early encounter with Roman remains had been an expedition in 1792 to see Hadrian's Wall in the north of England, an excursion which gave him 'a stupendous idea of the perseverance of its founders'. Like other antiquaries, he was struck by the sight of Roman inscriptions built into more recent structures. This had been a trip (as he told William Clerk, grandson of Scotland's most eminent antiquary of his day, Sir John Clerk of Penicuik) to delight 'the very cockles of your heart'.[13] A later encounter with the 'ruin'd rampart' led him to think whimsically (as several of his antiquarian-minded countrymen had done throughout the eighteenth century) about the symbolism of the Wall in terms of conquest and independence:

> Where, the sons of freedom braving,
> Rome's imperial standards flew.[14]

The find of a Roman artefact—or, more probably, a *supposedly* Roman one—excited him, for he had himself become a 'hobbyhorsical antiquary'.[15] As a young man at the Bar, he had started to catalogue the Roman coins in the possession of the Faculty of Advocates.[16] A farm purchased and added to Scott's Abbotsford estate was land which, he believed, included 'a fine old Roman station', whence 'unquestionably Roman' artefacts had been unearthed. A friend mischievously said that these specious associations had added additional and compelling value to the ground, at any rate in Scott's antiquarian mind.[17] At Abbotsford he had Roman altars built into his garden wall, but he can have known little of the full extent of the Roman presence at Newstead, near Melrose. Most traces of the fort and marching camps at the site beneath the triple-summited Eildon Hills, which had been known in antiquity as Trimontium, had long-since disappeared under the plough. It would be later generations that would really relish the notion of the great Romans in their Borders neighbourhood.

A set of prints of Roman monuments and *vedute*, inherited from his uncle, which Scott described as 'Piranesi's views by Clérisseau', hung in his Edinburgh house in North Castle Street until 1826; though Scott wrote of them that year in terms that do not suggest any great interest in representations of ancient Rome, and in so doing he implies, perhaps, that such things were out of fashion in a new world of Romance.[18] A few 'classical' antiquities added to his 'gabions' at Abbotsford—this was the arcane name that he gave to his miscellaneous assemblage of curiosities in general—did not seem to have stirred his antiquarian blood to an undue extent: referring to himself in the context of such comparative exoticism as 'the Hermit on Tweedside', he mentioned almost in passing the 'handle of a Grecian sword and two or three specimens of marble' which had been sent to him by a Scottish family resident in Naples.[19] On the other hand, Dom Bernard de Montfaucon's famous *L'Antiquité expliquée et representée en figures,* pleased him greatly. However, in Scott's particular mention of it in his 'house catalogue', as a 'most copious and invaluable work upon antiquities, the merit of which is acknowledged in all parts of the world', one may suspect that his enthusiasm for the superb scarlet morocco-bound set of the original work of 1719 (five volumes in ten) and its 1724 *Supplement* (in a further five volumes) was due more to its being a gift from King George IV than any intrinsic merit as a thesaurus or 'paper museum' of the material remains of antiquity as illustrative of classical literature.[20]

Not long before he at last set foot on classic ground, Scott had acquired the pioneering, if eccentric, work by Gilbert Laing Meason on landscape architecture and its relation to the works of the Italian old masters. Laing Meason was a fellow member of the Bannatyne Club, and Scott was later to meet and keep company with him in Naples. This remarkable book informed him of the opulent villas at

Baiae, where the ancient Roman rich had disported themselves, and where those who came after them on that beautiful stretch of coast had found it convenient to build their seaside houses on indestructible Roman foundations.[21]

Yet all this did not make Scott a man particularly classically-inclined. He admitted as much to Lady Abercorn in 1822. In fact, having told her that he thought of going to Berlin or Dresden the next spring to collect Walter, and that he hoped he might return via Vienna and the north of Italy, he confessed in an off-hand way: 'It is a pity to miss Rome but I am not very classical and time will not serve me.'[22] This remark alone puts an apparently unbridgeable distance between Scott's mind-set and the mentality of the most characteristic upholders of the old Grand Tour ethos.

Scott was not entirely positive about Italy in general, either then or even when on the very verge of actually setting foot there: the fault, he recognised, lay chiefly in himself, rather than in the 'classic ground' of the Grand Tour tradition. 'I fear I shall not be able to appreciate Italy as it deserves, as I understand little of painting, and nothing of music.'[23] In fact, he had previously been damning of Italian music, asserting that he was neither a judge nor an admirer of it, and that he really could not appreciate what it was all about.[24] But he had, rather surprisingly, obtained a copy of Stendhal's *Histoire de la pienture en Italie*, not a very likely acquisition for someone of his limited aesthetic or art-historical sensibility, and an uncommon one given that even the Advocates' Library did not have the book. This may perhaps be evidence that he was beginning to think he really *should* go to Italy in order to see what it was that the Grand Tourists had seen.[25]

Stendhal was later to present Scott with a copy of his *De l'amour*.[26] If Scott ever read this, he would have noted what Stendhal termed the process of 'cristallisation' (crystallisation) whereby, in a new relationship, love developed from (as it were) the indifference one might feel in, say, Bologna, to the overwhelming passion one might find on seeing Rome after a journey there through the Apennines, in which love grew and developed. So might he, Scott, learn to like, even to love Italy. But when outlining for the reader the literary education and attainments of his first fictional hero, Edward Waverley, Scott made a comment which is, perhaps, a little barbed. In the realm of Italian literature, the young man had acquired a familiarity with the productions of 'the genius of that elegant though luxurious nation'. It sounds rather as if Scott was both attracted to, and yet repelled by, Italy's sensuous culture. And if he allowed Waverley to speak for himself in this regard, his fictional hero did not really reflect Scott's own modest classical attainments—in which Edward appears to have left the 'Author of Waverley' somewhat behind, having 'made the usual progress, and read the usual authors'.[27]

Negative feeling towards the classical past persisted even when Scott was at sea on his voyage to the Mediterranean in 1831. He wrote gloomily to his last publisher, Robert Cadell: '... I am sure the tumult of Naples would drive me mad. I care very little for classical antiquities and probably shall hardly go to Rome where they keep an indifferent kind of London or Paris.'[28] That is a most telling phrase. To the man who used it, *an indifferent kind of London or Paris* implies a place of secondary, even tertiary importance as a travelling destination. It presupposes a likely dissatisfaction when the traveller at last arrives in Rome to see its (perhaps over-vaunted) sights and experience its (probably inferior) social and intellectual life. It hardly represents the view of key exponents of the Grand Tour in its prime, of Scots who were prominent in the promotion of Rome as uniquely inspiring and magnificent: Sir John Clerk, for instance, for whom the city had stood as the absolute queen of travelling destinations; or Robert Adam (architect uncle of Scott's friend William Adam of Blair Adam), for whom it had been 'the most glorious place in the universal world'.[29] When Scott did, at last, set foot on Italian ground, he was fond of saying that John Morritt and others had 'frequently tried to drive classical antiquities into his head but they had always found his "skull too thick", for within that cranium lay (as he once put it facetiously) 'the brain of a half-lettered Goth'.[30]

Sir William Gell, who described himself as Scott's 'keeper' while in Italy, was one of the great figures in British classical scholarship of the early nineteenth century. This telamon of topographical studies in the Troad, the Aegean and in southern Italy ('I leave topography to Classic Gell', Byron had jested in 'English Bards and Scotch Reviewers') found himself both shocked at, yet clear-eyed about, Scott's fundamental lack of concern for the classical world. It must have astonished Gell's correspondents in the Society of Dilettanti—the very epicentre of British philhellenism, with members who were stalwarts of the Grand Tour tradition, and who joined in its famous toast of 'Grecian Taste and Roman Spirit'—to be told how little Scott actually cared for Greece and Rome, and that not even residence in Greece itself would have caused him (in Gell's words) to 'become Classical'.[31] Writing to his patron saint, Marguerite, Countess of Blessington, whom he had known well in Naples, Willam Gell attempted to explain his principles governing what he chose to focus on (and what to omit) in his memoir of the time he spent with Scott in Italy. It was the *Classicism* issue that was the sticking-point. Gell just could not comprehend or fully express the oddity of Scott's 'total want of classical taste and knowledge': this on the part of a man he called the 'hero'. Gell was trying to 'explain away and render less ridiculous' Scott's attitude 'in a situation full of classical recollections', and to do so in such as way as Scott 'might not seem insensible to its real merits.' These facts notwithstanding, Gell confided that he

perceived that the account of the last days of so distinguished a person was really interesting when told with strict regard to truth. The circumstances of his illness having changed his mind, or deprived it of its consistency ... might be judged of from his way of treating the subjects of conversation which presented themselves, and this alone would be of consequence to his numerous friends.[32]

*　　*　　*　　*　　*

Greece as a potential travelling destination—however remote a possibility this might be—had been mentioned by Scott to Matthew Weld Hartstonge in the spring of 1816.[33] But he had in fact already shared some second-hand knowledge of Greece with Hartstonge rather earlier: he had confided the fact that John Morritt had told him before this of the so-called Treasury of Atreus at Mycenae, a 'beehive' tomb constructed of stone laid in overlapping horizontal courses finely-cut to a curve, and not perhaps the most likely of antiquities for them to have discussed.[34] Scott, of course, saw somewhat tenuous architectural parallels with Highland brochs as 'very ancient Dwellings ... constructed by a People unacquainted with cement ...', but whose skill in relatively sophisticated masonry was, in its way, admirable.

However, there is ample evidence of Scott's admission of his lack of relevant linguistic knowledge: he told various correspondents that he was 'no Grecian'; that he was 'almost entirely ignorant of that noble language'.[35] In January 1824, Archibald Constable presented him with a magnificent and comprehensive collection of the best editions of the Greek and Latin authors, in 140 volumes, with commentaries: *Libri Classici cum Notis Variorum*, as Scott distinguished the assemblage in the description of his 'gabions'. This was by way of 'handseling the new library' of Abbotsford—that is, as an inaugural gift to mark a fresh undertaking or enterprise, or to celebrate a new possession. Delighted, honoured and flattered, but also perhaps slightly embarrassed, Scott thanked the donor profusely while offering this confession and assurance:

> Who knows what new ideas the Classics may suggest for I am determined to shake off the rust which years has contracted and to read at least some of the most capital of the ancients before I die.

He knew he was but a poor classic, and he thought the less of himself on that account. But Constable's books, handsomely bound (like George IV's presentation copies of Montfaucon's *L'Antiquité expliquée*) looked good on the Abbotsford shelves, and (as Scott said) 'set me up in the line of classical antiquities', even if he had to admit that he was 'an author not very worthy of [the gift]'. This remark led him to borrow—and, though quoting it inaccurately, to apply to himself—the aside of Thomas Warton:

> For long, enamoured of a barbarous age
> A faithless truant to the Classic page...[36]

But one material relic of antiquity stirred him even more than magnificent sets of Greek and Latin authors. Friendship with Byron resulted in Scott's receiving, in 1815, a remarkable present. 'Like the old heroes in Homer, we exchanged gifts', Scott told Thomas Moore. Byron sent him a 'large sepulchral vase of silver. It was full of dead men's bones, and had inscriptions on two sides of the base. One ran thus:—"The bones contained in this urn were found in certain ancient sepulchres within the long walls of Athens, in the month of February 1811."'[37] Scott went on to say that the other face bore a version of a line from the tenth Satire of Juvenal's fourth book, to the effect that the mighty dust which remains can scarcely represent what a great man had been. In translation, the quotation continues: 'Death alone shows how insignificant are the fragile bodies of human beings.' Byron's urn took pride of place in the library at Abbotsford, Scott commissioning for it from George Bullock a stand of exceptional design and of idiosyncratic classical inspiration.

Scott knew that he *ought* to make a late Grand Tour—or what might now substitute for the great institution of old—if only to have the name and status of having done so. Still, his imagination could more than make up for lack of personal familiarity with classic ground; and, in any case, classic ground was not the rock on which his fiction, and indeed all his imaginative writing, was founded. In 1818 Scott had described Greece as 'the country whose sun, so long set, has yet left on the horizon of the world such a blaze of splendour.'[38] Such was his lip-service to Antiquity. The Greece that was more to his taste, perhaps, was the one touched by swashbuckling Venetian adventurers such as Francesco Morosini, 'Peloponnesiacus', a memoir of whose campaign against the Ottomans in the Morea he owned; and doubtless it was easy to overlook that puissant general's unfortunate near-destruction of the Parthenon in 1687. Even when, out of the Aegean blue, came a copy (presented by the publishers in 1819) of Edward Dodwell's important *Classical and Topographical Tour through Greece*, to prick Scott into contemplating lands beyond the traditional ambit of the Grand Tour, he was not to be tempted for another dozen years to follow in Dodwell's footsteps.[39] Then, in 1824, Scott was approached by John Carne, of Queen's College, Cambridge, for permission to allow him to dedicate to Scott the work that became Carne's *Letters from the East*. Replying, Scott was gracious, and accepted, though pleading his unworthiness as a traveller, or a traveller manqué:

> ... although I have no title to the compliment your kindness proposes me in inscribing your Grecian travels with my name yet I cannot decline out of a sense of my own demerits what you so handsomely offer. If the travels be as interesting

as the specimens which you had the goodness to give us at Abbotsford they cannot but command the general attention of the publick.[40]

A curiosity of Scott's library at Abbotsford was the seven-volume, 1817 French edition of Jean-Jacques Barthélemy's *Voyage du jeune Anacharsis en Grèce*. This imaginary account of the travels of a young Scythian, which actually presents a comprehensive 'encyclopaedia' of information on every aspect of ancient Greek life, is supposed to have been compiled and committed to parchment by 'Anacharsis' on his return to his Black Sea homeland. It will have informed Scott, in a palatable and intriguing way—rather similar to his own assumption of various aliases and his presentation, through them, of historical narrative or the establishment of a social setting—of many essential aspects of classical culture. As the London edition states, the reader is induced 'to imagine he is perusing a work of mere amusement, invention and fancy', when in fact all was supported by ancient authority. Scott must have been attracted by the account of Athens, where 'every thing is animate, every thing speaks to the eyes of the attentive spectator.' 'It is a source of the highest pleasure to a traveller, to have enjoyed a number of pleasing and lively emotions, the remembrance of which is perpetually recurring during the course of his whole life…'. Particularly appealing was, doubtless, the evocation of 'The Library of an Athenian', with its discourses on booksellers and such topics.[41] This idea of memories of travelling experience remaining with one ever afterwards may have motivated Scott to retain at least the notion that he, too, might one day voyage to the eastern Mediterranean, and that he might record his 'pleasing and lively emotions' in the sort of travel book that (as we shall see) he hoped to write, and which his publishers very much wanted to extract from him.

*   *   *   *   *

Encouragement to go South had come from Byron:

> Why don't you take a turn in Italy—you would find yourself as well-known as in the Highlands among the natives. As for the English you would be with them as in London … I am building a little cutter at Genoa to go a cruising in the summer—I know *you* like the sea too.[42]

Byron appears to suggest that there were so many Britons in Italy that Scott might either feel at home, or (alternatively) feel threatened by the press of fellow-nationals. As has been noted above, the British were already acquiring a certain notoriety on the Italian scene, and not for the best of reasons.

Discouragement, of a kind, came from Maria Edgeworth, who had been to France at the Peace of Amiens and again in 1821, and who now, in 1824, wrote cynically of acquaintances bound for the Continent

to see the Rhine, and the *Venus*, and the *Apollo* and all that must be seen nowadays before people can be happy at home. But they will only stay one year away, and then come to the old end of the fairy tale: 'And so they lived very happily all the rest of their days'—at home must have been always omitted at the end of this sentence; but it could have been nowhere else. [43]

Maria Edgeworth was at the time contemplating a novel, to be called *Travellers*, in which the 'faults, follies, humours' of various classes of such people would be exposed. She asked Scott to 'throw her a few hints out of your abundance.'[44] Scott thought the idea 'delicious'. 'John Bully is so uncommonly diverting in his travelling frolics that he will furnish you with a rich variety of matter.' He cited the anecdote, once retailed to him by William Clerk, of the Cockney broker whose travels were dictated not by what was best, or most convenient, or most interesting, but merely by the advantages (or otherwise) of the prevailing rate of exchange. Clerk had encountered this man among a sightseeing party in Rome. Their leader, a gentleman of rank and education, and an antiquary above the common run of *ciceroni*, conducted the party to the Pantheon. Scott takes up the story: 'The Italians, with little else left to be proud of, are still proud of their works of ancient art...'. The immense rotunda demanded a dignified silence, and a sense of awe in its beholders. All, that is, except the Cockney stock-jobber. With hands in pockets, and an Aye! and an Umph!, the Londoner at last expostulated: '"Pray, Senior, did you ever see our Pantheon in Oxford road[?]." Imagine the shame and horror of his countrymen. Sudden death would have been too slight a punishment for the vulgar dog—protracted and with tortures it might have been some petty expiation. Such are the frolics we play in the face of Europe.'[45]

This splendid anecdote seems a perfect illustration of the general point about Grand Tour attitudes and the respect (or otherwise) for European societies that the institution bred in its participants, one made effectively, if cynically, by Paul Langford: 'There was some scepticism about the value of an experience which involved [young aristocrats] disgracing themselves and their country in front of their hosts.'[46] This jibe has plenty of contemporary evidence to support it, and many instances will have been well known to Scott: Lady Mary Wortley Montagu's assertion that all over Italy the British were known as 'Golden Asses'; or Smollett's contemptuous onslaught on the 'raw boys, whom Britain seems to have poured forth on purpose to bring her national character into contempt: ignorant, petulant, rash and profligate ... [who] return finished connoisseurs and coxcombs, to their own country.'[47]

Scott was well aware of the new type he mocked: those who assumed the mantle of 'Grand Tourists' while lacking the traditional basis of gentility, education and receptiveness to the new and the foreign. The figure of the archetypical 'Cockney' enters with increasing frequency into the literature of the period of the end of the Grand Tour. Many social commentators and wits enjoyed mocking the 'Cockney' type as one who would not previously, for good or ill, have been encountered on the loose in Europe. And it was not just lower-middle-class characters who were parodied. Gentlemen who should have known better, or would-be gentlemen, played the same or a similar character all too well. Increasingly the presence abroad of the *nouveau riche* 'John Bull' was not seen to enhance the standing of Britain in the eyes of the world. James Simpson recalled having seen the British ridiculed in Paris in 1815 at the Théâtre des Variétés in an act featuring 'Jean Bool'.[48] David Carey had great fun in his *Life in Paris* ... of 1822, with the Rambles, Sprees, and Amours of Messrs Wildfire, Jenkins and O'Shuffleton. During a fracas in a Parisian *caveau* over a *fille de joie*, her regular beau, himself a rough enough creature, cries 'Jean Bull! Jean Brute! Jean Bête!'[49] Mary Shelley also referred to 'the mere traveller, or true John Bull' as a type who did not fully appreciate the magic of Italy.[50]

Thackeray was soon to mock the type further—and further afield, in Anatolia and the Levant—to devastating effect.

> Wherever the steamboat touches the shore adventure retreats into the interior, and what is called romance vanishes. It won't bear the vulgar gaze; or rather the light of common day puts it out, and it is only in the dark that it shines at all. There is no cursing and insulting of *Giaours* now. If a Cockney looks or behaves in a particularly ridiculous way, the little Turks come out and laugh at him. A Londoner is no longer a spitoon for true believers ... Byronism becomes absurd instead of sublime, and is only a foolish expression of cockney wonder.[51]

That 'spitoon' makes one think back to Scott's comment on every London citizen making Loch Lomond his washpot.[52] The mockery of vulgar travellers abroad was matched by a similar and growing ridicule of the type among home tourists. Lockhart and others condemned 'Cockney visitants' to Scottish sites of historic interest and scenic splendour, and 'steam-boat parties' of 'Cockneys' invading the Highland setting of Scott's latest novel, *Rob Roy*.[53] Seeking to get beneath the skin of such contemporatry comments, Ian Duncan assesses the matter crisply: 'To jeer at bad taste is to acknowledge good...'.[54] As Gerald Newman has well put it, 'the [Grand] Tour's educational value fell as its social value was strip-mined.'[55]

*   *   *   *   *

Sicily had begun to exert an attraction. Sir James Hall of Dunglass, an eminent geologist and chemist, was Scott's predecessor as President of the Royal Society of Edinburgh. He was the father of Scott's friend Captain Basil Hall, who would play a key part in arranging Scott's voyage to the Mediterranean in 1831. Sir James had been to Sicily, in pursuit of his geological researches, in the 1780s. Basil Hall had been there as well, as had his younger brother, James, an advocate and 'gentleman' painter connected artistically with Scott: James, indeed, had travelled all over the island in 1822 as part of a very remarkable late Grand Tour that had taken him to Spain, all over France and Italy, and then through Germany.[56] Now, in 1827, Scott conceived the idea that he, too, might like to go to Sicily. He told Mary Hughes as much, confiding to her that—money worries permitting—he was resolved to visit the Continent.

> I am sure I am much more accustomed to endure any species of fatigue where my lameness does not impede me than most people & have slept on the heather as soundly as ever I did in my bed so have great hopes I may get to the top of Etna. Lockhart will tell you that even in my age I can climb like a cat and in my boyhood was one of the boldest *craigs-men* in the High School as the Cats-nick on Salisbury Crags & the Kittle Nine Steps on the Castle rock could tell if they would speak. So I may get to the top of Etna yet.[57]

When Scott thought of Mount Etna or, indeed, of Mount Vesuvius, he might well have referred to them, facetiously, as 'volcanuses', the term he had heard used by 'a travelled lady' of his acquaintance in speaking of the distinctive geological features of southern Italy.[58] Beyond that, again, was the childhood exercise of 1782, the manuscript proudly preserved and annotated by Scott's mother as his first literary composition.[59] The subject was an eruption of Etna, translated, in rhyming couplets, from Virgil's description in the *Aeneid*, Book III, 571-580. Doubtless Scott would have discussed with James Skene the possibilities and prospects, not least the logistics, of ascending Italian volcanoes. Skene, for his part, had recorded his contempt for the feeble guide who had offered to pull him up Vesuvius: 'The idea amused me much—a sallow son of Italy to teach a hardy Scot how to climb a mountain.'[60]

Scott had heard of life in Palermo and its environs from his friend Lady Compton (later Marchioness of Northampton), who had experienced a dramatic earthquake in the city. What she said of Sicilian art and literature piqued his curiosity: she described the attraction of the island for 'lovers of the antiquity of the middle ages', and wrote of a luxuriant land and a kind people.[61] The Northamptons lived in Italy and Sicily for ten years; Palermo was a favourite wintering-spot. In 1828 she wrote:

Pray pray if you ever did a really wise & clever thing in your life (& some you have done, I believe) spend next winter there too—you will find it a perfect mine, much more so to you than Italy... [62]

By this phrase she meant a 'mine' of historical information and interest, particularly mediaeval—and so rather more to Scott's *gusto*—and also a treasure-house of literary inspiration.

Replying, Scott betrayed something extremely important about his historical and literary method in relation to the likely benefit of travelling to potentially book-inspiring locations, which he saw as the main purpose of such expeditions. This was that 'autopsy'—as his generation might have termed personal inspection (using the word in its literal Greek sense)—was not necessary for his imagination to work, and his prose to flow. He used the analogy of the optical devices regularly employed by Grand Tour sketchers for capturing scenes of 'picturesque' landscape encountered en route.

> As for Palermo ... you shall tell me a great deal about it and I am confident it will make a much better subject than if I had seen it myself. There are you know many artists who paint rather from reflection of the subject in a bright mirror (a dull one wont do) than from the actual object. I think there is something like this in composition for I would rather write from the account given me by a friend of taste and judgement than from hasty and superficial information picked up in a hurried tour. Seriously I have often thought of setting to work on Sicily. It is a noble subject for a tale of the middle ages and these normans and saracens the bravest and most romantic of men run strongly in my head.[63]

Unfortunately, however, in using this analogy, Scott actually got muddled, because one of these devices—that which he most likely had in mind, namely the 'Claude glass'—was, in fact, a tinted mirror which gave a mellow tinge to the view. He was, perhaps, further confused by the notion of the *camera obscura* and even (just possibly) by that of the newer *camera lucida*. The camera obscura would have cast a bright image; and this may be what he really meant.

The mixing-up of ideas in contemporary optical technology is not, however, important. The really significant point is that Scott was stressing the relevance, to him, of the *reflected* view or mediated image of a place, or of a series of scenes. With these he could become familiar through the images of artists or, equally, by means of the written descriptions of travellers: people who had actually been to the spot, and whose graphic or verbal accounts he could use as the basis for topographical description of his own. One may think of the striking passage in *Redgauntlet* where Scott has Alan Fairford refer to 'what artists call a Claude Lorraine glass, which spreads its own particular hue over the whole landscape which you see through it'. Alan says this in order to seek a metaphor for what he regards as the way Darsie Latimer—just like Scott himself, in fact—'gets a touch of the wonderful and the sublime from [his] own rich imagination ...'. Darsie, like Scott again, beholds 'ordinary events just through such a medium.'[64]

Scott did not actually *have* to travel *himself* in order to know the lands of the Grand Tour: others might voyage for him, and convey the information for his later exploitation in the way he could do best. 'Autopsy' might indeed distort, or dull, an image which was already distorted through the medium of the vicarious view.

9

A Cast in a King's Ship

'Still I am zealous for the Mediterranean when the season comes', Scott confided to his journal on 20 May 1829. The end of that year was in his mind; but the long-postponed tour was, perhaps unsurprisingly, postponed once more.

Reluctantly, in the course of the hard years 1830 and 1831, he began to accept that his literary powers were fading. He experienced serious problems in completing the novel *Count Robert of Paris* to his own very moderate satisfaction, not to mention the major reservations of a squeamish printer (James Ballantyne) concerned at what he perceived as impropriety in the plot, and a publisher (Robert Cadell) alarmed lest Scott's wizard wand be irreparably broken. He had begun this novel in September 1830, and the contentious and troublesome task of completing it dragged on until it was finished 'after a fashion'(as Eric Anderson tactfully put it) in August 1831. Journal entries throughout 1830-31 chronicle the painful progress.[1] But the hard fact could not be gainsaid: 'I have lost it is plain the power of interesting the country', he admitted to Cadell, 'and ought in justice to all parties to retire while I have some credit.' So he thought again of 'a trip to the Continent'. That might now, in the changed circumstances of his life, easily be for a year or two.[2] This was in December 1830. To his journal he admitted: 'I caught the alarm of my critics and announced my purpose of going to a warmer climate to ward of[f] the blow of fate.'[3] On the same day as he had written these words to Cadell, he also told Ballantyne that any potential trip might be merely for 'a few months', adding the deeply affecting qualification, 'if I hold together as long.' He continued with a sobering thought for his great predecessors who themselves had died abroad, and whose lives he had already written, with an ill-concealed sense of foreboding in the mention of their dissolution: 'So ended the fathers of the Novel Fielding & Smollet [*sic*] and it would be no unprofessional finish.'[4]

It then became abundantly clear to Scott that Cadell, whose rapacity was ill-concealed, expected him *not* to go abroad, certainly for the present. 'Selfish regret' was how Scott assessed, in part at least, Cadell's concern.[5] Regret, that is, lest there be no more novels and thus no more publishing profits for Robert Cadell. On 10 December 1830 Cadell wrote both to wheedle and cajole:

> We [that is James Ballantyne and himself] agree that laying aside Count Robert is out of the question, it would not do in any way, were you once to lay aside a Novel I question if you could be induced to write another under any circumstances ... There are so many points requiring your presence in this Country, the Notes to the Novels [that is authorial notes for the 'Magnum Opus' edition, then in course of publication], not to mention these several at press ... that I would tremble were you absent for more than a few months. Independent of this the Continent is no very comfortable place to go to, and very probably will not be for a long time to come. [Cadell was thinking of the revolutions sweeping Europe, notably France and Belgium, but also the political unrest in Italy and elsewhere that year.] For a few months from April to October you might find the Continent agreeable, while you move about from place to place, but for any thing permanent I trust I shall never see you anywhere but at Abbotsford. The whole associations connected with it are attached to your name & fame & I do hope you will never think of leaving it [but] for some pleasure tour.[6]

So Scott remained doggedly at his post, struggling on until the autumn of 1831—despite having suffered at least three strokes between February 1830 and April 1831—labouring on the notes and additions for the Magnum edition of the novels, on the vexatious *Count Robert*, on his new tale *Castle Dangerous*, and on other work encouraged by the persuasive, self-regarding Cadell.

The Magnum edition of *The Fair Maid of Perth* includes a whimsical note, dated August 1831, on the relative merits of the River Tay and the River Tiber. In this Scott suggests that he might soon be in a position to judge the Tiber in 'the surer language of personal conviction': in other words, he hoped soon to see Italy for himself.[7] Indeed, such a trip to the warmer south had become essential if his health (or what remained of it), and with it his peace of mind, was to be assured.

In July 1831 he had suggested to his elder son Walter that they might go south as far as Naples, where Charles Scott, his younger son, was attached to the British legation as a fledgling diplomat on the first rung of a professional ladder. The proposed route was ill-defined, but their return would be through parts of the rest of Italy and, having traversed the Tyrol, they then might 'take [in] as much of Germany as we could manage.' The 'we' here was perhaps to be extended to embrace Walter and his wife and possibly others, such as one or both of Scott's daughters, and Lockhart: a family party was in his mind, and his letter betrayed the loneliness and uncertainly of an elderly, unwell man wary of hazarding Europe without company. 'If ... you would take as much of the little tour as you can with us it would encourage me for what pleasure can I possibly expect in seeing things by myself.'[8] But this prospective trip was immediately postponed till later in the year, though Scott's determination was now to start southwards through Germany. Indeed, his ideas for the route, and for the trip as a whole, become rather confused and contradictory in the correspondence with his sons and with others. His mind ranged hither and thither over the travelling possibilities before him, and over the pros and cons of this or that itinerary or destination. In December 1830 he had told Charles despondently that he thought he would never actually see Naples.[9] Not long afterwards, however, Naples had again become a real possibility in his mind.

An old friend, the poet, dramatist and translator William Sotheby, had been to Italy in 1816. His visit resulted in several poems on Italian themes with which Scott was familiar. One might assume, therefore, that the company of this fellow man of letters would be stimulating and inspiring to a host thinking of going to Italy himself. Sotheby's visit, with his wife and daughter, to Abbotsford in August 1829 failed, however, to produce the expected fillip. On the contrary, Scott told his son (having assured him that *Sotheby* was not Robert *Southey*: Walter Scott the younger was not really a literary man) that the Sothebys had 'sate down upon [me] like a Coroner's jury upon a smothered man'. Maybe William Sotheby had talked *too* much of Italy and, in so doing had put Scott off the notion of travelling there. We can never know. But certainly he had smothered rather than inspired. To that extent, a visit that might have been just what was needed as encouragement failed in its purpose.[10]

What does seem abundantly clear is that Scott felt he had seen enough of France, and thus was not keen on Charles's suggestion of his sailing down the Rhône from Lyon to Marseille, and then by sea to Leghorn (Livorno) and Genoa, a city Charles recommended strongly, having been delighted with his own very short visit on his way out to Naples.[11] Abundantly clear, that is, unless one reads Scott's letter to his old French friend and *cicerone*, Jean Baptiste Le Chevalier, to whom he admitted that his serious illness had 'disconcerted a fine plan I had to visit the continent and my friends at Paris on my way further south.'[12] So he appeared both inclined and disinclined to experience France once more. It is indeed strange, but utterly characteristic of Scott's capricious attitude to European travel in general, that he could hold diametrically opposed views in rapid succession, or even concurrently. Seven years previously, he had shown enthusiasm for the very country he had now turned against—if indeed he had actually done so. Then, he had praised the verbal and visual portrait of the Rhône and Provence by Charles's Oxford mentor, John Hughes, to the extent of insinuating mention of Hughes's book by name into the Introduction to *Quentin Durward*.[13] Now, there was an apparent wish for a last renewal of Parisian and other French contacts. And yet, on the other hand, he did not want to journey through France... Whatever his real intentions, and whether he did or did not want to see Paris and other regions of France again, his apology to Le Chevalier ended with the sad factual admission: 'But it cannot be. My diminution of strength will not permit.' In concluding his letter of February 1831, Scott alluded to the affecting passage in Horace's sixth Satire of Book II, line 62, and had expressed the wish 'to cherish the "... iucunda oblivia vitae..."'. Unspecified and unquoted was the passage in this poem that precedes the tag; and if he did not actually mention Abbotsford, it was surely in his mind as he dredged his un-classical memory for some suitable classical reference to offer a learned French scholar. For Abbotsford must always be regarded as possessing a kind of power and personality of its own in the story of Scott's travelling life. Abbotsford was both an excuse not to venture abroad, and a better place than those he might ever find, were he actually to go to the Continent.

> O country home, when shall I look on you again! When shall I be allowed, between my library of classics and sleep and hours of idleness, to drink the sweet draughts that make us forget the troubles of life!

When in a positive mood, Scott's curiosity seemed now to direct him up the Rhine to Mayence (Mainz), from which point they might take a carriage over the Simplon Pass. Hundreds of miles lay between these points, but—not for the last time—his capacity to telescope distance seemed both remarkable and alarming in one contemplating a Continental excursion. The Rhine, as he imagined it (and as he told Walter) was 'the most beautiful country in the world'.[14] To see the Rhine had, indeed, become a major desideratum among British travellers in Europe.[15] Henry Cockburn sailed up-river in 1823, only to think that it was no finer than 'the Tweed below Melrose, or the Tay below Perth' and the surrounding hills no more dramatic than the Pentlands—sentiments which would surely have struck a chord with Scott.[16] Many people, however, preferred to sail *down* the Rhine as a pleasing finale to a European tour begun by some other route, rather than to work their way *up* it as the initial stage of a Continental trip. Young James Hall enjoyed a kind of travelling ecstasy in descending the stream through its castellated and craggy landscape.[17]

Scott, for his part, once over the Alps and into Piedmont or Lombardy, would go on south, not stopping (as he told Charles) 'till I shall [shake or take] you by the hand in Naples ... I believe old Daedalus can find *wings* for the whole party Icarus included ... I expect also to find you quite qualified for a cicerone.' With his customary self-deprecation, Scott was, presumably, likening himself to the man who flew too close to the sun and who fell to earth:

a metaphor for a literary career in trouble, but a career of which something—
and including also this Icarus's life—might yet, perhaps, be saved by a sojourn
in the South.[18] A few weeks later, Scott wrote to Charles, now with the definite
thought of Italy, and especially Naples, as the place to pass 'the dead months
of winter':

> The idea of your being my guide through these classical regions is a very pleasant
> pro[s]pect so you must get well acquainted [with them] ... I shou[ld] like to see
> some thing of Sicily but when I think of Vesuvius and Aetna it is too late a week
> in life for visiting the Cyclops her reverence. Here is something to speak about
> and how you will bear your old padre pick a back like father Anchises.[19]

Splendid confusion of classical reference apart, one cannot but reflect on the
contrast this letter provides with the optimistic tone of that to Mary Hughes,
written on Christmas Day 1825, when Scott had entertained visions of himself
scrambling up Etna like the schoolboy he had been some forty years before.

But Scott also tried to be bright and hopeful, writing thus to the Duke of
Buccleuch (aged thirty-one): 'I am going to try whether the air of Naples will
make an old fellow of sixty young again.' What must have been in Scott's
mind, however, was that the Duke's father (the 4th Duke, Scott's great friend)
had died in Portugal, where he had gone for his health.[20] He was also well
aware, through the experience of a fellow Clerk of Session, Colin Mackenzie,
who had gone South for a cure, that no such panacea was guaranteed: 'Alas!',
Scott recorded, 'long seated complaints defy Italian climate.'[21] He knew he
would be lucky if he made it back to Abbotsford. 'Nature is calling for her
tribute', he had said, a little melodramatically, to Charlotte Eaton—alluding
to his fast-declining health—in course of an interchange of correspondence
about a copy of her *At Home and Abroad* destined for him, but which the
publisher seems never, in fact, to have sent. In this letter to Mrs Eaton he made
no mention of any wish or plan to go to Italy, which seems strange given the
context of the exchange of letters was that of continental travel, at any rate as
much as Mrs Eaton represented the topic in her new fact-based novel.[22]

An interesting correspondence with Samuel Rogers materialised in January
and February 1831. Rogers had been to France on either side of periods of
conflict, and he had travelled in Italy first in 1814-15. He returned in 1821.
Out of these visits emerged his long poem *Italy*. This failed to succeed, in
either of its two parts, until Rogers brought out the famous illustrated edition
of 1830, with steel engravings after works by Thomas Stothard and J. M. W.
Turner. In its new guise as a drawing-room gift-book, rather of the 'Landscape
Annual' kind, this was an outstanding commercial success, and it became
famous. It may also have given Scott pause for thought, and stirred him to
attempt to push forward the illustrative part of a major project of his own.

In acknowledging the gift of a copy of the new edition, Scott wrote in gratitude to Rogers:

> ... your beautiful verses on Italy which [are] embellished by such beautiful specimens of architecture as form a rare specimen of the manner in which the art of poetry can awaken the muse of painting. It is in every respect a bijou and yet more valued as the mark of your regard than either for its literary attractions or those which it derives from art although justly distinguished for both ... It is this that makes me look at your volume with particular interest ...

Scott took the opportunity, also, to explain that he was not well, and had demitted office as Clerk of Session. The current state of his health made a visit to Italy, long pondered, seem unlikely; and, this being so, illustrated travel books would have to stand for actual experience and personal inspection. It is significant that he sought to tempt Rogers to Scotland, implying that, in his heart, it was Scotland that still held for him a greater appeal than Italy or indeed anywhere 'furth of the realm'.

> I had promised myself the pleasure of seeing some part of the continent and the thought of visiting the well sung scenes of Italy. I am now so helpless in the way of moving about that I think I must be satisfied with the admirable substitute you have so kindly sent me which must be my consolation for not seeing with my own eyes what I can read so picturesquely described. I sometimes hope I shall pick up heart of grace and come to my daughter Lockhart [Sophia Scott, then living with her husband John Lockhart in London] in spring another time I think I had best keep my madness in the background like the confidant of Tilburina in The Critick [R. B. Sheridan's *The Critic*, Act III, Scene 1] at all events I wish I could draw you o'er the Border in Summer or Autumn when at least we could visit places which though not very romantic in landscape every valley has its battle and every stream its song.[23]

Rogers's response compounds the idea that, for Scott, 'abroad' was best enjoyed when 'packaged' for him by others. Scott might then re-package the landscape and the atmosphere, and give them back to a public hungry to know the world but unable to see it for themselves. He might even render a similar service to those more fortunate members of society who had themselves made a Grand Tour-style pilgrimage, and who now wished to re-live the experience, so to speak, at the hands of a master scene-setter. 'Happy should I be', wrote Rogers, 'if I thought the Picture-book I sent you, could give any pleasure at Abbotsford, & still happier if it would induce you to lay your scenes in Italy & transport <u>us</u> thither, though you will not go yourself.'[24]

The success of Rogers's *Italy* in its new illustrated form prompted Scott to impress on Robert Cadell the need to push forward with the visual element of the new edition of his collected verse, for which Turner was working on the illustrations. These, in their engraved form, might lack the glamour of the plates in Rogers's book, but they were clearly close to Scott's heart—and to his and Cadell's pockets, too. Scott urged haste. 'The success of Mr Rogers by dint of beautiful illustration will not have escaped the Trade who will make eager attempts to imitate it & it is in such a race that the Devil catches the hindmost ... Therefore Carpe Diem...'.[25]

Scott had read Samuel Rogers, and must have imagined that he might find in Italy a route to his own revivification. In one of the prose passages that intersperse his verse vignettes (the piece is entitled simply 'Foreign Travel'), Rogers had described how indulgence in travelling 'restores to us in a great degree what we have lost ... All is new and strange. We surrender ourselves, and feel once again as children.' And Rogers continued:

> Would he who sat in a corner of his library, poring over books and maps, learn more or so much in the time, as he who, with his eyes and his heart open, is receiving impressions all day long from the things themselves?

Albeit this passage appears to contradict Scott's proven and preferred method of absorbing both information and atmosphere, it also expresses the notion that a tour, and sights seen for himself, might just, after all, enable Scott to retrieve a childlike sense of wonder at the world, and feed anew the life of his imagination.[26]

Broken in physical health though Scott was, and all but played-out in imagination as a writer of fiction, he still entertained an idea that a work of some sort might emerge from his forthcoming trip. This would be a travel book of a kind, possibly a 'journal' or, more likely, a series of ostensible 'letters' from the Continent. As mentioned previously (see above, Chapter 3), a scheme along such lines had first been mooted in 1818 by John Ballantyne and Archibald Constable, both now dead. But now, in 1831, there was an understanding with Robert Cadell that a journal, or some such other record, of the tour would be (as Scott put it) 'visible one day'—ominous words, perhaps suggesting a posthumous publication which would, very likely, be a commercial success as the memoir of a great man's search for strength, health, diversion and solace at the end of life, and on the European tour he had never before attempted.[27]

Thomas Moore dined with Scott in London on 14 October 1831 shortly before he actually departed on his long-contemplated journey to the Mediterranean sun. Moore supposed that

> The great object in sending him abroad is to *disengage* [my italics] his mind from the strong wish to *write* by which he is haunted; eternally making efforts

to produce something without being able to bring his mind collectively to bear upon it—the *multum cupit, nihil potest*. Alas, alas![28]

Yet on 18 October 1831, Scott made two very different observations about the likely literary results of any projected foreign excursion. To Robert Cadell he confided his hopes for 'an instructive voyage ... I have little doubt to get stuff for our work [the travel book, of whatever form that might assume] if the climate restores me a little elasticity.'[29] But in the privacy of his journal he was much more candid. 'The time is gone of sages who traveld to collect wisdom as well as heroes to reap honour. Men think and fight for money.'[30]

The apophthegm, though actually applied by Scott in another context, has personal relevance to his own current dilemma as to what he *might*, and what he *could* write during or after his impending voyage. Scott himself, surely nearing sagehood, would be journeying to collect ideas and themes for those letters, or for a journal, or indeed for whatever might emerge, in whatever form, from his travels: that much would be the result of wisdom collected. His honour involved the working-off of his debts: therein lay his heroism in adversity. Wherever, and however, he travelled, he would have to think of money: his journey would, he hoped, produce published books—and the sale of books would pay his creditors.

*   *   *   *   *

Everyone could see that a trip to warmer climes was essential to Scott's continued well-being. This would not be so much a latter-day Grand Tour as an attempt at a grand salvation of a great man and the remains of a once-great mind. The imponderables regarding routes, destinations and duration of a possible voyage and sojourn somewhere in the south of Europe were suddenly brought into alignment when, in a fortunate turn of events concluded with remarkable speed, an ideal solution was hit upon. Captain Basil Hall, RN, described this as 'the most favourable resource, and one which seemed obvious to every person but the Great Unknown himself'. It was nothing less than 'passage in a ship of war.'[31]

John Wilson Croker, until 1830 Secretary of the Admiralty, suggested to J. G. Lockhart that their Lordships of the Board of Admiralty might be persuaded to offer Scott free passage in a warship bound for the Mediterranean. Robert Cadell took it upon himself to write to Captain Hall in London, asking how this might be obtained. Hall went immediately—literally so: the entire arrangement was conceived and concluded within two days, starting in the evening of 13 September 1831—to Sir James Graham, First Lord of the Admiralty. Lockhart later recorded Hall's suggestion to Sir James that it would be 'a fit and graceful thing' to place a frigate at Scott's disposal for a voyage to the Mediterranean.[32]

Hall told Graham that his assistance 'might essentially contribute to preserve one of the most valuable lives in the country.' Graham said that a ship was shortly to sail for Malta, and that a passage for Scott 'might be considered certain': HMS *Barham* (50 guns, Captain Hugh Pigot) was actually under sailing orders.[33] Whenever Scott might find it convenient to come south from Abbotsford, the vessel would be 'prepared for his reception.'[34] Graham sought, and received on the spot, the personal endorsement of King William IV—'the Sailor King'—to the proposal. And on 15 September the First Lord of the Admiralty wrote to Scott, whom quite clearly he viewed as the First Lord of Literature, conveying the King's actual words of satisfaction at being able to provide assistance in a cause as noble as was Scott's salvation. Speaking personally, Graham espressed himself pleased to have the opportunity of 'evincing that respect which in common with the nation I feel, and which from me, as a Borderer [he was a Graham of Netherby] is due to the Wizard of my native hills.' [35]

The one matter to be overcome was Scott's diffidence about taking advantage of the offer, and his perennial doubts about 'abroad'. Hall summarised the circumstances acutely. It was Scott's

> secret reluctance to root himself up from his house and home, his dearly beloved black-letter library, his musty papers, and his cherished plantations, in which he took infinitely more delight than in all the society and scenery of the rest of the world besides.[36]

This one perceptive statement epitomises the essential problem of Scott and his participation in Continental travel.

The appeal of seeing Malta, and of visiting the fabled place in this comparatively easy, leisured and (importantly) economical way, was probably the deciding factor that persuaded Scott to accede to the proposal. But how reluctant and indifferent a Grand Tourist Scott now appeared is clear from his remarks first to James Elliot Shortreed and then to Cadell:

> The Doctors have prescribed a foreign country as a thing necessary to mend my very indifferent health and I am willing at least to give it a trial though at the melancholy expence of changing all my habits at a late period of life…

> For myself I would rather stay [at Abbotsford] than go & expect little from a change of climate and would be content to die where I am. But for the sake of my family I am willing to make an exertion for experiments sake.[37]

Malta! The thought gave him courage: an island fortress in the sun, a place steeped in history and chivalric derring-do. Of Malta he had read since in his teens, when he had devoured René Aubert, l'Abbé de Vertot's history of the Knights Hospitallers of St John of Jerusalem, sometime of Rhodes and latterly of Malta. This work, which he read in the English translation of 1728, had been 'exceedingly dear' to him, as he confessed in the Ashestiel Fragment of autobiography, precisely because it 'hovered between history and romance'.[38]

It is not necessary to go quite as far as Edgar Johnson in suggesting that 'The entire country rang with applause of the generous offer' of the complimentary cruise to the Mediterranean in the Royal Navy warship.[39] Nevertheless, it is true to say that Scott's unique status as (in that hackneyed modern phrase) a 'national treasure' did mean that, to a very real extent, his voyage in pursuit of health and respite carried the hopes of a nation, or at least of its literary classes. William Wordsworth, visiting Abbotsford to pay farewell, wrote a sonnet on Scott's departure. It includes the lines

> ... the might
> Of the whole world's good wishes with him goes; ...

and it concludes thus:

> ... Be true
> Ye winds of ocean, and the midland sea
> Wafting your Charge to soft Parthenope!

Little known is an anonymous poem addressed to HMS *Barham* herself, which contains the following passage:

> ... Bright sun of Italy! soft southern clime!
> Ye gales that breathe of health, refresh his fame!
> Not yet consummated his glorious aim;
> Forms yet unseen, the beauteous, the sublime.
> From his creative spirit, life implore—[40]

A. N. Wilson has evoked touchingly and memorably the departure from Abbotsford, and has given us a wonderfully imaginative picture of Scott on the eve of leaving for Italy.[41] Scott's late-in-life Southern European tour, and the circumstances in which he undertook it, moved even the most hardened of travellers. Many shared, as it were, in his experience. In reading of his coming excursion they were themselves rejuvenated, reinventing their own past journeys and joining vicariously in what remained of the old rite of passage that had been the Grand Tour.

When, fourteen years previously, Mrs Marianne Maclean Clephane had been thinking of going to Italy to see her daughter Margaret, Lady Compton,

Scott had been enthusiastic. He appeared to wear his unmerited guise of the experienced and worldly-wise European traveller.

> I much approve of your going to Italy by sea: indeed it is the only way you ought to think of it. What a famous thing it would be to get a cast [variously meaning an opportunity, a chance, a help or a 'lift'] in a King's Ship—perhaps Captain Clephane might arrange such a matter for you. It would save expence, and then the having it in your power to land here and there would render the voyage so interesting.[42]

Now Scott was himself fortunate in getting his own 'cast' in a Royal Navy frigate.

There is no doubt Scott was facing the distinct possibility that he might die abroad. This much is clear from a letter of farewell to Charles Kirkpatrick Sharpe, written when the much-anticipated European trip had become a reality soon to take actual form:

> I am just setting off for the Mediterranean, a singular instance of a change of luck, for I have no sooner put my damaged fortune into as good a condition as I could desire, than my health... has failed so utterly in point of strength, that while it will not allow me to amuse myself by travelling, neither will it permit me to stay at home. I should like to have shaken hands with you, as there are few I regret so much to part with. But it may not be. I will keep my eyes dry if possible, and therefore content myself with bidding you a long (perhaps an eternal) farewell. But I may find my way home again, improved as a Dutch skipper from a whale fishing. I am very happy that I am like to see Malta.
> Always yours, well or ill—[43]

The workaday simile of the Dutch whaler is unexpected in a literary man embarking on a Continental tour in search of cultural enlightenment. The symbolism is not even Mediterranean, but rather that of Northern seas. These were doubtless dangerous in their ways; but prospective Grand Tourists might have been more wary of falling into the volcanic Solfatara near Pozzuoli, or of being overcome by the *mal'aria* of the Pontine Marshes in the Roman Campagna. In its flippant tone it is characteristic of Scott's enduring view of foreign travel. But then Scott was not a regular Grand Tourist, and any late-in-life 'improvement' was to be regarded as purely incidental.

*   *   *   *   *

In London, before departure for Portsmouth to board HMS *Barham*, Scott completed the Introductory Address, in the name of the pseudonymous

Jedediah Cleishbotham, to what was to appear as the Fourth and Last Series of *Tales of My Landlord*, that is the two novels *Count Robert of Paris* and *Castle Dangerous*. These were published together under the *Tales of My Landlord* general title in December 1831 (though the volumes are actually dated 1832). J. G. Lockhart quotes what he terms the final passages of this 'preface'; but what Lockhart actually cites is the very much shorter piece of prose that had been reconstructed, and much altered, from Scott's original text by Robert Cadell so as to form a short postscript to *Castle Dangerous*. This bears an entirely valedictory character.

> The gentle reader is acquainted, that these are, in all probability, the last tales which it will be the lot of the Author to submit to the public. He is now on the eve of visiting foreign parts; a ship of war is commissioned by its Royal Master to carry the Author of Waverley to climates in which he may possibly obtain such a restoration of health as may serve him to spin his thread to an end in his own country.

If mental and bodily powers should not decline unduly, Scott mused, he hoped that he might meet his public 'if not exactly in his old fashion of literature, at least in some branch [here he was surely thinking of the putative travel book], which may not call forth the remark, that—"Superfluous lags the veteran on the stage."'[44]

The writer of the 'Critical Notice' [i.e. a review] of the Fourth and Last Series of *Tales of My Landlord*, published in *The Border Magazine* for December 1831, expatiated on the finality of Scott's, eve-of-departure, leave-taking by adding another gratuitous, and even more sombre, note of termination. If Scott himself was hoping to spin his thread to an end contentedly at home, having survived his desperately-needed time at sea and in the sun, then this anonymous doomsayer envisaged a more likely and less happy outcome:

> ... he the mighty magician, oppressed by the burdens of age, is now seeking in a foreign and milder clime relief from pain, where perhaps he will find a stranger's grave.[45]

Captain Basil Hall, who had been instrumental in pulling together arrangements for Scott to be conveyed at the Admiralty's pleasure, was one of the greatest travellers of his age. He knew South Africa, Java, Korea, and South and North America. He had written extensively about these countries and regions of the world. He had met Napoleon in his exile on remote St Helena. Yet Basil Hall recorded his emotional involvement in the mechanics of Scott's departure in terms that are remarkable. Of all the voyages and travels he had ever made, Hall asserted, the most interesting by far was the

trip with Scott from London to Portsmouth to assist him in embarkation.
Hall noted how Scott had been entertained by re-acquainting himself with
Henry Fielding's *Journal of a Voyage to Lisbon*—but also how Scott had been
much affected by the thought that Fielding and Tobias Smollett had both died
abroad, each having journeyed south in unrequited search of health.[46] Henry
Matthews, the literary invalid, had been forced to set out on 'a wild goose
chase after health, and try, like honest Tristram Shandy, whether it be possible
to run away from death…'. And Robert Semple had observed that 'there [was]
always something affecting in the sight of the grave of a fellow countryman in
a foreign land; how much more when they are crouded so thickly together' as
in the English burying-ground in Lisbon where Fielding lay, the spot (as Henry
Matthews discovered) unmarked.[47]

*   *   *   *   *

Scott was to be accompanied on his Mediterannean voyage by his younger
daughter Anne and by his elder son Walter, now promoted Major, who had
been granted special leave from his regiment and who was to travel without
his wife. In Naples the three were to meet with Charles Scott, the younger son.
Together, as a family, this little group would make one of the more unusual
of British 'Grand Tour' parties. It was riven by difficulties of all kinds. If Sir
Walter was a sick man, then neither was his daughter a well woman. Elder
brother and younger sister did not get on. Both were stressed by their father's
condition. Major Walter Scott was taciturn but dictatorial, boorish yet (in
Naples at least) a smooth British sort-of *cicisbeo* figure, who developed an
unbecoming interest in a flirtatious, married Englishwoman. Charles Scott, in
his own way both ill and ineffectual, did not add much to the happy family
mix in 'soft Parthenope'. The often acerbic, but acute, Marianne Talbot could
not conceal her unflattering view of the Scott siblings. She included Charles
Scott, diplomat or not, in her damning judgement on the family. 'What an
extraordinary thing it is that such a Man as Sir Walter is should have children
so little like him.' According to the émigré Glaswegian doctor, Edward Hogg,
who attended them in Naples, the Abbotsford travelling party formed 'quite
an ordinary Scotch family in their interior [that is, when at home, in their
Neapolitan apartment]. They storm & scold & swear!'[48]
    Naturally, Scott had hoped he might find his son Charles 'quite qualified
for a cicerone.' In that aspiration he was to be disappointed. Charles himself
had seen little of Naples, and nothing of the ancient sites in the surrounding
countryside. Writing to a friend, Charles had admitted that, though he had
been in his post nearly a year, he had not 'seen any of the lions here not even
Pompeii.' He complained that he was 'nearly all day in the Chancellerie—
employed about trifles.' He followed this confession with the statement of

resolution that 'as soon as my father arrives [I] intend to see Pompeii & all the other lions before I return to the Land of Fogs [that is, Great Britain].'⁴⁹ The 'lions' were the great sights and sites of Europe, which the Grand Tourists of tradition had been accustomed to tick off in their guidebooks. Now, his father's impending visit reminded Charles just what he himself had not, as yet, got to know. It must have been with a sense of embarrassment that he had written to his sister Sophia to the effect that it was 'just as well there is so much to be seen here, for Books'—he seemed to imply that his father's real interest in Naples would be in the bookshops and libraries—'are not to be got in this Kingdom.'⁵⁰ To some extent he would be proved right, in the direction of Scott's interests; but also wrong, in the matter of his being unable to satisfy those same inclinations, for Sir Walter bought many books, and also delved in the Bourbon royal library.

Immediately upon his father's arrival in Naples, however, Charles, together with his brother Walter and Captain Hugh Pigot of HMS *Barham*, made an impulsive night-time assault on Mount Vesuvius in eruption. The three had been at the opera on 26 December 1831 and, coming out of the Teatro di San Carlo, had seen the volcano glowing and belching fire and smoke. In a rather surreal episode, they hailed a carriage to take them out of the city and as far up the mountain as possible, and continued on foot in midnight darkness. Pigot was forced to give up, exhausted; but Charles and Walter pressed on to the crater, wading through hot ashes and with streams of lava flowing around them. The following morning, equally impulsively—but now refreshed and fortified by excellent wine and ham at a local hostelry—they carried on to Pompeii. After this double expedition, Charles wrote something so interesting and noteworthy about Pompeii that his father, had he known of it, would surely have been impressed. Charles's diary entry is cryptic, barely legible and difficult to interpret due to the obscurity and abbreviated nature of his reference. Flying visit though this was, it appears to have occurred to him that touring the ruins of Pompeii was somewhat akin to another flying visit: the tale told by Alain-René Le Sage in *Le Diable boiteux* (1707). In this story, by one of Walter Scott's literary heroes, the character Don Cleophas is taken by the 'Devil upon Two Sticks', Asmodeus, on a demonic flight over the roof-tops of Madrid, and is able to look through them into the rooms of the houses below. Anyone who knows Pompeii can appreciate immediately what Charles Scott meant when he noted the idea of a town opened to the gaze of the visitor because the roofs of the buildings were not present, and can only be impressed by Charles's imaginative, if recondite, allusion.⁵¹ Who else had then, or has since, used this simile in writing of the buried cities of Vesuvius? It is the kind of conceit that Sir Walter Scott, devotee of Le Sage, might have been pleased to think of for himself.

*　　*　　*　　*　　*

At Portsmouth on 25 October Scott opened his heart to his journal:

> Here I am going on a long and curious tour without ability to walk a quarter
> of a mile. Quaere what hope of recovery? I think and think in vain when
> attempting to trace the progress of this disease, and so gradually has my health
> declined that I believe it has been acting upon me for ten years gradually
> diminishing my strength. My mental faculties may perhaps recover; my bodily
> stren[g]th cannot return unless climate has an effect on the human frame which
> I cannot possibly believe or comprehend. The safe resolution is to try no foolish
> experiments but make myself as easy as I can—without suffering myself to be
> vexd about what I cannot help. If I sit on the deck and look at Vesuvius it will
> be all I ought to think of.[52]

Scott's lawyer, John Gibson, had at least been able to tell him that all three
assurance companies with which his life was insured had given him 'leave …
to go abroad', two of them, however, stipulating an additional premium of
ten shillings per cent [*sic*]. The Norwich Union had made no such demand.
Gibson thought fit to share with Scott the 'very handsome letter' from Richard
Morgan, actuary of that life office. This read:

> The Directors have much pleasure in conceding to Sir Walter the permission
> requested. They make no charge—and offer their sincere and warm good wishes
> for the restoration to health of the greatest genius of the age.[53]

10

'The Glory of Scotland, Sent to Visit Strangers'

For most Grand Tourists, the sites they visited were already familiar through word and image. As HMS *Barham* stood off Gibraltar, Scott encapsulated succinctly in his journal something of the essence of the 'Grand Tour' experience. Here was, indeed, a place that he and his companions had, in a sense, known or at least 'heard of all our lives': to see it now in actuality was, therefore, akin to meeting an old friend. Scott had entertained an idea of the rock fortress 'from prints, panoramas and so forth'. Reality proved not so very different from imagination.[1] Personal inspection or acquaintance with sites might result in emotions ranging from the comfort of actually seeing for themselves what they already knew, to the satisfaction of having their excited expectations confirmed. Alternatively, tourists might succumb to a measure of disappointment when they found that the buildings of ancient and modern Rome, for example, did not appear quite so majestically vast in scale as Piranesi had rendered them in his artfully contrived and, in perspectival terms, daring *vedute*. Awe might be tempered by actuality. Joseph Forsyth had written of

That rage for embellishing, which is implanted in every artist [and which] has thrown so much composition into the engraved views of Rome, has so exaggerated its ruins and architecture, or so expanded the space in which they stand, that a stranger, arriving ... with the expectations raised by those prints, will be infallibly disappointed.[2]

Off south-west Sicily *Barham* hove-to so that Scott might visit 'Graham Island'. This was the geological phenomenon, part of the underwater volcanic mass of what is now known as 'Empedocles', that had suddenly arisen from the sea in the summer of 1831. It had been claimed by the Royal Navy for Great Britain, and named first for Vice-Admiral Sir Henry Hotham, Commander-in-Chief in the Mediterranean. A later landing by the Royal Navy saw Hotham displaced (as it were) by his political superior, and the upstart volcanic 'island' renamed in honour of the First Lord of the Admiralty, Sir James Graham, Scott's benefactor in facilitating the passage to the Mediterranean. In London before his departure, Scott had spoken of being anxious to see 'Graham Island'—if (as he put it) 'it would wait for him'.[3] It did. In his journal he referred to it as 'the Burning island' noting, perhaps with some regret, that it did not make its 'terrors visible'.[4] Italian volcanoes in eruption held much attraction for Grand Tourists as examples of the stupendous power of nature and the sublimity of spectacle, as shown by the paintings of Pierre-Jacques Volaire, or the engravings of Pietro Fabris which illustrated the superb work of Sir William Hamilton, *Campi Phlegraei*. Even mortal danger, such as Captain Basil Hall had experienced when caught in a sudden, violent eruption on the slopes of Vesuvius and showered by red-hot stones and lava bombs, could be made much of in retrospect.[5] Now Scott was carried on the back of a sturdy sailor all over the steaming and suphur-reeking 'island', just as Grand Tourists of the past were in the habit of being carried through flooded Roman structures on the shore of Lake Avernus or at Baiae; James Hall, indeed, recorded just such an experience only a few years before.[6]

The 'island' was to subside as suddenly as it had emerged, soon after Scott's visit—but not before he had written an account of it, which he sent to James Skene so that it might be read before the Royal Society of Edinburgh. A synopsis of Scott's whimsical offering to the (doubtless surprised) learned men of Edinburgh is included in two letters to Robert Cadell, written from Naples and in the knowledge that the 'island' phenomenon was no more. Scott and his fellow travellers had been, he mused, 'possibly the last who imprinted the footsteps of inhabitants belonging to the upper earth upon materials which have now been reclaimed by the unfathomable caverns of Ocean.' The disappearance of the island 'would be a fine subject for an Ode to the tune of "Molly [*sic*] put the Kettle on"'. His 'paper' was best 'termed the last speech, dying words & expressions of the new island'.[7]

Although Scott does not say as much, one wonders whether a comparison had not flashed through his mind as he 'rode' over Graham Island: a transient land-mass—just as a glittering career—might rise from nothing, burst into heat and flame and bubbling effervescence attracting the world's fascinated admiration, yet subside and vanish as suddenly as it had appeared, because its internal structure could not sustain its eminence. In some ways, Scott's landing on Graham Island is an unrecognised metaphor for what he described to Skene (in the letter of 25 November 1831, cited above: see note 7) as his 'defects' and 'deficiencies' so evident on a journey 'undertaken late in life'.[8]

After receiving Scott's 'paper' on Graham Island, and having presented it to the Royal Society of Edinburgh, James Skene wrote a long letter to Scott that refers back to Scott's account of the phenomenon and, beyond that again, back to the benefits of travel. Skene also sought to find a connection between Scott's recent reportage and his wider, past literary career:

> Your account of the hide and seek island was very interesting. I read it to a most numerous assemblage of the Royal Society <u>the day after</u> the arrival of your letter which added not a little to the gratification of the Society to find that the first notice of you which had reached Scotland should contain so kind a remembrance of them.

Scott's letter on Graham Island, Skene wisely and tactfully judged, was neither intended nor strictly suitable for publication by the Royal Society. Rather, he consigned it to the realm of what one might term the Transactions of Whimsy than to any actual Proceedings of a scientific academy:

> The time will come when it may be considered a curious document, when all memory of Graham's Island has passed away, and a somewhat remarkable feature in your Geological Annals, that after having filled the world with a whole phantasmagoria of imaginary scenes, it should be your fate to commence Geologist by the description of the next thing to an apparition, which seemed to wait for the waving of your rod to vanish from existence.

As to the world of the traveller, Skene shared thoughts founded on a lifetime of wide experience. This ended on a cheerful note of refreshment and renewal, and with the hope of a coming reunion with a dear old friend:

> I have always found myself revived by a foreign trip, and have no doubt but that you will experience the same; there was something to me in the change of diet and mode of life, and the succession of agreeable excitements which made the machine turn smoothly on all its pivots, and then the being removed out of the way of all the little bothers that get time to gather round us when dozing at home. One feels justified in seeking for amusement alone, and whether you will find it or not, the very search is pleasure and the indifference as [to] the result prepares one to get, in point of health, the full benefit of change of climate. So that I am quite confident of again seeing you tramping it with renewed vigour in your old haunts of Abbotsford.[9]

*   *   *   *   *

Just over three weeks were spent in Malta. As has been indicated in the Preface to this book, the period began with a time in quarantine. 'It is in the capacity of Quarantine prisoners that we now inhabit the decayd grandeur of a magnificent old Spanish palace', he told James Skene of his party's confinement, rather as a 'contraband commodity', in Fort Manoel.[10] Two of his visitors were daughters of friends and colleagues at the Scottish Bar, which must have helped the time pass more agreeably. One was Mrs John Davy (née Fletcher, daughter of an advocate who had actually lived in Castle Street, not far from Scott's former house). Her views on the discomfort of a quarantine have also been quoted in the Preface. The other, Euphemia Dawson, was the daughter of William Erskine, Lord Kinedder, dedicatee of the Third Canto of *Marmion*, and who had been one of Scott's companions on the 'lighthouse cruise' of the summer of 1814 and, before and after that time, one of his greatest literary confidants. Scott had known Mrs Dawson since her childhood. There was much to chat about. If Scott was thus enabled to feel at home—whatever Scott might say against 'herding' with one's compatriots—so too must these particular Scotswomen have been reminded of what Lady Nairne called 'hame and infancy'. Mrs Davy recorded Scott's appearance, improbable as it was for the central Mediterranean. With his stick, his shepherd-tartan trousers, his voice 'so home-like a sound in this strange land' and his talk of his 'own Tweedside', he was an apparition that she said brought to life the Charles Robert Leslie portrait, which she knew in its engraved form.[11]

The offer of a home from home was uppermost in the mind of Sir John Stoddart, who wrote to Scott as soon as *Barham* dropped anchor in the quarantine harbour. Stoddart, Chief Justice of the island, lost no time in reminding Scott that he was 'the oldest friend you have at Malta, and that I shall insist on my rights as such.' Both Stoddart's town and country houses were immediately offered for Scott's use or accommodation and, as if to tempt him further, Stoddart added this: 'Lady Stoddart, you know, is an old Scotchwoman, and will know how to prepare for you the comforts to which you have been used, so far as they can be supplied at Malta.' One imagines stocks of haggis, sheep's-heid, Glenlivet and black bun being laid in or searched for in Valletta... But Stoddart also pressed a literary button. He mentioned that he had just received a letter from Wordsworth—Stoddart had, in fact, first brought the two poets together—and recalled also how he had given hospitality to Coleridge twenty five years previously, during his first period of legal service in the island.[12]

Above all, in Malta there was John Hookham Frere, who with his late wife had retired there some years previously: 'the captive', as Lockhart put it, 'of the enchanting climate and the romantic monuments of the old chivalry.'[13] Sir Walter wrote to Mrs Scott of Harden that Frere was 'one of the most entertaining men I know'.[14] It was Frere whom (as we have seen) Scott had hoped to join in Spain in 1808. Thus there is a certain completeness to the story of Scott's European travel history, either wished-for or accomplished, in keeping company with Frere in Malta; a circle had been described, as in the ancient *ouroboros* symbol.

The most striking memoral of knightly power in the island, the armoury of the Grand Master's Palace, will surely have struck a chord with the owner of an historical collection of arms and armour at Abbotsford. And for one who delighted in heraldic display, as Scott did on a rather more modest scale in the hall of his country house, the Cathedral Church of St John (today the Co-Cathedral of Valletta), with its spectacular display of chivalric consequence—its incomparable armorial pavement, and the opulent chapels of the various national and regional *Langues*—will have been an inspiration if, that is, the experience was not simply overwhelming.

Had Scott been a 'regular' Grand Tourist of the old school he would, on reaching the lands of the Mediterranean, have fallen under the influence of the architecture of classical antiquity. The memory of this or that structure might have led him to build a classical garden pavilion, perhaps, or a lodge gate. But Scott was not one such, and his house was Abbotsford. In the higgledy-piggledy streets of Valletta, however, where the buildings leaned on each other 'in such a bold, picturesque and uncommon manner', he found 'some ideas for finishing Abbotsford by a screen on the west side of the old Barn with a fanciful wall decorated with towers to enclose the Bleaching Green ornamented with watch tower[s] such as these, of which I can get drawings while I am here.'[15]

But all was not contentment in the winter Mediterranean sun. Scott was deeply concerned for his financial position, and distressed by the thought that the expenses of the trip might be dishonoured by his bankers. He was desperate to hear news from Robert Cadell of the success (or otherwise, as Scott feared) of his latest novels. Upon those sales depended his ease of mind. Dark and cryptic entries in his journal suggest that he was contemplating the most radical of solutions to his financial predicament: suicide. This is what the sinister phrases 'some strong measure', 'meditating a sad purpose in case of my being disgraced', and 'self Agency' indeed suggest.[16] He was conscious that any such action would prejudice the payment of insurance policies on his life. He had known men who had died by their own hand. But, at last, he heard from Cadell of the improbable triumph of *Count Robert of Paris* and *Castle Dangerous*. He could breathe again with relative ease.

Landscape, history and topography apart, Malta inspired him in a literary direction. His prospective novel, *The Siege of Malta*, with 'much description & some real history', made good progress. In Valletta there were fine libraries to consult. The very fact that he had nose in book, and pen in hand once again, caused him to look with some optimism to the future. Thus he mused to himself: 'I think if I continue it [the new novel] will be ready in a very short time and I will then get the opinion of others and if my charms hold I will be able to get home through Italy—and take up my own trade again.'[17]

Writing to James Skene, Scott managed something of the old fire of descriptive ability:

> It is pipers' news [stale or out-of-date news] to tell of the splendid beauties of what is called the Channel of Malta, which is one of the most glorious scenes, with the assistance of the Great Mongibello [Mount Etna], which I ever saw in my life. Certainly if landscape various as the heart of man can conceive could atone for a curious want of national character, this land has it all to show for itself ... Their former great men of literature were indeed giants in the land, but they live less in the hearts of their own countrymen than the much inferior personages of our own. Robert Burns, Allan Ramsay even, and less men than even the last, have received fully their meed from their countrymen. I myself have every right to be grateful to my countrymen, and I will say in your ear that I have not been undeserving of good-will at their hands, particularly those who in a matter-of-fact age enough are much acted upon by the feelings of the very imaginative one which preceded us.[18]

Circumstances had not in the end permitted a diversion to Sicily—Captain Pigot could do only so much for his famous passenger, and even without landfall in Sicily the voyage from Malta to Naples, courtesy of the Royal Navy, was more than Scott had necessarily accepted as a certainty. And although it was indeed 'a week too late in life for visiting the Cyclops her reverence' (as he had joked with Charles in August), he continued to hope that there might just be the chance to see the island by some means as an excursion from Naples, or on a yet-to-be-determined extension of his Mediterranean tour. Skene had written to Scott of his hope that he might

> be able to visit the <u>whole</u> line of the eastern coast of Sicily. I traversed it foot by foot. It is full of interest. I was made prisioner in Syracuse & confined for three weeks, but it is needless to talk of scenes which will become as familiar to yourself. The day I hope will come when we shall traverse it together at the fireside of Abbotsford.[19]

*   *   *   *   *

The periods Scott spent in Naples (three months and three weeks) and thereafter in Rome (where he remained for some twenty-two days)—*loci classici* of the Grand Tour, the latter being its heart, soul and intellectual essence; the former the seat of incomparable natural beauty, gaiety, and a full-blown exoticism—were not simply the most interesting episodes of his journey: they furnished, also, certainly the most moving moments of his European experience as a whole. John Scott of Gala had been sure that his great kinsman would find much of interest in Naples and its vicinity, and was concerned only that he might find it *too* exciting.[20] When, within a couple of days of disembarkation, Sir Walter and his daughter were nearly killed in a run-away carriage, this presentiment was almost proved correct. The 'soft Parthenope' of the Romantic poets had a hard and fearsome edge.

Scott was amused that his arrival in the Bay of Naples should coincide with a spectacular eruption. It was as if Vesuvius were paying tribute to the 'Monarch of Parnassus', as Byron had called him long before. Scott had confessed to Robert Cadell that he thought the tumult of Naples might drive him mad.[21] All his reading in the years before his Mediterranean jaunt—and he had a surprisingly large number of works on Neapolitan history and topography in his library—will certainly have conveyed a picture of a city of bustle and beauty. Only Marianna Starke, whose *Information and Directions for Travellers on the Continent* he had bought in its sixth edition (presumably in anticipation of the visit on which he was now embarked) offered an opinion on the character and demeanour of the Neapolitans more charitable than other writers, for whom the city always seemed what one might call a Janus-faced place poised on the edge of chaos.[22] Joseph Forsyth had written memorably of the Neapolitan crowds: 'a general tide rolling up and down, and in the middle of this tide a hundred eddies of men. Here you are swept on by the current, there you are wheeled round by the vortex.'[23] Henry Matthews had warned of the 'eternal bustle and worry of the streets', and of the English visitor surrounded by a crowd of applicants 'as ravenous as birds of prey about a carcass;—all anxious to have their share of the carrion.'[24] For Jane Waldie, the *lazzaroni* were contemptible. Sin, want, crowds, homelessness, profligacy, falsehood, crime, cowardice, cruelty, lack of all decency and all cleanliness: such were characteristics of Naples, a failing state tainted to the very core.[25] Viewed 'within', thought Anna Jameson, 'Naples gives me the idea of a vast Bartholomew fair ... It is a crowd which has no cessation ... The whole population seems poured into the streets and squares ... such wild physiognomies, picturesque dresses, attitudes and groups—and eyes— no! I never saw such eyes before ... half langour and half fire...'.[26] Forsyth juxtaposed a nobility 'pure both in heraldry and opinion' with the lower orders in their 'paradise inhabited by devils'; 'a delicious climate, high spirits, a facility of satisfying every appetite, a conscience which gives no pain, a convenient ignorance of their duty, and a church which ensures heaven to every ruffian that has faith.'[27]

But the setting and physical appearance of Naples were universally praised, and Scott must have looked forward to seeing for himself what his travel books had described. Anna Jameson had written of how the city 'Viewed from the sea ... appears like an amphitheatre of palaces, temples and castles, raised one above the other by the wand of a necromancer...'.[28] It sounded an ideal destination for 'the Wizard of the North'. Forsyth dismissed the churches as 'harlequins in marble, quite ugly with decoration … They delight in the crooked, the piebald, the gaudy, and push irregularity to its farthest bourn…'.[29] Scott would have been unconcerned: he did not like the Baroque anyway, although he was partial to the irregularity of the Gothic, and tried hard to achieve it in Abbotsford. But the landscape was incomparable. This Scott would, and indeed did, appreciate. As Forsyth had put it:

> To a mere student of nature, to an artist, to a man of pleasure, to any man that can be happy among people who seldom affect virtue, perhaps there is no residence in Europe so tempting as Naples and its environs.—What variety of attractions!—a climate where heaven's breath smells sweet and wooingly— the most beautiful interchange of sea and land—wines, fruits, provisions, in their highest excellence—a vigorous and luxuriant nature, unparalleled in its productions and processes—all the wonders of volcanic power spent or in action—antiquities different from all antiquities on earth—a coast which was once a fairy-land of poets, and the favourite retreat of great men. Even the tyrants of the creation loved this alluring region, spared it, adorned it, lived in it, died in it.[30]

*   *   *   *   *

The letter James Skene had sent to Scott in the hope that it would catch him in Malta was, in fact and by coincidence, written the very day Scott disembarked at Naples: 26 December 1831. In this letter, Skene had expressed doubt as to whether Scott would like Naples: 'the winter climate is often disagreeable, and rather an overdoze of society.'[31] To some extent, Scott found both these statements true. About the climate he could do nothing; and as far as Society went, it devoured him as both a celebrity (on the strength of his reputation and past achievement) and a curiosity (owing to his present condition and circumstances). As in Paris on both his visits, so now in Naples Scott was fêted by royalty and the great world. Newly released from abbreviated quarantine, and settled in his lodgings, he must have been both flattered and amused to learn that ladies at a Neapolitan ball on New Year's Day 1832 would be wearing dresses modelled on Waverley Novel characters. In fact there is no conclusive evidence that he himself attended the event: he and his daughter were rather shaken by the near-disastrous carriage accident just beforehand. There seem actually to have been not one but two Waverley balls in Naples that month. Charles Scott (who must surely have known what was going on in society and diplomatic circles) reported to a friend on 20 January that

> the Austrian Minister gives a grand fancy ball of characters taken from the Governor's [that is, his father's] novels. All the pretty women English and foreign

are fighting and crying as is usual before these affairs. One beautiful Italian
woman has been in tears for the last week because her family are too Catholick
to allow her to take the character of Rebecca the Jewess [in *Ivanhoe*].[32] -

Further flattery came in the form of welcomes and solicitations of various
kinds from members of the British community. Thomas James Mathias,
an English scholar of Italian literature who had met Scott in London on a
number of occasions, greeted him first with a fulsome manuscript ode in
Latin, 'Viro per Europam celeberrimo Gualtero Scott: patriae ornamento
poetae historico...'.[33] This was then printed in Naples and given to Scott for
the Abbotsford library, where it remains along with other works by Mathias,
some also presented in Naples. These were accompanied by an epistolary
tribute to one 'who has so long instructed, informed and gratified more nations
than his own'. Mathias hoped Naples would restore Sir Walter's health,

> that you may be enabled to encrease more and more the publick stock of that
> ennobling and dignified pleasure which your genius, learning, and unexampled
> fertility of invention, and your reverential regard to the publick morality, have so
> eminently qualified you to offer to your own country and to Europe.[34]

This makes it sound, first, as if the fertile volcanic soil of Campania might
increase Scott's literary production; and, second, that his influence might even
be able to reform the morality of a basically immoral (or even amoral) city.

Yet Scott was wise enough to appreciate the strangeness of his position
as a fish somewhat out of mainstream Grand Tour waters. Writing in a long
letter from Naples to the fourteen-year-old Charles Scott of Sunderland Hall
(for whom he stood guardian) he offered an interesting series of thoughts of
guidance for the young man's future, whichever direction he might happen to
take. Near its conclusion there occurs this passage:

> Music, for which I think you have a natural turn, is an art which renders you
> delightful in society and enables you to enjoy it yourself. The languages for
> which your classick studies have laid an excellent foundation will I think one
> day enable you to qualify yourself for foreign travel, which I am now practising
> at the advanced age of sixty one, and in the character of a dumb beggar—a very
> amusing character in society.[35]

Shortly after Carnival, Scott made a report on his Neapolitan life to his
kinswoman, Mrs Scott of Harden, who was of German birth.

> The society is very numerous and gay, and somewhat too frivolous for my time
> of life and infirmities; however there are exceptions; especially poor Sir William

Gell, a very accomplished scholar, who is lamer than I am, and never out of humour ... It has been carnival time, and the balls are without number, besides being pelted to death with sugar-plums, which is quite the rage. But now lent is approaching to sober us after all our gaiety, and every one seems ashamed of being happy, and preparing to look grave with all his might.[36]

By March, Scott was evidently feeling that what he assessed as the prevailing characteristic of Naples—its frivolity—dominated even its 'singular mixture of good nature and savageness'. A city 'certainly one of the gayest in the world' was 'abominably frivolous'. 'Society' was a perpetual round of dancing: hard enough for a lame man in the prime of life, let alone for one in Scott's physical condition. 'I am perhaps more disgusted at an amusement from which I am excluded yet I think I should be the same were [I] as light a foot in the ballroom as any of my neighbours [in the Neapolitan social whirl.]'[37]

An even less jolly picture of Scott in Neapolitan society is furnished by Owen Blayney Cole who recalled watching him, at a *conversazione* at 'Palazzo' Garnier, standing 'helplessly' between rooms, the one full of company, the other empty and silent: the scene, thought Cole, was 'memorable as an eclipse'. Yet there was something 'granitic' about Scott's bearing; and Cole was not alone among the British in Naples to remark on his 'roughness'. He seemed almost like a 'gentleman farmer' in those gilded salons, possessing (in what Cole termed his 'Caledonian Club' dress) more of a 'baronial than a literary appearance.'[38] The verses—as far as is known his last original composition—which Scott wrote at the request of the Russian Princess Zenaide Wolkonsky (otherwise Zinaida Volkonsky) served to demonstrate his sadly diminished mental and physical capacity. They contain, however, not just a recondite biblical reference but one that Scott seems to turn into a perceptive and gently mocking self-assessment in the lines

> Say can fair Wolkonsky expect
> Fruit from a withered Scottish thorn?[39]

Early nineteenth-century travellers of the appropriate strata of society were urged not to overlook the benefits of bringing along a uniform. Not only was such a dress considered the proper attire for presentation to royalty and princes of the Church, but it also demonstrated the wearer's status as a man of importance. In Paris in 1815—clad in the regimentals of the Royal Edinburgh Volunteer Light Dragoons—Walter Scott, Esquire, had met the Tsar of Russia. Now in Naples in 1832, as Sir Walter Scott of Abbotsford, Baronet—accoutred in the somewhat grander uniform of a Brigadier in the Royal Company of Archers (King's Body Guard for Scotland)—he was presented to Ferdinand the Second, King of the Two Sicilies, looking (as Scott himself recorded) 'as well as sixty could make it out when sworded and featherd *comme il fault*. I passd well enough. Very much afraid of a fall on the slippy floor but escaped that disgrazia.'[40]

Physical infirmity, however, limited him greatly. As he told Skene:

> I admire the face of the country extremely about Naples but, alas! I can no longer crawl up the hills on pony back, at which no man on earth would ever have defeated me, and it would be quite folly under all the circumstances to hope to acquire such dexterity again. I can have a pony cart, and we may have a race of gigs if we wish to revive old frolics …[41]

With genuine sadness and concern for Scott's condition, both physical and mental, Marianne Talbot recorded her feelings in her private journal. 'Reports say he is in a state of imbecility; I trust not to the extent said.' She met him as soon as he had come out of quarantine. Her immediate reaction was one of pity at the spectacle before her of 'poor Sir Walter.' Miss Talbot, in her shocked state of feeling, had to explain herself to her own journal:

> Think of saying 'Poor Sir Walter'! He could hardly rise from his chair to welcome me, & his speech was so defective that I could hardly hear him … How sad to see genius & imagination brought so low—for a man in the state Sir Walter is in throws a chill over a whole society; it is impossible not to watch him & and to attend to him … It is most melancholy to see the glory of England & Scotland sent to visit Strangers & appear thus.[42]

She later noted that, in Scott's Neapolitan rooms, there was ' cruel deal of gossip after he goes to Bed…', the gossipers presumably being the Scott sons and daughter, none of whom Marianne Talbot liked. She continued: 'Scandal reigns in that Palazzo Caramanico [Palazzo d'Aquino di Caramanico al Chiatamone, below Pizzofalcone, where Scott and his family had taken rooms after leaving their temporary quarters in the Hotel Gran Bretagna] & lies innumerable are circulated. Still it is life, & at home is death now.'[43]

It was with some relief that she noted occasions when Scott's condition seemed better and his mind appeared firmer. Nevertheless, it was the fact that though his memory was 'as accurate as ever for distant events connected with Scotland or Litterature [*sic*]' it was 'but faulty for every day events.' And his 'speech struggled with his imagination.'[44] She also—and most tellingly—observed that, in company, 'he seemed tired with heat & light & foreigners.' These three essential elements of the Grand Tour experience appeared not to agree with him.[45]

Marianne Talbot's record of Scott's mental state echoes that of Thomas Moore, who had been in Scott's company in London prior to his departure for the Mediterranean. On that melancholy occasion Moore had been shocked to see and hear Scott, whose 'looks and utterance' showed signs of paralysis. He contributed little to the conversation. Moore was 'painfully struck by the utter vacancy of his look. How dreadful if he should live to survive that mighty mind of his! It seems hardly right to assemble company round him in this state.' Moore noted, nevertheless, that it was 'charming to see how Scott's good temper and good nature continue unchanged through the sad wreck of almost every thing else that belonged to him.'[46] Flashes of that temperament, although decreasing evidence of the once-mighty mind, were apparent in Naples.

Thomas Moore may be the source of some comments (by one 'M—') about Scott in 'his pride and prime' which entertained a dinner-party given by Marguerite, Countess of Blessington, in London, probably in the winter of 1833-4. The language and sentiments are so similar to those of Moore quoted above that it seems very likely that the words were his. The speaker recalled 'the most manly and natural character in the world. You felt when with him, that he was the soul of truth and heartiness'. His hospitality was as 'simple and open as the day'. 'M—' contrasted this with the condition in which he had found Scott when in London on his way to Italy, 'broken quite down in mind and body'.

The recorder of this table-talk was the young American man of letters Nathaniel Parker Willis. In his *Pencillings by the Way*, Willis also gives a long account of a fascinating episode in Naples that is not to be found in any other original source.[47] His information was derived from Lady Blessington, doyenne of Anglo-Neapolitan society during her residence there in the 1820s. She in turn alleged that the anecdote was taken from the account written by Sir William Gell of his relations with Scott in Naples. But, as the passage does not occur in Gell's own retained copy of his reminiscences, this may be suspect. However, Gell did add passages to his account and sent them to Lady Blessington when, convinced that Lockhart would not do justice to his memoir of Scott, he was encouraging the Countess to find a British publisher *instanter* (as he put it) for his account as an independent work.[48] As J. C. Corson dryly observed, the Blessington copy of Gell's memoir 'must have been fuller' than Gell's copy, if the account by Willis 'does not contain his [Willis's] own or Lady Blessington's embellishments'. Either accurate, and deriving ultimately from Gell's memoir, or else fanciful and embroidered, what Willis wrote is nevertheless worthy of resurrection from a little-known byway of gossipy travel literature or the obscurity of a learned endnote.[49]

In his memoir, which Willis described as 'a melancholy chronicle of [Scott's] weakened intellect and ruined health', William Gell unquestionably stated that

When Sir Walter visited the Library at the Museum, the Literati of Naples crowded round him to catch a sight of so celebrated a person, and they shewed him every mark of attention in their power, by creating him honorary member of their learned societies.[50]

Under Willis's gushing pen, however, what is very probably the same episode has become hugely elaborated and infused by every possible trait (or rather *caratteristica*) of Neapolitan exuberance and emotion.

… Sir Walter went with his physician and one or two friends to the great museum. It happened that on the same day a large collection of students and Italian literati were assembled, in one of the rooms, to discuss some newly discovered manuscripts. It was soon known that the "Wizard of the North" was there, and a deputation was sent immediately to request him to honour them by presiding at their session. At this time Scott was a wreck, with a memory that retained nothing for a moment, and limbs almost as helpless as an infant's. He was dragging about among the relics of Pompeii, taking no interest in anything he saw, when their request was made known to him through his physician. 'No, no', said he, 'I know nothing of their lingo. Tell them I am not well enough to come.' He loitered on, and in about half an hour after, he turned to Dr. H.[i.e. Edward Hogg] and said, 'Who was that you said wanted to see me?'. The Doctor explained. 'I'll go', said he; 'they shall see me if they wish it;' and against the advice of his friends, who feared it would be too much for his strength, he mounted the staircase, and made his appearance at the door. A burst of enthusiastic cheers welcomed him on the threshold, and forming in two lines, many of them on their knees, they seized his hands as he passed; kissed them, thanked him in their passionate language for the delight with which he had filled the world, and placed him in the chair with the most fervent expressions of gratitude for his condescension. The discussion went on; but not understanding a syllable of the language, Scott soon wearied, and his friends, observing it, pleaded the state of his health as an apology, and he rose to take his leave. These enthusiastic children of the south crowded once more around him, and with exclamations of affection and even tears, kissed his hands once more, assisted his tottering steps, and sent after him a confused murmur of blessings as the door closed on his retiring form. It is described by the writer as the most affecting scene he had ever witnessed.[51]

Writing to Lockhart about the spectacle of the Bay of Naples, Scott described a scene 'closed by Vesuvio of the one hand and the romantic island of Capreae [Capri] on the other'.[52] There is no evidence that he visited Capri, which he would surely have loved, though he would also have found its vertiginous slopes and steeply stepped lanes too much for him. The taxing ascent of Vesuvius was clearly out of the question, even with porters and chairs to carry him, no matter how much he might reminisce about erstwhile agility and climbing feats of yore. There is no evidence, either, that he visited Sorrento and the northern shore of the Sorrentine peninsula, or the spectacular Amalfi coast on the southern side of that delicious finger of land projecting into the Tyrrhenian Sea. When he wrote 'Sarentum' in his journal, he certainly meant to write 'Salerno', through which he indeed passed on his excursion to Paestum: his description of the landscape, with its buffalo pastures, unquestionably fits that of the region south of Salerno, and undoubtedly not that of Sorrento.[53] But the wider Sorrento locality would surely have attracted him, had he been able to tour it, on many counts: the mediaeval history, and the later English literary allusions, of the maritime state of Amalfi; the incomparable natural beauty of the rugged scenery; the sea-girt, cliff-top villages clinging to the rocks. But even if he does not appear ever to have visited Sorrento, his name and reputation did attach themselves, however erroneously, to the place; and, to some degree, both live on. Today—in an egregious instance of wishful-thinking that claims a famous traveller for itself—the distinguished old Tramontano Hotel (built on the site of Tasso's house) lists him among its illustrious Romantic-era guests, both in traditional, faded inscribed form in its saloon, and now also on its website.

The food and wine that people have enjoyed on holiday is one of the great retrospective talking-points. Grand Tourists shared some of this interest, albeit in a less pronounced way than today. And when they did write or talk about the food in France or Italy, it was all too often in derogatory terms. Scott, as we have seen, rather enjoyed the food and wine of France, though he was still quite pleased to stop eating and drinking *à la française* and to live more in a traditional Scottish manner once again. But by the time he went to the Mediterranean, his health was so poor that his doctors had cautioned against any form of over-indulgence. He had greatly moderated his intake of wine and spirits, had lessened his consumption of any form of rich food, and had cut back on after-dinner 'segars'. But in Malta there had been too many dinner parties, and too much Champagne. Later, and on the return journey, he sought distraction and release from the numerous, varied stresses of travel and, beyond that, from the mental disturbance his worsening condition brought on: his children, and others, noted with alarm his abandonment of prudence with regard to all food and drink. Much was pressed on him, and he made a Grand Tour of the dinner tables of Rome. But now, in Naples, he was relatively restrained, and generally stuck within limits. He certainly experienced the unaccustomed delights of the Vesuvian Lachryma Christi, but was equally able to hold back in favour of moderation. It was with some self-satisfaction that he told Cadell about his diet: bread and butter, and a bunch of grapes for breakfast; little meat; and 'my mess of vegetables, and macaroni', which 'keeps me in excellent order.'[54]

The most noteworthy aspect of Scott's Neapolitan experience was the frequency with which he compared the scenes and sights encountered with the more familiar ones of Scotland. Comparisons with home ground were, quite naturally, by no means uncommon for British participants in the Grand Tour to make; but Scott's constant evocation, when abroad, of his native heath is particularly striking. 'The country [around the Bay of Naples] is the most beautiful I ever saw', he confessed to William Laidlaw, 'but I would often give it all for a sight of Tweedside.' Marianne Talbot had hinted at his enduring memory of Scotland, if not of much else. Scott's was, she freely admitted, 'the finest imagination we have'; yet his head was 'even now full of old Legends & Knights & Ladies & of the good old time' in Scotland: he could repeat Border ballads, 'but grew puzzled about the present time.' He liked to talk much of King George IV's visit to Scotland in 1822, for which he had been pageant-master and for which (as she said, with just a hint of waspishness) he took 'great credit to himself for the management of Lords & Ladies, Highlanders, Taylors & persons of all tempers & all degrees whose obstinacy would have spoiled the Show.'[55]

Marianne Talbot also remarked that 'What seems to give him most pleasure at Naples are some vile little prints of the scotch lakes hung up in his bed room in the Caramanico.'[56] It is an intriguing thought that the Scotts must have brought these prints—poignant reminders of home—with them as part of their travelling equipage in order to use them to decorate any potential lodging, whether that be Sir Walter's cabin in HMS *Barham*, hotel rooms taken on first arrival in a place, or the apartments in baroque palaces rented for more extended stays. This seems more probable than that a cache of 'Scotch views' was chanced upon and acquired in Naples. Perhaps Anne Scott extracted the images from her 'beautiful Albums' which Miss Talbot admired and which included, besides drawings, the manuscript of Wordsworth's verse quoted above. If so, one wonders how many, if any, British Grand Tourists did a similar thing. The vast majority of travellers would surely have acquired views of the countries and cities through which they passed—an aspect of the traditional Grand Tour acquisition of art en route—rather than taking with them to Europe such graphic reminders of the homeland whence they had come.

Sir William Gell, who called himself Scott's 'keeper', was the principal recorder of Scott's observations when in Naples (the word 'keeper' being no doubt a nod to the traditional role of the Grand Tour bear-leader, who had featured in many a young man's journal or many an old man's satire). Scott, in turn, dubbed Gell the 'Coyphæus' of his party when they went to Pompeii, thus exhibiting sufficient familiarity with the terminology of the Attic theatre to call to mind this technical term for one who lead a chorus in its stylised dance and recitation.[57] Scott's condition, however, would scarcely allow him to walk let alone dance; and his lack of enthusiasm for most of what Gell showed him in the realm of archaeological remains did not encourage much verbal expression on his part.

Gell made much of Scott's repeated recollections of and allusions to Scotland. He noted how, among the most picturesque scenery that the Grand Tour had to offer, and at sites redolent of the very essence of classical history and mythology, Scott would often turn the conversation to Scottish history and landscape, or see Scottish parallels and symbolism when or where such thoughts might not readily occur to others.

Gell thought this trait significant enough to wish to add a passage to his *Reminiscences* that would illustrate Scott's enduring fixation on Scotland. At one moment he would talk in support of the refutation, by Gilbert Laing Meason, of the authenticity of Macpherson's 'Ossian' because names had been taken from modern maps, including some place-names of comparatively recent coining. At another time, he would be anxious to describe the ancient megalithic monuments of Orkney (Laing Meason's home territory) which Scott himself had seen on his 'Lighthouse cruise' in 1814: the Stones of Stenness, and the outlier from the henge circle itself, the mysterious Stone of Odin, with its perforation that made it so significant in local folklore. Improbable as it seems, Scott appears to have had with him in Naples a drawing of the Stones of Stenness—did this come from among his 'Scotch views', or from Anne's albums?—which he gave to Gell.[58]

Of course Scott was far from alone among his contemporaries in the way he tended to see Europe in 'Scottish' terms, or to make comparisons in which Scotland did rather well for itself and punched above its weight in aesthetic terms, not to mention intellectual and social ones. Henry Cockburn was a notable example of just such a tendency: a disposition, as Karl Miller has well put it, 'to read Europe in terms of Scotland, in terms of an indefatigable series of homely comparisons, invidious or otherwise.' Having memorably described Cocky's 'Scotching of the Rhine', Miller wryly notes 'the persistence of Scottish comparisons. There in the midst of these foreign parts', namely (in Cockburn's case) Venice and the north of Italy, 'were Arbroaths and Dalkeiths.'[59] So Scott's specific reaction to Italian scenery was part of a national pattern, even if in the environs of Naples he carried it further than most of his compatriots.

Lago d'Agnano, in the evocative volcanic region of the Phlegraean Fields or Campi Flegrei ('Fiery Fields') west of the city of Naples, is a case in point. It reminded Scott immediately of a Scottish loch. This, said Gell, was indeed Scott's chief gratification in visiting Agnano, 'for I afterwards found that his only pleasure in seeing new places arose from the poetical ideas they inspired, as applicable to other scenes with which his mind was more familiar.'[60] At the monastery of La Trinità della Cava, at Cava de' Tirreni on the neck of land between the gulfs of Naples and Salerno, Scott was moved to recite the whole of 'Jock of Hazeldean' on account of some resemblance he perceived in the landscape which reminded him of home. Early manuscripts in the convent library piqued his interest, for to the mediaeval (as Gell regretfully conceded) 'he is more addicted than to Greeks & Romans.'[61] At Pozzuoli and at Cumae, in the heart of the Phlegraean Fields, and even when William Gell asked him if he had noted the names of the numinous spots they had seen—and whether he remembered the places they had visited—Scott's mind immediately reverted to Scottish ground and Scottish history, especially that tinged with Jacobite sentiment. Gell thought this a 'strange commentary' on all he had been saying about legendary Lake Avernus and other sites. 'As an antiquary', sniffed Gell, 'I felt that my citadel of Cumae and my Greek and Roman tombs had produced little ef[f]ect on the mind of the poet, and we therefore returned to Pozzuoli to an excellent dinner…'.[62]

It is interesting to note that Scott's son-in-law, J. G. Lockhart, was, in his turn, equally disappointed by the lakes of the Phlegraean Fields. Perhaps unconsciously, Scott's views, as recorded by Gell, had lodged in Lockhart's mind only to surface in a letter to a friend from Naples in 1843. Classicist though he was, Lockhart wrote that Lake Avernus, fabled mythical entrance to the underworld, was 'very like a third-rate Highland loch'.[63]

*   *   *   *   *

Gell was equally disappointed by Scott's reaction to the ruins of Pompeii, to which he appeared 'generally nearly insensible, viewing the whole and not the parts, with the eye not of an antiquary but a poet, and exclaiming frequently "The City of the Dead", without any other remark.'[64] The Street of the Tombs was Scott's introduction to the site. William Gell supplied the touching reminiscence that here, because Scott was tired and walking with difficulty, Gell offered the chair in which he himself—Gell was also lame—was to be carried around: a chair on poles, almost like an open sedan chair, rather of the kind which was also used to manhandle tourists up Vesuvius. Another chair was procured and both were tied together with cords and handkerchiefs, so that the two British knights might ride side-by-side over the basalt-paved streets. In the forum, a large table was set for luncheon; and, like tourists everywhere when refreshment is provided during a respite from physically taxing and mentally tiring sightseeing, Scott seemed (as Gell noted) 'cheerful and pleased'.[65] Henry Baillie, on whose arm Scott lent as he shuffled round a smoother part of the site, confirmed the comment about 'The City of the Dead', which saying Scott uttered repeatedly.

Scott's phrase has been remembered, and it has done his memory little good. Yet it is possible that he can be considered as not just a tired, bored old man, with 'underlying health issues', visiting an archaeological site when he would rather have been having a *riposo* (siesta). He can, indeed, be viewed as a leader of a changing aesthetic. Modern scholarship now perceives the unfortunate 'City of the Dead' refrain, once regarded as so banal and pedestrian, in a different and a better light. Scott's Pompeiian 'rehabilitation' began in 1979, with an essay by Laurence Goldstein:

> Though a passionate antiquarian who had turned an entire generation's eyes towards the vivid scenery of the past, he now seemed indifferent both to the excavations in progress and to the archaeological history which his guide, Sir William Gell, recited at length. Instead he limped dejectedly through the ruins, muttering 'The City of the Dead, the City of the Dead', as if claiming a place of burial. His poetic phrase, a cliché from that moment if not before, elevated Pompeii from a romantic stop on the Grand Tour ... to a place of profound symbolic character. Travelers became increasingly fascinated with the ambiguous spot where ... 'Life and Death/ [Are] Wedded'.

Goldstein goes on to assess Pompeii's 'sacramental quality' as a place chosen, as it were, 'by history to intrigue the modern consciousness'. He interprets Scott's visit—so easily written off—as the beginning of a new way of seeing, thinking about, and being moved by Pompeii. It would be for Charles Dickens a dozen years later, and others before Dickens and after him, to put into fuller words sentiments Scott only just touched upon.[66]

More recent scholars since Goldstein have taken up the theme of Scott's significance as a new type of 'discoverer' of Pompeii:

> The encroachment of romantic sensibility onto more detached and abstract antiquarian turf neatly crystallized in 1832, when Sir Walter Scott (himself dying) visited Pompeii ... in the company of the eminent archaeologist Sir William Gell ... This episode was widely reported, and it demonstrates that a frisson of delight and horror at the prospect of so much death in such an idyllic setting was as valid a response to the site[s] as antiquarian reflection.

The same writers continue: 'Narratives centering on the trauma of horrific destruction of the cities became the predominant approach in the nineteenth century as Scott's "City of the Dead" supplanted the antiquarian vision of the sites.'[67] With Giuseppe Fiorelli's astonishing plaster casts of bodies, thirty years later, 'catalyzing and performing for a broad public the terror of Vesuvius's eruption as they revivified the dead in their final moments ...[a]... shocking physical manifestation of the ghosts of antiquity', Scott's apparently pedestrian reaction has been vindicated in retrospect.[68]

But, at the time, Henry Baillie, himself a huge enthusiast for classical antiquity, could not understand 'the small amount of interest' displayed by his great countryman in what was shown to him, and was astonished that Scott made no remarks about anything. 'Sir Walter's whole heart', Baillie recorded, 'was in the Middle Ages'—a period in which Baillie himself happened to evince little interest.[69] In all probability, Scott was ill-prepared for his visit. Although he had bought Major J. P. Cockburn's views of Switzerland on their appearance in 1820, he had not thought to acquire the previous year the same author-artist's *Delineations of Pompeii* when John Murray started to issue the first parts of a work which was, in fact, soon abandoned.[70] But more to the point, and more embarrassing in view of William Gell's role as companion and *cicerone*, was the fact that Scott had never added to his antiquarian library Gell's own extremely important *Pompeiana: The Topography, Edifices and Ornaments of Pompeii*, written in conjunction with John Peter Gandy and published in parts by Rodwell & Martin between 1817 and 1819. With his interest in the Claude glass and the camera obscura as aids to conveying images of landscape and structures, Scott should have been intrigued to see what Gell and Gandy had been able to achieve by use of the camera obscura as a method of recording the discoveries at the site.[71] But of course he was not to know that he would ever go round the site with its distinguished chronicler and interpreter.

A pleasing detail of both Gell's and Baillie's accounts of Scott's visit to Pompeii is that an excavation had been 'ordered for him'. This was probably the dig to which Scott makes reference in a letter to Robert Cadell: 'The King [Ferdinand] has been particularly civil & offered to make an excavation at Pompeii expressly in my name.' This produced the sort of utilitarian objects as were found every day—ironically just the sort of artefacts that, earlier, Scott would have been delighted to see turned up by the plough on his land at Abbotsford.[72]

In the year of Scott's visit to 'The City of the Dead', the American poet Sumner Lincoln Fairfield published his extensive, three-canto *The Last Night of Pompeii*, with a love-interest in Mariamne, the Hebrew slave, and Pansa, the Roman soldier. It had a theme that was really a religious allegory, with a sort-of classical version of the biblical flood, heaven-sent destruction, and the remaking of the world. Pompeii was a licentious city destroyed as a result of its own wickedness. The excavations, Fairfield suggested in his Preface, 'have furnished the tourist, the antiquarian, the novelist, and the poet, with many a subject of *picturesque* and glowing description.' Fairfield used the same phrase, 'the cities of the dead', this epithet comprehending also Herculaneum, which Scott did not visit—but neither had Fairfield seen them, in actuality. These places, Fairfield wrote, 'have not wanted frequent and often faithful historians; every disinterred temple, theatre, statue, pillar, tomb, and painting, has found admirers.'[73] Only two years separate Scott's visit to Pompeii and Fairfield's poem (both 1832), and the publication of Edward Bulwer-

Lytton's novel *The Last Days of Pompeii* in 1834.[74] (Fairfield felt he had been plagiarised by Bulwer-Lytton.) The site clearly had the emotional power to inspire both a poet and a novelist; but that poet and novelist was not to be Sir Walter Scott, who would in all probability not have written on such a subject even in his prime. For places or objects to interest (or inspire) him, as it has recently been observed, 'these had, directly or through his imagination, to fit into the landscape in his mind created over previous decades.'[75]

The tour of Pompeii had a very strange and almost contemporary afterlife. In 1835, the alpinist and geologist John Auldjo (who had known Scott in Naples) reported to Lady Blessington that a sketch of a fictitious visit to Pompeii had been published in the Neapolitan literary magazine *L'Omnibus*. This, by one 'Bonnucci', purported to be the story of the Countess's going to the site accompanied by Scott, Byron, Madame Juliette Récamier and various others in a *mélange* that is, of course, both absurd and chronologically impossible. It went one better than Scott's actual visit, for the party toured the ruins by romantic moonlight. Scott is made to hobble for a while before being given a crutch—which may actually have been a human one in the form of Lady Blessington herself. The author's fantasy includes a vignette of Scott speaking *cattino Inglese*—bad English—because *il facile e gentile idioma gli era affato ignota*: meaning, roughly, that easy and polite language was entirely unknown to him! Scott was, furthermore (as Auldjo reported, paraphrasing the Neapolitan author's nonsense), 'sulky' because he was *zoppo*, lame, like Byron, Bulwer-Lytton—'what will he say to this libel?', Auldjo interjected— Chateaubriand [did Bonnucci mean Talleyrand?] and George Canning. Auldjo continued his precis of Bonnucci's bizarre *jeu d'esprit*:

> However, poor Sir Walter takes little notice of anything, being buried as it were in his own past dreams, as one called from the grave, and only kept with them [the rest of the party] by the enchanting smiles of the beautiful genuis [sic], who hung upon his, the delighted author's, arm![76]

Scott's lack of interest in classical antiquities is further illustrated by his attitude to some characteristic wall-paintings from Pompeii. These had been removed from their original locations, and were displayed in an apartment where a meeting of the Royal Society of Naples—the Società Reale Borbonica, the national academy of the Kingdom of the Two Sicilies—was taking place. The President of the Royal Society of Edinburgh, Scotland's national academy, asked naively what might be 'all those red things on the wall'.[77] The great collections of classical art in the Museo Borbonico, otherwise known as the Palazzo degli Studi or just 'the Studi', left him unmoved. Probably his reading of Marianna Starke put him off: sightseeing in the museum—as indeed later in the Capitoline and Vatican collections in Rome—was just too formidable a proposition, if one were to follow Miss Starke's pioneering system of exclamation marks (! to !!!) and her laboriously detailed lists of the sculptures in these great collections.

*   *   *   *   *

Yet, despite his Laodicean attitude to antiquity, Naples had given Scott himself the sort of fillip he believed should recommend travel to others. With a moment's enthusiasm for the Naples area that he did not always exhibit, Scott suggested to Lockhart that he 'would really like this country extremely you cannot tread on it but you set your foot upon some ancient history...'. In his time, Lockhart did like the country, and the coastal scenery of the Bay of Naples from Baiae to Castellammare di Stabia. 'You can't conceive anything richer, grander, or more beautiful, certainly nothing more curious, for every rock is pierced with Roman brick, and you can see arches and pedestals creeping everywhere into the sea.'[78]

As for Scott himself, he had researched and written a fair amount: further literary works were in active preparation, or at least under consideration. To William Laidlaw he wrote cheerfully: 'I have been busy stuffing my head with information and have enough new information to block out at least £10,000 of entertaining literature.' The initial interest shown in a prospective novel set in Malta was sustained in Naples, and indeed the thought of that, and research for it in Neapolitan libraries, buoyed him to an extent while in the city. Marianne Talbot, who helped him with translation and who supplied books for his use, said that he was 'full of his Maltese book', and that though it was pathetic to see that he showed little concern for much around him, Malta did spark some real interest.[79] William Gell also commented on Scott's having 'already got a Malta romance in hand & almost finished & a poem & other things in view.' Although not blind to Scott's mental and physical deficiencies, Gell also reported to the Dilettanti in February 1832 that he was 'by no means in an unenjoyable state but very chatty & amiable.'[80] To Lady Blessington he confided a month later that he thought Scott 'in much better health; in short I would say recovered, and all the better since his arrival here ... He is very agreeable in a drive or *tête-à-tête*, but lost in parties of twenty, to which he is invited.'[81]

Gell told Lady Blessington that his memoir of Scott's time in Italy would owe much of its likely interest to what he could say of Scott's 'future literary projects'. He reckoned his 'Reminiscences' much less 'barren of interest' than he had expected when he began to set them down on paper. Indeed, Gell thought that only he could supply information on the genesis and progress of these very late literary plans of Scott's.[82] The idea of a work on Rhodes was prime among them: this will be touched upon shortly. Scott's other project was the travel book. An old idea had been revived, and it was now certain—so Scott asserted, with a backwards glance to his successful *Paul's Letters to his Kinsfolk*—to be a series of letters in the form of another 'tour of Paul'. Initially this was mentioned as likely to make a work of three volumes; but only a little more than a fortnight later it was being described as a potential book of perhaps double that size. 'If the burn [stream] does not burst and the banks bide [remain, or hold fast] we will have the letters from Italy amounting as it may fall to five or six volumes of epistolary letters.' Clearly Scott was ebullient when he gave thought to where his current and prospective travels might lead in publishing terms. But, just as clearly, his over-optimism was in the ascendant. 'I feel myself so alert and well', he told Cadell, with a rodomontade almost worthy of the most boastful of Italian literary characters—though his verbal repetition in this very sentence may tell another story—'that I am not ashamed to say that I feel myself as well able to work as when I began Waverley.' In part, this mood of cavalier over-confidence was because wider shores had beckoned: he might now visit the Ionian Islands, mainland Greece and the Aegean for perhaps a month, and perhaps even venture beyond, 'which if I make it will greatly add to my collection of letters.'[83]

A Continental travel journal; another 'Tour of Paul' in a series of ostensible letters; some other form of diary or memoir: whatever might have emerged from Scott's Mediterranean journey would be almost wholly reliant for its sales and its success upon the mystique of his name. Surely it would have to be known to be *his* journal or *his* letters. The market was flooded with 'Continental journals', so something to set yet another of the genre apart would be essential. Anonymity would not do, as it had sufficed in 1815. But there was also the far more fundamental issue of what he could possibly have to say that others had not said; and, furthermore, of how he could quite manage to do so in his diminished mental and physical condition. Writing in the specific context of the epicentre of the old Grand Tour, Henry Matthews had made a perceptive observation. 'Of the sights at Rome', he had written in 1820, 'it is impossible to say nothing—and it is difficult to say anything new. What so many have told, who would tell again?'[84] Taking up from Matthews's acute assessment of the late-Georgian travel writer's essential problem, Stephen Cheeke has expounded further on a predicament that would certainly have been Scott's, writing of

> the romantic trope of inexpressibility, of the ineffable, [that] runs up against the sheer weight of history ... [What Matthews says] is true, but it is also itself a commonplace. 'What can I say that isn't a cliché' is itself a cliché in Rome. What can I say that hasn't been said a thousand times before? The refusal to speak like an antiquarian and the awareness of the burden of too much history are gestures not invented by Goethe, but which inevitably accompany a city with

an ancient past ... Hostility to connoisseurship, anti-antiquarianism, and search for archaeological knowledge, were important parts of the sensibility of visitors such as Byron and Shelley in Rome...[85]

And of Walter Scott, too. His antiquarianism was not of a precise, pedantic kind. He viewed the classical scenes of the Grand Tour with the eye of a Romantic. But his brain, in 1831-32, was simply not up to the task of distilling new thoughts in new ways for his old readership.

*   *   *   *   *

When Scott and his printer James Ballantyne had been correcting proofs of *The Talisman* (1825)—that novel which, with *The Betrothed*, constituted the Waverley Novels sub-set entitled *Tales of the Crusaders*—an important admission was conceded by the author.

> One thing is certain that I am so far from dreading that I do most solemnly reverence any criticism founded on a superior knowledge of the subject treated of to that which I possess ... if my tale be false I would in every case desire my manners to be true and it is therefore I fear these Asiatics whom you keep *routing* for—they are a sort of folks of whom I know nothing but from books & with whom many are now acquainted by actually [*sic*: he meant 'actual'] observation.[86]

Some six years later, in July 1831, Scott had been engaged in revising *The Talisman* for the Magnum Edition. In the novel (which had been a considerable success) he was writing, as he now freely and publicly admitted in the new Introduction, about a part of the world of which he was 'almost totally unacquainted', save for early *Arabian Nights* recollections. By contrast, many of his contemporaries were experienced in precisely the way he was not.

> The love of travelling had pervaded all ranks, and carried the subjects of Britain into all quarters of the world. Greece, so attractive by the remains of its art, by its struggles for freedom against a Mahomedan tyrant, by its very name, where every fountain had its classical legend; Palestine ... had been of late surveyed by British eyes, and described by recent travellers. Had I, therefore, attempted the difficult task of substituting manners of my own invention, instead of the genuine costume of the East, almost every traveller I met, who had extended his route beyond what was anciently called 'The Grand Tour', had acquired a right, by ocular inspection, to chastise me for my presumption. Every member of the Travellers' Club ... constituted my lawful critic and corrector.[87]

Here he may, perhaps, have had in mind certain droll comments made by Lord Normanby in *The English in Italy*. Writing of what he lampooned as the 'pride of travel', Normanby discussed the imagined gradation of rank among travellers. Those who had been to Geneva thought themselves superior to those who had been only to Paris; those who had got to Naples superior to those who had only reached Florence; and so on. Even Italy was now much less prestigious than, say, northern travel in the Baltic region. Normanby amused himself—and doubtless Scott—by envisaging military ranks in travel. Italian travellers were subalterns; Baltic voyagers were captains; but those who ventured to Egypt or the far reaches of Greece were field officers, and the most adventurous of all were 'Knights Grand Cross of the peripatetic order'.[88] To what rank among travellers could a mere sometime Quartermaster of the Edinburgh Volunteer Light Dragoons, albeit one now advanced to a Baronet of the United Kingdom, aspire? Charlotte Eaton's character Mr Bredalbane, in *Continental Adventures*, made what she described as 'the modern Grand Tour, which begins where the ancient Grand Tour used to end.' Thus Bredalbane, like 'other accomplished and adventurous youths of the present day', set off from Naples bound for Greece. That much Scott, disadvantaged by age and infirmity, might just have seen his way to accomplishing, even if the rest of the itinerary prescribed by Mrs Eaton for her imaginary traveller—one almost inconceivable in its range and exoticism—was far beyond either Scott's present capabilities or his wildest desires.[89]

Scott accepted that, whereas he still looked to Italy as the apex of his travelling plans, others—who might subsequently write of their experiences—had moved beyond: to Greece, the Levant, and further. Had he missed the boat completely; or might he still catch up with the new trend? And so even he began to yearn to see, for himself, beyond the Western Mediterranean. This was not an easy step. Going to Greece, as Robert Holland had observed, 'called for a mental as much as a physical leap over and beyond any visit to Italy.'[90]

Even before he left Portsmouth in HMS *Barham*, Scott had been speaking of perhaps seeing Alexandria, and the Pyramids; and of getting as far as Athens, even Constantinople.[91] Indeed, he had even mused airily about going on from Malta to Alexandria if his curiosity—specifically a wish to 'expiscate' [a splendid Scottish term for finding out something by skilful means or close examination] the answer to a question about oriental magic then intriguing him—so directed his course.[92] In Naples, his intentions became more narrowly focused: first, on Corfu, where General Sir Frederick Adam, son of his old friend Willam Adam of Blair Adam, was British High Commissioner of the Ionian Islands, and to which transport might be provided in Adam's steamboat; and, second, on Rhodes, which had become, in his mind, the setting of a narrative poem. The cycle of his literary life would thus be complete: narrative verse, to prose fiction, and to romantic poetry once again. He wrote confidently to Lockhart that Sir Frederick 'will give me a cast in a steam boat to visit Greece ... We will return to Europe'—Greece was clearly considered to lie effectively outwith the European Continent—'through Germany and see what peradventure we shall behold.' In one rather confused letter, Adam's craft 'for carrying me to any part of Greece I may wish to visit' had become, in his excited mind, a naval vessel of an interesting kind, namely 'a good armd gun steam brig, so we shall be in full state.'[93] To Robert Cadell he wrote optimistically: 'I have not a complaint of any kind, and am as able to endure travel as ever I was in my life.'[94] But Scott had not fully appreciated how far Rhodes lay from Corfu. References to his projected travels were invariably buoyant: he would certainly go to Corfu, to Athens, to Corinth, to Rhodes, 'and other places great in Antient story, with great content, ease and safety'; maybe even to 'Stamboul', if another Royal Navy frigate were to be available. His daughter, Anne, thought that Vice-Admiral Sir Henry Hotham, Commander-in-Chief on the Mediterranean Station, would oblige by providing another vessel, 'which will make travelling easy... In that country I hope to pick up a great deal that is new and interesting.'[95] As a result of 'expiscation' there would be further scope for fresh reportage and new anecdote.

Although he meant *Corfu*, Scott had actually written *Corunna* in his letter to Cadell of 13 February 1832: it was almost as if, in his imagination, he had returned to his earliest foreign scheme, that of visiting the scene of the war in the Iberian Peninsula. But now he was hoping that some time in Sicily might also be worked in: still he thought of Sicily, his appetite sharpened by Skene's recent description and, before that, by what he had heard from Lady Northampton. Alternatively, if he went immediately to Rome, Sir Frederick Adam would send a steamer to Brindisi—the geography became somewhat mixed-up in Scott's mind—for 'the promised peep at Greece which is in great confusion [the politics of the country, that is] but it is little I will care for that as I do not mean to expose myself to the least danger.' As demonstrated so often before, he was no Byron. The Greek war of independence was dragging on, and at the time Scott was fantasising about a possible visit to Athens there was fighting in the city and the Acropolis was again in Ottoman hands.

In March, Sir Frederick Adam wrote both to clarify the position and to offer Scott a further possibility for wider travel.[96] In doing so, he introduced a famous name—Sir John Franklin—into the story of Scott's putative venture beyond the lands of the traditional Grand Tour. Rather than confirming the offer of his own steam-boat, Adam now assured Scott that, with the connivance of Admiral Hotham, a man-of-war would indeed be at his disposal. 'My friend Sir John Franklin (the traveller) is very anxious to be allowed to bring you here [Corfu] & will be equally glad to carry you on to

Greece.' Franklin was captain of HMS *Rainbow*, then on the Mediterranean station. He was, moreover, interested in ancient sites and would have been an excellent *cicerone* had he in the end been able to escort Scott through the Greek islands.[97]

Adam went on to express the hope that events in Greece would have assumed

> a more quiet aspect ... for in truth the accounts of the state of that Country...
> scarse were such as would have made me more than doubt the prudence of any
> body going there for pleasure & gratification of curiosity. As to your coming
> to any Adriatic port of the Kingdom of Naples to embark it is quite out of
> the question, the accommodation is such & the roads in such a state as not to
> be encountered by any females. We had good proof of this on our journey to
> Brindisi which we got through but not without very serious inconvenience from
> which our party suffered considerably...

Adam was not a man to make a fuss about nothing. He had commanded a brigade at Waterloo and was engaged in the climactic action of the day, so when he reckoned conditions were difficult on some Apulian back-roads and in wayside *osterie* we can take his word for it. Scott, on his part, was unlikely to have been stirred by mention of Brindisi. Otranto, the next port down the coast, might have been more attractive to him, given its association with the Gothic romance of Horace Walpole.

Adam concluded with the hope that the Admiral's arrangements with Franklin would see Scott taken to Corfu by the end of April, 'the season of our greatest beauty & enable you to see Greece also just at the most propitious moment; before the heats are inconvenient...'. This may be one of the first recorded instances of the weather as a recommendation in favour of tourism in Greece at particular times of the year! Adam, however, was not a travel agent: he was a British Government servant, concerned with weightier issues; and so, remembering this, he concluded with the hope that 'the political heats will have subsided owing to the appointment of the sovereign'—that is the Bavarian implant, King Otto—allowing Scott freedom to see in safety whatever he desired.

One by one, however, Scott's dreams faded. Adam was now to be posted to Madras, so the Corfu scheme would come to nothing. With it went Athens, even if it were just a case of gazing at the city from the sea; so too, as he lamented, his 'vision of Rhodes goes to the Devil'. By mid-April, Scott had not yet heard anything further of his hoped-for passage to the Ionian Islands and the Aegean; no vessel seemed in prospect, though (as he said) 'I am on the lookout anxiously for one.'[98] Sir William Gell, however, obligingly provided Scott with 'as much topography as was necessary'—thus Gell described the matter in his *Reminiscences*—and indeed with 'more information ... than in the existing state of his infirmities he could have collected himself on the spot.'[99] As so often before, the first-hand travel memories of others, and factual material furnished by friends, might substitute for Scott's personal experience and 'autopsy', and might allow him to construct literary work relating to foreign parts on this 'at-one-remove' basis.

Scott would have loved Rhodes. But it would fall to Thackeray, a traveller even more than Scott at the attenuated end of the prolonged Grand Tour tradition, to put into words something of what Scott might have felt there; and, in doing so, Thackeray, in a magnificent interpretation of the tide of history, would tip his hat to Scott as romantic historical story-teller. But first he set the scene:

> The chivalrous relics at Rhodes are very superb ... beautiful and aristocratic: you see that they must have been high-bred gentlemen who built them ... they have this advantage over modern fortifications, that they are a thousand times more picturesque. Ancient war condescended to ornament itself ... whereas to judge from Gibraltar and Malta, nothing can be less romantic than the modern military architecture; which sternly regards the fighting, without in the least heeding the war-paint.

Thackeray went on to discuss, acutely, the 'double decay' of both Western chivalry and of the Ottoman Empire. But, retrospectively, he sympathised with Muslims in the era of the Crusades: they seemed, as he perversely suggested, 'the best Christians of the two...'. He continued: 'As far as I can get at the authentic story, Saladin is a pearl of refinement compared to the brutal beef-eating Richard—about whom Sir Walter Scott has led all the world astray' with his 'good-humoured pageant'. What was needed now—and what, presumably, Scott could not have provided in any poetic romance—was 'a real authentic story to instruct and frighten honest people of the present day, and make them thankful that the grocer governs the world in place of the baron.' Meanwhile, Thackeray went on,

> a man of tender feelings may be pardoned for twaddling a little over this sad spectacle of the decay of two of the great institutions of the world. Knighthood is gone—Amen; it expired with dignity, its face to the foe; and old Mahometanism is lingering, just about ready to drop.[100]

One feels Scott might have written, and certainly would like to have written, in that manner, of a place he longed to see. But Scott was the past, and Thackeray was the future.[101]

Genuine sympathy for a man he liked was tinged with an element of mild cynicism, even sarcasm, in William Gell's dismissal of Scott's Eastern Aegean fantasy. In late February 1832 Gell had informed his Society of Dilettanti friends that Scott 'thinks he is now going to Greece, which considering how little he cares for Greece & Rome is certainly not worth the trouble to him. But he seems to like sailing & so Greece is very well for that in a good Kings Ship.'[102] But in mid-March Gell wrote again to the Dilettanti in these terms:

> ... I hope I shall persuade him not to go to Greece for which He is quite unprepared to take any interest & and for which his health is quite unequal. He has an idea of a poem on Rhodes ... but as I go about a good deal with him & observe how he sees things, I can tell him more about Rhodes, than he will ever learn if he goes & am now making him a little collection of notes, sketches & hints which I trust will render the voyage useless [by which Gell means 'unnecessary']. The fact is that though he is very well & much better since he has been here, a case might arise when he might be lost in a few minutes for want of a Doctor which as He is now quite free from all debt, if he will go, he will I hope take with him.[103]

Gell had said elsewhere this that he believed—erroneously, as it happened—that Scott had now paid 'every shilling of his debts' and so could, presumably, afford to employ a private physician.

Four things stand out in these remarks. First is the repetition of the idea that Scott could work as well—indeed, perhaps, more easily—from secondary published sources and hand-me-down information as he could from personal observation and direct acquaintance with actual places. Second is the notion that such free financial resources as Scott now possessed could best be invested in what we might describe as travelling medical care of the kind that today gives assurance to elderly (and wealthy) passengers on cruise ships. Third is the real traveller's dismissal of the motives and methods of those whom they perceive as not essentially interested in what they might see or where they might sail, but who go 'to have the name of it', and for the sake of the sea-voyage. Indeed Scott is categorised by Gell almost as the archetypal, mass-market 'cruise ship passenger' of today: those people who like sailing, and doing so in luxury, but who do not, perhaps, mind very much where they go, and who voyage without profound understanding or even great appreciation of the seas, coasts, islands and landfalls through, along and to which such a cruise might take them. Fourth is the strong idea that the traditional but passé Grand Tour, and the spirit of adventure that it exemplified and was embodied in it, might now be curtailed and constrained by such practical considerations of health such as Gell mentioned in the case of Scott having a doctor on call. The era of the organised, package excursion and the Cook's tour—on which particpants could feel safe and secure, and have their path smoothed by couriers—was fast approaching.

*   *   *   *   *

William Gell detected an increasingly urgent wish on Scott's part to return to Abbotsford. Lockhart's assertion was that his father-in-law had learned of the passing of Goethe, which had unsettled him: 'Alas for Goethe! but he at least died at home—Let us to Abbotsford.' The anecdote, affecting as it is, has long been discredited by Donald Sultana and others, John Sutherland going as far in justified cynicism as to label it one of Lockhart's 'more beautiful' inventions.[104]

But, by now, Scott probably had indeed had enough of 'abroad'. Walter the younger had returned to military duty in Britain. Charles and Anne Scott would escort their father back. Not only was there a pressing wish to see home again; there was perhaps another, sadly prosaic, reason why Scott did not pursue his notions of more exotic travelling in the Ionian and the Aegean seas. This is revealed in fascinating, unpublished transcripts of letters among the 'Grierson Rejects' in the National Library of Scotland.[105] We have already seen that there was a scheme for Captain Sir John Franklin to take Scott first to Corfu and then round the Peloponnese into the Aegean, there to show him whatever might be seen from the safety of the poop deck of HMS *Rainbow*. Franklin may have been a name synonymous with adventure and discovery, but Scott was now facing realities the very reverse of such a spirit of derring-do. In a letter to Robert Cadell, Scott explained that his lawyer, John Gibson, was worried that one of the insurers of Scott's life—the Edinburgh Life Assurance Company—would now quibble if he were to venture any further.

Knowing this, Sophia Lockhart had written anxiously to her sister Anne Scott in Naples. Her letter was addressed to their father, but it was clearly intended for Anne's eyes first and foremost. 'Mr Gibson understands', she wrote, 'that

> Papa's plan is to visit Greece… and that in consequence he [Gibson] has written to the insurance offices… to obtain the necessary permission, but until he obtains this permission Papa must not set foot in either <u>Asia</u> or <u>Africa</u> or the money will be gone.

John Gibson, Sophia added, 'begs us [that is herself and J. G. Lockhart] to write to put Papa on his guard.' Charles Scott later confided to Lockhart: 'I hope something will prevent the Greek expedition'[106]

For his part, Scott insisted to Robert Cadell—arguably the man with even more to lose by any premature end to Scott's life—that he did not

> intend to travel but merely to look ashore at some respectable places I can see from the sea. Do not fear I shall keep myself out of all scrapes and if the affairs of

Greece mend for at present they look gloomy I shall come home by some other method.

Scott shared with Cadell his hopes—reflecting those of Adam and Hotham—that, if the situation in Greece were to 'mend', and if Franklin should actually be able to convey him from Naples to Corfu and thence into Greek waters proper, and thereafter to 'any place I may wish to see which will be only what I can see easily and safely', he would be prepared to take the risk; but, 'if the insure[r]s object I will hold my course northward and look at Italy and return by Venice and the Tyrol,' and then though Germany, where I have many friends.' To set Cadell at his ease, the assurance was given that Scott would be sure always to travel 'hooly and fairly'—hooly (or 'huilie') being a Scots word for slowly, carefully or gently.[107]

Scott's 'Grand Tour' was thus ending in a strangely subfusc, unromantic, almost 'Victorian' world of insurance policies and 'risk'. Indeed, this letter might well betoken the absolute, definitive end of the Grand Tour itself, as an institution based upon the premises of excitement and discovery, one where young men had traditionally grown to maturity despite all manner of rollicking adventures and risk-taking of every description from the religious, intellectual and political to the physical, moral and sexual, and even brushes with the Grim Reaper. Here now, instead, was a sick old man with a life policy, and a careful Edinburgh solicitor to raise issues of prudence and precaution.

Things changed fast. On 10 April Marianne Talbot noted in *her* journal that Anne Scott 'goes to Greece & Constantinople with her Father'; but on 15 April Scott confided to *his* that 'The Greek skeeme is blown up'. The starkly impressive temples of Paestum—'simple, chaste and inconceivably grand ... of the most awful species of classick architecture', as he noted in his journal, and 'particularly worth the while wonders' as he described them to Lockhart—which he had visited on an excursion from Naples would have to exemplify those temples of Greece which he was never to visit. And they surely stood as mockeries of the Greek Revival buildings of his own 'Athens of the North': 'pillars to which any that ever I saw are like pipe staples in point of size and scarce any other wise imperfect than in being roofless ... nothing I have yet seen have so much reality about them.'[108] (A 'pipe-stapple' or '-staple' was a term used in the Scottish borders for the stem of a clay tobacco pipe.)

A 'small closing carriage, warra[n]ted new and English' had been bought; 'we start tomorrow for Rome after which we shall be home ward steering.'[109] Gamely he had told Willie Laidlaw at Abbotsford that he would 'strive to fight round by Rimini and Venice', and so to Britain by the Tyrol, the Rhine and Holland. That was a much better way, he thought, than sailing from Naples to Marseille and thence up the Rhône: 'This is a horrid dull route and I dislike France very much.'[110] Of HMS *Rainbow* and Sir John Franklin no more was heard, though Charles Scott continued to hope that the ship would somehow put into Civitavecchia and so waft them away from the port of Rome—but to where?— given that insurance issues and urgency now directed the party northwards rather than on some ill-defined extension to their Mediterranean journey. Meetings in Naples with John Auldjo, and a presentation copy of Auldjo's *Narrative of an Ascent to the Summit of Mont Blanc*, did not tempt Scott to hazard a western Alpine route into France, despite half a lifetime's apparent wish to see such spectacular mountain scenery.[111] Even at the last, his views on various travelling itineraries and destinations were as fickle and capricious as ever.

*   *   *   *   *

Rome—'that Rome of which I have read so much', the place which Scott had several times told friends that he must somehow see in order to feel complete[112]—he did indeed see; but his time there proved largely an anti-climax. A city, in which Grand Tourists of the past, and of course pilgrims through the ages, might have spent many months or even a few years, detained him for just over three weeks. It is ironic that the epicentre of the Grand Tour tradition was reduced to a glorified staging-post on Scott's way home.

The travel literature he had read will have prepared him. Whereas Naples captured the senses, thought Jane Waldie, 'Rome occupies the soul.'[113] Mrs Jameson, similarly, considered it the 'city of the soul' and the home of art and artists.[114] Always trenchant, Joseph Forsyth was sure that the traveller's attention would be 'divided between magnificence and filth.' The churches were 'horrible with the works of faith'; in the palaces 'the grand object is the picturesque. Nothing is done for the comfortable...'. But the villas were 'the pretty eyes of Italy', the gardens formal with 'walks of laurel, porticos of ilex, green scutcheons, and clipt coronets vegetating over half an acre, theatres of jets d'eaux, geometrical terraces, built rocks, and measured cascades!'[115] Charlotte Waldie had briefed Scott to find that 'the people live in flats, and have a common stair, as in Edinburgh; a plan by no means confined to that much-vilified city ... Though by no means conducive to cleanliness or comfort, it is highly favourable to grandeur of appearance, and architectural effect. For by this means the houses are built upon so much larger a scale, that their exterior is susceptible of fine design and ornament...'.[116] She might almost have been describing Scott's former home at 39 North Castle Street, where whole, relatively small three-floored houses, with entirely separate flats above, were disguised as a unified 'palace-fronted' block which, in its totality, gave the appearance of a much grander level of accommodation than in fact existed behind its splendid, bowed, pilastered, pedimented and balustered façade.

As previously in Naples, Scott again had the benefit of Sir William Gell as companion and *cicerone*. When resident in Rome, Gell lived in an eccentric villa on the Palatine Hill shared with Charles Andrew Mills. It had a delicious garden, and was situated in the ruins of Domitian's palace. At least some thought the garden delicious. The Hon. Henry Edward Fox considered that, with its bowers of roses, it possessed 'too many littlenesses and prettinesses for such a spot as the classical and splendid one on which [Gell] lives.'[117] Originally the Villa Mattei or Villa Spada, it was sometimes known as *Boschetto Gellio*.[118] It later assumed the name of the Villa Mills. Charles Mills had transformed the building into a Strawberry Hill-Gothic creation, of a style which was also known in Rome as 'Scotch Gothic'—doubtless under the influence of Scott himself and the 'baronial' style he was seen to have championed. Here Scott was entertained, and here he must have felt strangely at home: Mills had introduced pinnacles, battlements, cloisters, and ornamental medallions representing the rose, thistle and shamrock; twin gate-piers sported large sculptured thistles.[119] The Farnese Gardens adjoined the Villa Mills and *Boschetto Gellio*. Charlotte Waldie had been very rude about these 'wretched gardens ... hideous summer houses and grottos, the deformity of which still impeaches the taste of their architect', and the whole forming 'a curious picture of ancient gardens and existing wretchedness. The casinos of popes mouldering upon the palaces of Roman emperors—pigs and peasants inhabiting a corner of these splendid ruins ... fragments of precious marbles and granites, of carved cornices and broken alabaster, scattered amongst the mould...'.[120] 'The novelty of the scene', remembered Gell, 'seemed to amuse him [Scott] much.'[121]

But Scott's mind was, if anything, perhaps less engaged even than in Naples. The mediaeval past of Rome, and of the surrounding Lazio countryside, was more attractive to him than was the classical past, although Gell asserted that the Cloaca Maxima and the Colosseum 'seem to have taken his fancy'. Gladiators and underground drains evidently exercised the imagination of the man who had written so much of single combat and dark dungeons. Gell described him as 'the Master Spirit of the history of the Middle Ages, of feudal times, of spectres, magic, abbeys, castles, subterraneous passages, and praeternatural appearances'.[122] Scott's preferences are surely illustrative of that change in interest and inclination to which Rosemary Sweet has rightly drawn attention when she writes of the ways in which 'the classical hegemony of the Grand Tour began to break down': the increasing concern of travellers with the mediaeval heritage of Italian cities, and the displacement in their intellectual priorities of the Graeco-Roman by the Gothic.[123]

The catacombs of the early Christians, however, failed to elicit Scott's interest. It is recorded that he declined to dismount from a fellow visitor's carriage on a drive out along the Appian Way, saying to the American lady who had asked him to accompany her on this occasion: 'No, I would hardly change my seat beside you for mouldering bones.' On this occasion the woman's brother, a sometime student at Edinburgh University, had kept Scott intrigued, distracted, or amused (perhaps all three) by reciting, from memory, passages from *The Lady of the Lake*.[124]

If ancient burial places did not prick his interest, neither did more recent ones. He did not go, with others, into the Protestant Cemetery, where lay the remains of Keats and Shelley. Jane Waldie had written elegiacally of 'the last homes of our countrymen in a foreign clime; which strike upon every tender feeling of our hearts, and make us mourn as friends for every individual who has sunk to rest in a land of strangers.'[125] Possibly Scott found it *too* affecting a place, and that it stirred notions of his own mortality, surely not long to be postponed. Scott might equally have become a Romantic legend had he died in Rome and been laid to rest in that corner of the cemetery in the shadow of the Pyramid of Cestius.

Edward Cheney, scion of a Shropshire gentry family and a former army officer, was a fixture on the British social scene in Rome at the time. Cheney sat with Scott in the carriage outside the cemetery. He later recorded (so Lockhart has it) that, on a visit to the castle of Bracciano, they had talked of Goethe, whom Cheney had visited and whom he thought had remained in possession of all his faculties. 'Of all his faculties!', Scott is supposed to have responded: '[I]t is much better to die than to survive them, and better still to die than to live in apprehension of it; but what is the worst of all would have been to have survived their partial loss, and yet to be conscious of his [i.e. a failing man's] state.' Of himself, Scott admitted that he was 'fast shuffling off the stage.'[126]

At some point during his time in Rome, Scott evidently gave Cheney a paper on which he had scrawled 'from recollection' lines that appear to have been giving comfort to him in his decline. This manuscript was later bought in Naples in 1906 by Archibald Philip Primrose, 5th Earl of Rosebery, the former Prime Minister and a leading man of letters (Rosebery owned a villa at nearby Posillipo, today the summer retreat of the President of Italy). 'A pathetic relic of Walter Scott', was how Lord Rosebery inscribed the envelope which now contains the paper. Scott himself had dated the lines, which show all too plainly that he could barely hold or control his pen, 'Rome May 1832'. This is, in all probability, the last substantial document he ever wrote (only two other brief letters of later date, both unsent, are known). In Naples and its surroundings he had recited Scots ballads and songs. Now, in Rome, his mind was also drawn to quotations which evoked memories of the Scottish past.

The paper is headed 'Verses on the ruins of Melrose'. Scott was recalling John Murdo (or Morvo, or Murray), a late mediaeval Scottish mason-architect of Parisian birth (hence perhaps 'Morveau') who worked on several Scottish ecclesiastical buildings such as St Andrews and Glasgow Cathedrals, and Melrose Abbey too, if a later inscription at Melrose commemorating him and his work to be believed.[127] A sculptured shield at Melrose, bearing the device of crossed compasses on a field with fleurs-de-lis, also alludes to Murdo and his profession. Scott transcribed the inscription from memory, tolerably accurately, and provided a description of the 'armorial' device and its location at Melrose. His text occupies the recto and verso of the first leaf of a small bifolium. Lines on the third page of the paper are also connected to Melrose. They give a version of another old inscription from the Abbey. This verse, which Scott had quoted to Samuel Rogers years before, had evidently lodged in Scott's memory:

> The Earth walks on the Earth,
>   Glistering like gold;
> The Earth goes to the Earth,
>   Sooner than it wold.
> The Earth builds on the Earth
> [Palaces, or Temples] and Towers;
> The Earth says to the Earth,
>   All shall be ours.

Thus, in Rome, as his life neared its end, Scott's thoughts were on a ruined building in Scotland close to his home at Abbotsford, elements of the architectural decoration of which had been inspired by Melrose Abbey.[128]

Sites and localities associated with the exiled Stuart dynasty in Rome and at Frascati interested him far more even than stupendous ancient ruins or mediaeval castles. Marianne Talbot reported that she had heard from Sir William Gell that Scott 'turns every thing to Prince Charles [Bonnie Prince Charlie] & sees nothing but the Pretender anywhere', in his confusion even conflating 'Albano' with 'Albany'.[129] Gell himself told the Dilettanti that 'nothing except that relates to the Stewarts seems to have any charm for him in this Country, & it is amusing to observe the ingenious contrivances by which he changes the conversation from any other subject' to that of the Jacobites.[130]

At the time of Scott's visit, the Villa Muti at Frascati—once the country residence of Prince Henry Benedict Stuart, Cardinal York, younger brother of 'Bonnie Prince Charlie', and thus sometimes known as the Villa York—was owned by Edward Cheney. Scott was particularly intrigued by one painting hanging there, a work in which we today share his interest. Indeed, Scott's keen observation of the picture, as noted by Cheney in the memoir he supplied to Lockhart for use in his biography, is the first record of it. This information provided fundamental evidence for the work's provenance when it was purchased by the Scottish National Portrait Gallery in 2000.[131]

The painting shows James, the 'Old Pretender' or the 'Chevalier de Saint George', receiving his younger son Prince Henry on the latter's appointment as a cardinal in July 1747. It is a highly significant image, not just in the catalogue of Jacobite iconography but in the story of the Jacobite movement itself. The Pretender and his son are depicted standing before the *facciata* or decorated false façade erected against a wall of the so-called Plazzo del Re, where the exiled Stuart family lived in Rome. Such a temporary *facciata* was required as a background to the *festa* held by Papal decree on the elevation of a new cardinal. As such, the painting chronicles a splendid piece of theatre. Scott reckoned, improbably, that he could identify several 'weel-kent' faces of Jacobite supporters and protagonists among the crowd of adherents and followers before the Palazzo del Re. He looked, in fact, at the painted record of the Jacobite presence in Rome very much as Grand Tourists of previous generations had eyed the Stuart court in flesh and blood. Formerly, travellers to Rome had ogled the princes and their retinue as historical and social curiosities: the exiled Stuarts and their hangers-on found themselves to be of just as much interest to loyal supporters of the Georgian monarchy of Great Britain as they were to attainted Jacobite fugitives and sympathisers. Now, in Scott's time, all that could be seen by tourists was a 'once and future' court captured on canvas, and the dream lent enchantment to the view. But the picture symbolises more than the grandeur and opulence of Papal Rome *in festa*. Prince Henry Benedict's decision to become a cardinal had put the cap— or rather the red hat—on any possibility that his family might ever actually now reclaim the British throne. The identification of the Stuart cause with the Roman Church and Continental absolutism was just too close. Even if Prince Charlie, 'the Young Chevalier', failed to gauge the tide, the Old Pretender and his second son knew this was the case. So, equally, did Walter Scott, sentimental Jacobite but Hanoverian realist.

Visiting the monument to the Stuarts in St Peter's Basilica was unquestionably a highlight of Scott's entire Grand Tour, and not just the Roman part of it. Commissioned by Pope Pius VII Chiaramonti in 1819, and paid for by George IV (Scott's 'fat friend') when Prince Regent, Canova's superb monument must have stirred for Scott so many memories, both of fact and of fiction. James Lees-Milne called Canova's superb creation 'perhaps the most successful neo-classical monument in the world'.[132] That is to exaggerate; but it is undeniably effective and—to British eyes—moving. Below the Royal Arms of the United Kingdom, and against the flat plane of the Greek-stele form of the stone, the portrait busts of the three Stuarts identified with Rome as their place of exile levitate over their titles: those titles once recognised only by the Papacy and by the enemies of Great Britain. James Francis Edward Stuart appears in armour, and with Garter riband, to the left: the 'Old Pretender', granted here the titular dignity of 'James III'. He faces his two sons. To the far right, also in armour and Gartered, is Charles Edward Stuart: 'Bonnie Prince Charlie', the 'Young Pretender', looking as dissolute as his Roman exile had made him and, most significantly, *not* accorded the style of 'Charles III', for the Papacy did not recognise his claim to the British throne on the death of James (whom it had considered legitimate). Between them appears James's second son, Cardinal Henry Benedict, in his ecclesiastical dress: titular Duke of York, and ultimately considered by surviving Jacobites as 'Henry IX', the last of the Stuart line. Three kings, in theory; but none wears a crown, though above their busts are carved three laurel wreaths and three floral swags. Angels with inverted torches stand guard on either side of the door of life, death and the hopes of an exiled dynasty.

The scene of Sir Walter Scott—teller of Jacobite tales, writer of Jacobite songs—or, at any rate, how posterity imagined or preserved the memory of the scene of Scott before the Stuart monument, was deeply affecting. The great romancer was brought face-to-face with the memorial to the most romantic of British national lost causes. His visit was observed by Richard Monckton Milnes, then aged twenty-two, a distant cousin of William Gell, who had presumably invited Milnes to join the party to the Basilica or to come along to witness the occasion. Milnes had arrived in Rome at the turn of the year. He had, by coincidence, been reading Scott's *Count Robert of Paris* on the journey there. The young *littérateur* confessed that 'St Peter's nearly knocked me down, the Vatican blinded me with its multitude of treasures'. But something else struck Milnes nearly as forcibly: the sight of Scott in juxtaposition to the monument. Within a dozen years, the episode had been made public by Milnes in his poem 'Sir Walter Scott at the Tomb of the Stuarts in St Peter's', with its theme of 'an alien pilgrim at an alien tomb'. Milnes noted in the Preface to *Memorials of Many Scenes* that he himself been 'sojourning in the bright countries of the south'.[133] But the note added to the poem by its author is obscure. Milnes states clearly that, for Scott, 'the history and localities of the Stuarts seemed to absorb all other objects of his interest.' More opaque is the following: 'The circumstance of this poem fell within the observation of the writer.' So unclear is this statement that Scott biographers, and others, have overlooked, ignored or misinterpreted it.[134] But it is clarified by Monckton Milnes's own biographer. We need to look forward to 1885, the year of Milnes's death. When in Rome that same year he had taken a young kinswoman to St Peter's and to the Stuart monument. 'Stand there, my dear', he had said. 'Now I want you always to remember that where you stand now *I* saw Sir Walter Scott standing when I was a boy.'[135]

For Milnes, Scott had given life back to the 'one heart-worshipped, fancy-haunted, name' of a doomed dynasty, exiled and peripatetic in Europe before settling, and dying out, in Rome:

... Once loud on earth, but now scarce else renowned
Than as the offspring of that stranger's fame.

There lie the Stuarts!—There lingers Walter Scott!
Strange congress of illustrious thoughts and things!
A plain old moral, still too oft forgot,—
The power of Genius and the fall of Kings ...

He rests his chin upon a study staff,
Historic as that sceptre, theirs no more;
His gaze is fixed; his thirsty heart can quaff,
For a short hour the spirit-draughts of yore ...

But purpled mantle, and blood-crimsoned shroud,
Exiles to suffer and returns to woo,
Are gone, like dreams by daylight disallowed;
And their historian,—he is sinking too!

A few more moments and that labouring brow
Cold as those royal busts and calm will lie;
And, as on them his thoughts are resting now,
His marbled form will meet the attentive eye.

Thus, face to face, the dying and the dead,
Bound in one solemn ever-living bond,
Communed; and I was sad that ancient head
Ever should pass those holy walls beyond.

Scott visited the Basilica with a glove tied round his stick to prevent him slipping on the polished marble pavement. Milnes's imagery casts Scott, with his 'sturdy staff', as some sort of hiker on the Road to the Isles. To tour the great church, equipped as Scott actually was, proved less taxing by far than it would have been to shuffle though the rooms of the Apostolic palace and the vast Vatican museums, where he did not venture. There, certainly, had he been sufficiently energetic, he would have seen some of the works restored after their return from exile in Paris: the sculptures which any self-respecting Grand Tourist of tradition would hardly have dared to admit he had not seen by daylight or (for greater effect) by the light of a flickering torch at night. But at least he may have taken the opportunity, before leaving for the Mediterranean, to leaf through the plates in his copy of Hakewill's *Picturesque Tour in Italy*, including elegant and detailed interior views of the cabinets and galleries of the Vatican (and of the Palazzo dei Conservatori and Palazzo Nouvo on the Campidoglio, too, for that matter) with all the sculptures shown in their places: a novelty in a work on Grand Tour travel.[136]

In Naples Scott had met the Russian Princess Zinaida Volkonsky. Having left Russia permanently, she had established herself in Rome in the villa which still bears her name—though the spelling 'Wolkonsky' is used in that context, and her actual house on the site of what had been the Vigna Falcone near the Lateran has been rebuilt. It is today the residence of the British Ambassador. Although it has recently been claimed that she embraced Scott in Rome, and that he became part of her salon, there is in fact no documentary evidence to support the notion. They may just possibly have met in Rome; but no such thing is related in the accounts of Scott's stay in the city by either William Gell or Edward Cheney. Indeed a certain amount of wishful thinking to support a supposed Russian connection in Rome has become accepted as fact.[137]

It has also been said, without any proof, that through the Princess, Scott met the Russian painter Karl Briulov (or Bryullov), that he frequented his studio and that he there saw the painter's vast, lurid and theatrical canvas imagining 'The Last Day of Pompeii'.[138] The painting was set in the very same Street of Tombs up which Scott had been carried on 9 February 1832.[139] Given how little interest Scott had actually shown in the site of Pompeii when he was there, the idea that he 'stood for more than an hour' in front of the painting—which was not in fact completed until the following year—is stretching credulity rather too far. Even if he had wanted to devote so much time and attention to the picture, his physical and mental condition would have made such a long period of concentration impossible. According to another imaginative account, he at least took the opportunity to *sit*—but to do so, still, for a full hour![140]

Maybe those who say Scott behaved in this way have read too much about what is called 'Stendhal (or Stendhal's) Syndrome', albeit a variant that struck and overwhelmed the viewer of a work of art in Rome rather than in Florence, the city where most victims are afflicted.[141] It is even claimed that Scott told Bryullov that he had 'created a true poem' with his picture; it would have been a poem of cataclysmic horror, not to say apocalyptic terror. Still, given that Scott is known to have appreciated some of the melodramatic works of John Martin, he might perhaps have been stuck by elements of Bryullov's nightmare vision. Paradoxically, it was actually Edward Bulwer-Lytton who was inspired to visit the site, and to write his *The Last Days of* Pompeii, by a direct encounter with Bryullov's painting.

The Princess is said to have commemorated Scott with a monument of sorts in her *Allée des Mémoires* in the beautiful garden of her villa, among the Roman ruins that lent the place much evocative charm. The monument— its form is uncertain—is supposed to have borne the inscription 'The quiet lamp of our conversations has been extinguished.' But this, too, seems either imaginative or speculative, and firm information is wholly lacking. Zinaida Volkonsky also published an essay on Scott. Despite its gushing hyperbole it is worth recording here as evidence, of a kind, of the effect Scott's brief acquaintance in Italy seems to have had.

> Walter Scott, our lovely dream of spring, our summer's shade, our autumn's rest, our long winter evenings, our castle in Spain always ready and complete: Walter Scott, the vagabond minstrel, to whom the gatekeeper's daughter will always open the door before he need knock! How much the people owe him, for having interested them without tiring them, instructed them without boring, amused them with no shame, for having frightened them, for having made them laugh and cry, while not making them blush for their tears, their laughter or their fears. Walter Scott, gentleman and popular writer, an aristocrat who loved the people, was one of them, wore their mourning, drank their wine, laughed with their happiness, spoke their language, loved with their love, sat carefree at their table, who fought, felt, was transported and then quiet again like them![142]

Scott lodged in Casa Bernini, in Via della Mercede, not far from Piazza di Spagna, heart of the Rome of the Grand Tour. Traditionally the area was known as the Ghetto degli Inglesi (the English ghetto), because so many British Grand Tourists based themselves in the vicinity. John Keats had died in 1821 in his little room in the house adjoining the Spanish Steps: a poet who, having gone south for his health, never made it back home. Today a marble plaque commemorates Scott's stay in the palazzo where Gian Lorenzo Bernini, the great sculptor, architect and painter of the Roman Baroque, had lived in his later years. Nearby, across the street, is the church of S. Andrea delle Fratte, a masterpiece by Borromini, Bernini's great rival, with some remarkable external features.[143] In this example of *seicento* architectural virtuosity Scott is unlikely to have shown much interest; nor, perhaps, might he have been much struck by the two superb Bernini statues of angels, carved by the master for the Ponte S. Angelo. But he might like to have known that, on the same site, had been an earlier church, also dedicated to St Andrew, which had belonged to the Scottish community in Rome before the Reformation.

It is in relation to sculpture that perhaps the most tender moment of Scott's Roman sojourn allegedly occurred. Only James Skene testifies to the details of this, and decorates the occasion with the tinsel of emotion. True or false, the episode deserves to be better known, although the actual facts are dubious; but, even if apocryphal, it is a good story. Scott had gone to see the great Danish sculptor, Bertel Thorvaldsen, in his studio. This atelier was certainly one of the sights of Rome, and a staple of Grand Tourists and British *cognoscenti* completing their Roman itineraries. Scott's Borders neighbour, the second Earl of Minto, for example, had visited it ten years previously.[144]

Both Thorvaldsen and Scott were elderly, distinguished men, who knew each other only by repute. Skene explains how, though they were

> impressed with mutual regard, they were altogether devoid of any common language of communication. Gazing at each other for a moment in silence, with inexpressible satisfaction beaming in their countenances, they embraced each other with fervour ... and after a short time of mutual contemplation without a word said, repeated their embrace and parted ...[145]

The meeting had been conducted by means of a 'pantomime' of simple words and gestures; but it was enough to allow the emotion of the moment to penetrate the obscurity of language, and surmount the difficulties of infirmity and age. This may be a garbled and romanticised version of the meeting between sculptor and man of letters which, as we know from other, independent evidence, indeed took place. The meeting was sufficient, too, for Thorvaldsen to capture a mental image of Scott, aided doubtless by hasty graphic records. From these sketches of the moment, Thorvaldsen went on to carve a bust of Scott, completed in 1833-4 from drawings and memory, rather than from a formal sitting during Scott's short time in Rome.[146] This marble, probably executed for Edward Cheney, who was a notable art-collector, ranks as almost the last portrait of Scott made from an *ad vivum* likeness, and it stands beside the few drawings of Scott done by young Roman 'gentlemen' artists at that time.

There is wider significance, however, in the meeting of Thorvaldsen and Scott because it illustrates an important aspect of 'Grand Tour' sensibility. To see what were sometimes called 'the lions'—the great sights of Europe— had long been the principal object of travelling, whether in the classic age of the Grand Tour proper or in the dimmer after-glow of the new age of travel that began in 1814-15.[147] Thus Scott himself saw, albeit in a sort of mentally semi-detached way, the 'lions' of Naples and Rome: Pompeii, the Phlegraean Fields and Paestum; the Colosseum, the Pantheon and St Peter's; and so on. Scott himself had used the term 'lions' for the Borders sites he often showed to visitors.[148] But he was, in his own person, a 'lion' of a different kind, and one of immense distinction: and in the course of his travels the literary lion saw the other 'lions', and was himself 'lionized' to a great degree. Travellers on their European tours of the eighteenth and early nineteenth centuries sought out living curiosities as well as inanimate ones. At the apogee of the Grand Tour, Lord Chesterfield had written of the 'constant collision with good company' from which a young man might benefit.[149] But not only might purely snobbish desires be satisfied on the Tour; so might a natural wish just to see the men and women of the day. European travelling frequently provided a two-way interaction: it was a case of 'see' and 'be seen'. As Alexander Pope had put it in

The Dunciad (Book IV, l. 294), 'Europe he saw, and Europe saw him too': his subtle *double entendre* offers a nuanced view of the way that the manners and modes of British tourists might be the subject of amusement or even contempt when abroad on what Scott would later call their 'frolics'. Though Scott did his fair share of gaping (in Paris especially, but also in Naples and in Rome) he, too, was the object of a great deal of curiosity on the part of celebrity-hunters.

He had become quite used to this phenomenon. He had been pursued by one particular 'lion huntress': the plain, persistent and insensitive New Yorker, Harriet Douglas, who, with American bravado, had once forced her way into Scott's Edinburgh lodgings. She subsequently turned up at Abbotsford. There she even helped herself to a cup and saucer from Scott's tea-set as a 'souvenir' of her visit. Scott described her as

> a professd lion huntress who travels the country to rouse the peaceful beasts out of their lair and insists on being hand in glove with all [the] leonine race ... I think I see her with javelin raised and buskind foot, a second Diana, rousing the hills of Westmoreland in quest of the lakers ...[150]

Of this particular 'Huntress of Lions' Scott would later write to Maria Edgeworth: 'She is [in] sad want however of some one to teach her some points of tact in society which are necessary to regulate the best feelings and to correct the enthusiasm of Columbian independence.'[151] He had the misfortune to find her in Naples in the spring of 1832, one of the 'horrid people' he encountered there, and one of those whom he hoped (with uncharacteristically uncharitable feelings) might be the first victims should the cholera visit the city.[152]

Marianne Talbot perceived the essential pity in this 'lion-hunting' interplay between those who wanted to see and meet Scott, and their unfortunate quarry. She saw that he was 'fast losing his intellect', and thought that, on this account, 'it seems terrible to have Sir Walter Scott exhibited to strangers so enclined to admire him ... he provokes the ridicule of strangers ... It is so sad, so cruel, to outlive great reputation.'[153]

Eleven years after Scott had been in Italy, Charles Dickens, then thirty-one years old, was contemplating a trip to and sojourn there. Writing to John Forster, Dickens displayed hopes rather similar to Scott's for such an excursion: it might help to 'enlarge my stock of description and observation by seeing countries new to me ... and you will be able to judge whether a new and authoritative book may not be made on such ground.' The difference was that Dickens really did want to go and to observe for himself, and to do so at an age when his powers were still vibrant, and when any proposed book was actually likely to emerge from a European tour. 'I was startled myself', Dickens confessed, 'when I first got this project of foreign travel into my head

...'. *Pictures from Italy* (1846) was the result. The younger writer held in his mind a vision of Scott's Italian tour. 'What would poor Scott have given to have gone abroad, of his own free will, a young man, instead of creeping there, a driveller, in his miserable decay!'[154]

A modern critic has interpreted Dickens's cruel judgement as 'a warning to those who waited too long before travelling'.[155] So it was; but it also failed to understand fully many of the peculiar circumstances underlying Scott's inability, reluctance, failure, or valid reason not to travel, at any given moment, and the consequent situation in which he found himself when, at last, he was able to go to the Mediterranean. For a complex series of reasons, Scott repeatedly found excuses why he should not travel at the age Dickens thought he should have gone south. Some were the faults of the times in which Scott had lived; some were the faults of his nature and his personal circumstances; some were the faults of his methods as a writer who did not wish to inhibit his imagination by actual experience; some were even (perhaps) the faults of an ingrained economy in spending-habits, which permitted him to wait until the Government gave him his great outward trip *gratis*, leaving him to pay only local costs of board, lodging, incidentals, and Continental and homeward travel. Scott's tragedy as a would-be 'Grand Tourist', or whatever kind of tourist had taken the field in the changed travelling world of the early nineteenth century, was that he made his move when he was too ill, and when it was too late to do any good to a career which was effectively over, and to an imagination that was spent. In after years (as even in his own day) everyone wanted to travel in Europe, on and off the beaten track, like Lord Byron; no one wanted to travel like Walter Scott.

That 'great reputation' of which Marianne Talbot had written with genuine concern and sympathy was a matter which also exercised Sir William Gell. After Scott's death, Gell was concerned how, and to what extent, Lockhart might use his memoirs of his time with Scott in Italy. But what Gell wrote initially for Anne Scott, and which Lockhart wished to draw upon for his biography of his father-in-law (and which Gell himself knew would very probably be used for that work), was, in fact, a charitable account of a great man in failing health. It opens with a clear, if bland, statement that Scott was a man whose actions and talents had excited the admiration and occupied the attention of his contemporaries: an incontrovertible truth. It closes with a statement of Gell's satisfaction at having been able to write his memoir of 'this great Genius and amiable man ... so celebrated and benevolent a personage ...', whose intellect 'had not suffered so severely as those who saw him seemed inclined to believe ...'.[156]

But in Gell's unguarded and unvarnished letters to his friends in the Society of Dilettanti he was very much more frank. At first sight, it may seem that Gell was lukewarm at best in his patronizing assessment of his friend. 'Some of his writings both in prose & Verse will however I think remain to posterity.'[157] But Gell was perceptive enough to realise that Lockhart wanted to 'make out that Sir Walter was a divine personage & free from the faults or infirmities of human nature'. The anecdotes and opinions of Gell as an observer of Scott in his decline, as he had witnessed his behaviour and watched his halting progress on this least grand of late Grand Tours, might well be disturbing to would-be hagiographers. Gell's assessment was cooly true, if bluntly delivered.

> First I very much doubt whether Sir Walter Scott was an extraordinary man, & secondly if he were so I think the history of his decay must be quite as interesting as the account of his glory, & would give an air of truth to the account which it must want without it ... The end therefore of the Life of Lockhart [i.e. the concluding chapters of Lockhart's biography, then in course of composition] will be vitiated by wanting truth in fact & in representation.[158]

This was written in early June 1834. Scott had died in September 1832; Gell himself died in 1836. Lockhart's great but flawed *Memoirs of the Life of Sir Walter Scott, Bart.* appeared in 1837-8. In his *Life*, Lockhart cut Gell's account radically, and used it with little regard for its integrity. No student of Lockhart and his controversial biographical method can ignore Gell's observations. This present study of Scott, his attitudes to travel and his late accession to the idea, and actual status, of being a latter-day Grand Tourist has shown Sir Walter's imperfections, in terms of vacillation and procrastination and lack of real interest, but also his humour, humanity and humility in facing up to a social and cultural tradition of European travel, outmoded as it was, to which he was not really attuned. Robert Holland has suggested that Byron's travels in the Mediterranean mark the start of 'a counter-impulse' to the spell of the Antique, and that they spell the 'end of deference' to 'classical deadness'.[159] Scott, as I have suggested, should really have relished this late-in-life experience; but he was simply too old, too ill, and too exhausted.

Thorvaldsen's bust of Scott carved in Rome was a neo-classical image of a Romantic icon. It is austere in the manner of the portraiture of the late Roman Republic or early Empire. The irony is that this classical vision was of a man who cared little for classical antiquity or its artistic tradition. As has been perceptively noted, the bust was sculpted by 'the last great artist of the very tradition which the novelist himself had played such a central part in vanquishing...'.[160] There is no better satire of this seismic shift from the Classic to the Romantic than is found in W. M. Thackeray's *The Paris Sketch Book* of 'Mr [Michael Angelo] Titmarsh'. It occurs in the essay 'On the French School of Painting'. Thackeray writes thus:

Jacques Louis David is dead ... The romanticism killed him. Walter Scott, from his Castle of Abbotsford, sent out a troop of gallant young Scottish adventurers, merry outlaws, valiant knights, and savage Highlanders, who ... did challenge, combat and overcome the heroes and demigods of Greece and Rome ... Sir Brian de Bois Guilbert has borne Hector of Troy clear out of his saddle. Andromache may weep; but her spouse is beyond the reach of physic. See Robin Hood twangs his bow, and the heathen gods fly, howling ... yonder are Leonidas and Romulus begging their lives of Rob Roy Macgregor. Classicism is dead. Sir John Froissart has taken Dr Lemprière by the nose and reigns sovereign.[161]

*   *   *   *   *

In 1853, J. G. Lockhart—also widowed, and with two of his three children dead, fast ageing and very ill—followed his late father-in-law to Rome. This was, in its own way, as sad a visit as Scott's had been. Lockhart told his surviving daughter, Charlotte Hope-Scott, on 15 March 1854: 'I am entirely satisfied that travel is insanity for a sick creature; and once established again in a home, however humble, I shall not be likely to quit it on any speculation.'[162]

Lockhart's view of a Mediterranean trip as a health cure for both mind and spirit was a jaundiced one: as so often in the past, sick men who went South to the sun, and to places where they hoped that the sadnesses of life might be forgotten, were often disappointed. This is the dark side of the Grand Tour tradition. Rome palled for Lockhart, as it had done for Walter Scott before him. Lockhart wrote to his daughter that 'Certainly I have now had enough, not of Rome, but of Piazza di Spagna Rome, to which fate at present binds me.'[163] He lived in the apartment of a Scottish friend in Via Gregoriana, near the Trinità dei Monti at the top of the Spanish Steps. What he meant was that the Rome of British high society, in their traditional, insular, stamping-ground of the 'Ghetto degli Inglesi' around Piazza di Spagna, or that of the aristocracy of Europe idly sightseeing each other at this very hub of the old Grand Tour, was cumulatively overwhelming and cloying. He put it more strongly still in a jingle appended to a letter to his friend Henry Hart Milman, Dean of St Paul's, written on the eve of his departure for home.

> Beds black with bugs,
> Monks fat as slugs,
> Beggars groaning,
> Thieves intoning,
> Leering models, lousy artists,
> Strutting, strumming Bonapartists;
> Mutton young, and stinking mullet,
> Wine sharp enough for Rossi's gullet.

Fancying these, make speed to Rome,
Curse beef and beer, law, truth and home;
For me I'd jump at once to [hell]
Before returning.[164]

Scott had prattled idly, and improbably, about returning to Rome the year after his visit. But he was flattered by Roman society of the highest rank, and was in his cups at their dinners. For Scott there was, of course, to be no second Roman spring. Within nine months of Lockhart's own visit, he too would die at Abbotsford, and be buried at Scott's feet at Dryburgh Abbey.

*   *   *   *   *

As coda to the story of Scott's short Roman sojourn, we may adduce Allan Massie's novel of 1994, *The Ragged Lion*. This purports to be the autobiographical memoir Scott composed towards the end of his life, much of it supposed to have been written in Italy. Massie would have us believe— and he does this with some credibility—that Scott left the manuscript of the memoir behind (by design or accident?) in Casa Bernini when he and his son and daughter quit Rome on their homeward journey. Charles Scott was supposed to have been handed it when he passed through Rome on his way back to the British legation in Naples in the latter part of 1832, where he had the manuscript copied in duplicate. One copy he transferred to Lockhart, who used it in writing his biography of Scott; the other he gave to an aristocratic Neapolitan lady. Her descendant eventually bequeathed the manuscript to Allan Massie.[165]

Of course, when one sees the actual effort Scott had to expend in order to write even a short document—such as the lines on Melrose, for Edward Cheney—and given that we know Scott made no addition to his journal after his first night in Rome, Massie's attempt to credit Scott with so much physical and mental ability is not wholly believable. But much of what he seeks to evoke of the inner workings of Scott's mind does ring true. Massie's Scott is moved by reminders—places and monuments—of the Stuarts. He thinks of what he might do at Abbotsford on his return, and of what additional land he might buy. He thinks of his family. He muses that his wife would like to have seen Rome: 'this of all cities was the one which she, who was normally content with her domestic circle, most longed to see'. Charlotte took no interest in history; yet she wanted Scott to take her to Rome. So Scott has come to Rome, perhaps to assuage his guilt that he—and Charlotte—had never done so on a Grand Tour in the prime of life. He thinks of her enjoying a *fête-champêtre* on the Palatine, as he himself had done. But otherwise, his mind dwells on Scotland, on its past, on its folk traditions and the supernatural, on the

Borders: in fact, on *home*. And it is a version of a song by Allan Cunningham (unacknowledged as such) that Massie puts into Scott's mouth for him to inscribe into this imaginary memoir.[166] Catching Scott's mood in Rome, this seems completely right:

> For it's hame, hame, hame, fain wad I be,
> Hame ance mair in my ain countrie.

11

'Let Us to Abbotsford'

The road from Rome—first Eric Quayle and then John Sutherland have well described it as Scott's *via dolorosa*—led north through beautiful countryside to Narni, Terni and Perugia to Florence.[1] The party left Rome on 11 May. For Charles Scott, the journey was marked by his father's 'obstinacy'. The carriage soon required some repairs, a common Grand Tour experience: it was, indeed, one amusingly listed by William Cowper, in 'The Progress of Error', as among the standard 'delights' of European travel and a fixture in its record: '... and where the chaise broke down ...'.

It was by moonlight that they saw the spectacular waterfalls at Terni, the Cascate delle Marmore, so beloved of Grand Tourists of the past, and so much painted by the artists who recorded the sites, sights and picturesque 'sublimity' of the Tour. In a letter Scott drafted, probably at Terni, but never actually sent to his elder daughter Sophia, he alluded to the 'moonlight journey through this famous country'. Moonlight sightseeing had loomed large in the sensibility of the Grand Tour, so some traditional experiences were Scott's, even at this late stage. However, the unsent letter subtly emphasises once and for all the fact that he really had neither taste nor temperament for one essential aspect of Grand Touring. To Sophia he wrote that he 'must leave the rest to Anne the rest to Anne [*sic*: the repetition is Scott's, perhaps due to his writing early in the morning after a long day on the road before that] who has learnd the cant of a [*sic*] amateur to the same purpose that most travellers do.'[2] If one interprets his words correctly, he seems to have maintained to the last, and until late in his own travels, a real distance from the Grand Tour aesthetic, and even to have held its sensibilities in something approaching distrust if not outright contempt. The 'cant of the amateur' is the exclusive language, and the cultural and aesthetic outlook, of the lover of the arts—literally an 'amateur'—that most Grand Tourists had sought to acquire, and which many did, at least to some extent. It is almost as if Scott deliberately shunned such acquisition of taste as mannered and affected. But the passage of the Apennines, in some remaining snow and among pines, reminded him of Scotland—and that was really what stirred his soul.

At Florence, Scott displayed some small appetite for limited research in libraries and archives. The Yankee lion-huntress, Harriet Douglas, was on his trail and she pursued him through northern Italy. At Florence she found him distracted by a manuscript of Scottish interest, and so unable or unwilling to pay her the attention she thought she deserved. By her own over-excited admission, Miss Douglas could hardly concentrate on the sights of the country for thinking about her next possible encounter with Sir Walter. Was he at Bologna, and, if so, at what hotel? In Venice? At Vicenza? Or in Verona? She wanted to travel with him. She chased Scott's party relentlessly, and continued into Austria in a 'game of hide and seek across Europe'.[3]

In Naples, Scott had shown interest in research on the subject of Andrea Ferrara, the legendary and eponymous maker of the fine sword-blades so much associated with the Jacobite cause.[4] 'Andrea (or 'Andrew') Ferraras', as a type of weapon, had featured in both *Waverley* and *The Antiquary*. Sadly, by the time Scott reached the city of Ferrara he was beyond care for such matters.

At Venice he spent only four nights, although its glorious sights evoked some genuine interest, the prisons of the Doge's Palace in particular. He was not to be deterred from scrambling with difficulty into these forbidding places across the Bridge of Sighs. Scott toured the Venice of Byron, and because of Byron. Anna Jameson had noted that Venice was a tree-less city, save for the 'few rows of dwarfish unhappy-looking shrubs parched by the sea breezes' and planted in the public gardens by the erstwhile French conquerors of the Serene Republic.[5] This fact was unlikely to have struck a chord with the great planter and author of 'Sylva Abbotsfordiensis', who thought his oaks would outlast his laurels.[6]

Another lion-hunter, though one less bold by far than Miss Douglas, was Owen Blayney Cole. This was the young man who had met and observed Scott in Naples, and who never tired of finding parallels between Scott and his characters, or of citing appropriate passages in the novels for situations current in Cole's Italian tour. Cole followed Scott north, through the same cities and towns, posting-halts and hotels. At least he and Scott spoke the same cultural language. His 'reward' was to be allowed to butter Scott's bread—literally—in the hotel in Vicenza, and to be instructed by him to see the tomb of the Scaligeri in Verona rather than the grave of Juliet.[7] It is significant that neither man preferred the magnificent Roman amphitheatre to these mediaeval monuments: their priorities echo that change of taste highlighted by Rosemary Sweet, though without reference to Scott or Cole.[8] The sight of Scott reading a large vellum-bound book while waiting in his carriage made Cole think of Mr Oldbuck, the immortal Antiquary, Scott's own favourite among his characters.[9] It is ironic that Alexander Gordon, once cited so admiringly (not to say amusingly) in *The Antiquary*, as author of the *Itinerarium Septentrionale* on the Roman antiquities of Scotland, should also have translated Scipione Maffei's treatise on ancient amphitheatres. It is, however, most unlikely that this was the book in which Scott, with his youthful Roman antiquarian days long behind him, happened to be engrossed when Cole observed him in Verona.

Yet it was Miss Douglas who secured the ultimate lion-hunter's trophy. Having run Scott to ground in a hotel in Augsburg, and having found him on that occasion friendly and hospitable to the extent that he called for wine to toast the fellow travellers in farewell, she contrived to keep the green hock-glass, or rummer, out of which he had drunk her health. Back home in New York, she had it encased in a web of silver thistles. In doing so, she created a mesh of silver flowers and leaves that (from photographic evidence) seems to recall, in a strange way, some elaborate basket hilt for a broadsword of the most opulent and showy kind, heavy with Jacobite iconography and symbolism. Scott himself might have liked the enmeshed glass and the idea behind it. Miss Douglas's intention was to ensure that that no other lip might ever sully it. Furthermore, her action ensured the safety of a 'relic'.[10]

*   *   *   *   *

Florence, Bologna, Vicenza, Verona, Venice: all were cities which the Grand Tourists of the past would have loved, or at any rate felt obliged, to visit, and in which much time might have been profitably (or sinfully) passed. But Scott's visits were not much more than mere restorative and recuperative halts on the journey home. Douglas Gifford has suggested that Italy gave Scott 'a last flair of colour and romance', and that his 'last and greatest foreign tour' afforded him 'some of the most vivid months of his life.'[11] There had not, in truth, been many foreign tours for this one to assume the status of the 'last and greatest'. Certainly it was the longest. But Paris in 1815 had been more of an occasion imbued with colour and romance, of which Scott had retained vivid recollections. Ireland in 1825 had been a successful and remarkably complete epitome of a whole world of contemporary travelling sentiment and practice. By contrast, a pall of incurable dolour hangs over the months in Italy. Had Scott been able to make his 'voyage of Italy' at the age and moment when the best of the Grand Tourists of the past were moulded by their experience—when (ideally) the 'liberal youth' of Britain acquired that polish and ease of manner, which the proponents of foreign travel reckoned the best way of fitting young men 'for the business and conversation of the world'[12]— then Italy would probably have rounded Scott and have added a measure of cosmopolitan sophistication to provincial precocity. But would it have made him ultimately a greater writer or a better man? Almost certainly not.

Charles Scott was dismissive of his father's wish to see what he could of Austria and Germany—Charles had, in fact, told Lockhart that he thought a return through Germany was 'out of the question', presumably because 'moving about seems always to make him [Sir Walter] nervous & unwell'— and confessed that he would be thankful if he 'ever gets over the Alps'.[13] But, having now positioned themselves in the Veneto, it made sense for the Scott party to cross the mountains by the nearest route, even if the Brenner Pass leading into the Tyrol offered less dramatic scenery than the western routes out of Lombardy or Piedmont-Savoy—the Mont Cenis, the Great St Bernard or the Simplon passes—would have afforded. There would be no sight of the Mer de Glace at Chamonix, nor of John Auldjo's Mont Blanc, 'this monarch of European hills' (as Henry Cockburn called it) for the Monarch of Parnassus.[14] Scott, however, had long expressed a stronger wish to see Germany than the north of Italy. The Brenner was the least formidable, lowest, quickest and easiest way there; and if it seems a pity that Scott—who had for so long wanted to see Alpine landscapes—should have thus missed the finest mountain scenery, or the opportunity to feel like Napoleon on the St Bernard route, or the chance to savour some of the classic Grand Tour psychological experience of sublimity and terror, this was by far the best compromise for a man as unwell as he was.[15]

The classicist William Gell reported that Scott had shown great interest in the possibility of seeing the celebrated chivalric statuary surrounding the cenotaph of the Emperor Maximilian, and associated monuments at Innsbruck. About these, Gell said a little sarcastically, Scott had 'raved' while surrounded by 'real' antiquity in Naples and Rome.[16] Scott also looked forward to seeing what he had called, in his life of Mrs Radcliffe, 'the frowning remains of feudal castles': Lockhart subsequently adopted and adapted Scott's phrasing when he wrote of Scott's party seeing 'the feudal ruins upon the Rhine'.[17] When the moment came, however, he was simply too weary, distressed and ill to absorb much.

En route, however, a touching scene unfolded in a bookseller's shop in Frankfurt. There he was shown a lithograph of a British country house. The shopman, knowing only that an 'English' party was in his premises, had brought out from his stock the one object he surely knew would be of interest—a print of Abbotsford. Scott, unrecognised, muttered 'I know that already, Sir', and hirpled away.[18]

*   *   *   *   *

Munich; Ulm; Augsburg; Heidelberg; Frankfurt. From the Fortress of Mainz, he penned the last words he is thought to have written. This was the note to Arthur Schopenhauer in which Scott alluded, perhaps dismissively, and in self-deprecation, to his 'little tour' (see above, Chapter 1).The Rhine, the joyful landscape of the German ballads of his youth, became to Scott, in age, a *flumen dolorosum*. At Nijmegen he suffered a major stroke.

Once across the Channel, the rush to return home was broken by Scott's being laid-up for several weeks in the St James's Hotel in Jermyn Street, London. The public was aware of his presence; stories of workmen asking where he was lying may not just be apocryphal. John Sutherland has described this melancholy time as 'a kind of lying-in-state.'[19] So in a way it was, albeit the subject of tribute was still alive.

A previously unpublished letter of Major Walter Scott to Captain Hugh Pigot RN, of HMS *Barham*, gives details that are touching in their frankness, if rather cold in the manner in which they are conveyed.[20] Scott wrote from the hotel to let Pigot know how 'your late passengers, guests, or if you will allow the term, friends, get on now.' He acquainted the Captain with what had happened since they had parted in Naples. Major Scott had returned home from Naples, leaving his younger brother and sister first to remain there with their father, then to accompany Sir Walter to Rome, and thereafter to escort him across Austria and Germany to Britain. But, picking up the story as he had heard it from his siblings, Major Scott narrated how his father had 'suddenly determined' to get to Rome; how he had then equally 'suddenly determined'— the repetition of the words somehow presses home the gravity of his father's irrational or aberrant behaviour—'to return home *instantly*' and, in 'such a state of irritability and anxiety', thus to insist on making the 'most earnest progress' northwards. On the road, his father had been 'eating and drinking as if he really wished to terminate his journey and life at the same time.' That the 'attack of paralysis' at Nijmegen should have occurred surprised no-one. His father was now 'in a state betwixt life and death ... his disease has taken a new and even more dreadful form than we should ever have anticipated and from the wandering & delirium of fever seems to be approaching towards insanity.' Anne Scott—on whom Captain Pigot had perhaps had some designs as a possible wife—was increasingly affected by nervous fits brought on by the anxiety of caring for her father, and of witnessing his condition. 'Such is our family state at present and a most melancholy one it is', the Major concluded—though the rest of his letter is about military duty, the progress of Reform, indiscipline in his regiment's ranks, and the failings of his commanding officer.

Walter wanted to give Hugh Pigot a 'complete copy' of his father's works: 'perhaps', he wrote, 'they may make a little addition to your cabin library and a trifling mark of esteem from the Author.' Even *in extremis* the man of letters wished his kinsfolk to pay his debt to those who had shown kindness, and who had supported him on his Grand Tour that was not really a Grand Tour. And what more appropriate way to do this than with a set of his collected works? Sir William Gell recorded how Anne Scott told him that 'the last intelligible command of her dying father' was that a set of Scott's works be sent also to him.[21]

T. B. Macaulay wrote to his sisters of how 'Poor Sir Walter Scott is going back to Scotland by sea tomorrow. All hope is over; and he has a restless wish to die at home.' Should he have expired in London, a public funeral had been considered. But, Macaulay reported, the Chancellor of the Exchequer, Lord Althorp, thought it would be better to give the Scott family the money that otherwise would have been expended on a 'one day's show'.[22] Either way, the measure of Scott's status as a national figure was powerfully demonstrated.

That summer Thomas Carlyle was writing to his brother John in Naples— 'the loveliest spot of Earth's surface', as he imagined it: '... had I one Oriental wishing-carpet, I were soon beside you ...'. The brothers had corresponded about intellectual and cultural life both there and in Rome. Men and places that Walter Scott had so recently known were discussed. Thomas told John how he had heard that Scott had been brought back from the Continent to London, 'struck with apoplexy, deprived of consciousness'; the fact that this 'Grand Tour' was, in all likelihood, ending so mundanely in a London hotel struck Carlyle particularly. From London, he reported, Scott had been conveyed to Edinburgh, and thence to the Borders, and so he 'greets his birthland, soon to be his grave! It is appointed for *all*.'[23]

No oriental magic carpet had carried Sir Walter Scott home from Rome, and no amount of wishing retrospectively could make his ultimate foreign visit a joyful one. According to Lockhart's romancing, the last sound Scott heard was, at least, that of the River Tweed purling over its pebbles. It might so easily have been the billows of the Bay of Naples, or the rushing of the yellow Tiber.

Notes and References

1 Fairy-Lands and Regions of Reality

1 *The Journal of Sir Walter Scott*, ed. W. E. K. Anderson (Oxford: Clarendon Press, 1972) [hereafter *Journal*], 65. Scott quotes the Border song 'Tweedside', by John Hay, second Marquess of Tweeddale, of which the line is the refrain in both stanzas.
2 Commenting on the mixture of real scenes with fictitious ones in *Continental Adventures*, Mary Shelley suggested that the book was 'not on a good plan', and that 'a guidebook and a romance form an incongruous mixture'. The two elements should have been separated. [Mary Shelley], 'The English in Italy', *The Westminster Review*, VI, no XII (October 1826), Art. IV, 337-9.
3 National Library of Scotland [hereafter NLS], MS. 3902, ff. 168-9, Charlotte Eaton to Walter Scott [hereafter WS], post-marked 1 April 1826.
4 The Eaton letters to Hurst, Robinson & Co. are NLS, Acc. 12462.
5 *The Letters of Sir Walter Scott*, ed. H. J. C. Grierson, assisted by Davidson Cook and W. M. Parker, 12 vols (London: Constable, 1932-37) [hereafter *Letters*], IX: 497, Walter Scott to the 'Author of Continental Adventures', i.e. Charlotte Eaton, 5 Apr. 1826.
6 NLS, Acc. 12462, Charlotte Eaton to Hurst, Robinson & Co., 18 Mar. 1826.
7 *Continental Adventures. A Novel*, 3 vols (London: Hurst, Robinson & Co., 1826), I: vii.
8 *Ibid.*, I: 2-3.
9 *Ibid.*, III: 24-25.
10 *Ibid.*, III: 287-88.
11 J. G. Lockhart, *[Memoirs of] The Life of Sir Walter Scott, Bart* [hereafter Lockhart], Edinburgh Edition, 10 vols (Edinburgh: T. C. and E.C. Jack, 1902-03), I: 129.
12 The expanded title of the three-volume work is *Rome in the Nineteenth Century; Containing a Complete Account of the Ruins of the Ancient City, the Remains of the Middle Ages, and the Monuments of Modern Times ... in a Series of Letters Written During a Residence at Rome in the Years 1817 and 1818* (Edinburgh: Archibald Constable, 1820). Scott had, in fact, received an inscribed presentation copy: it remains at Abbotsford. In her book the author wrote thus: 'I had one advantage, which I am taking special care you shall never enjoy—that of arriving at Rome in perfect ignorance of all it contained, for which I thank Heaven. I only knew that the Coliseum was in ruins, that

the very name of the Capitol had passed away, and that the Forum had been degraded into a cattle-market, and was called the Campo Vaccino.' (I: 123). For her opinions of the local guides, see vol. I: 130, 228; for those of her British contemporaries, see vol. I: vi-vii.

13 'Prefatory Memoir to Mrs Ann Radcliffe', was written in 1824 and first published in *Ballantyne's Novelist's Library*, vol X. For convenience, see Walter Scott, *Lives of the Novelists*, with an introduction by Austin Dobson (London: Oxford University Press, 1906), 302- 42.

14 'Mrs Ann Radcliffe', 316, 335, 341, 337-8.

15 *Ibid.*, 325.

16 Gerald Newman, *The Rise of English Nationalism. A Cultural History 1740-1830*, new edn (Basingstoke: Macmillan, 1997), 12-13.

17 Vicesimus Knox, *Liberal Education: or, a Practical Treatise on the Methods of Acquiring Useful and Polite Learning*, 10th edn, two vols (London: Charles Dilly, 1789), II: Section LX, 'On Foreign Travel', 297-99; 302-4.

18 Jean-Bernard, l'Abbé Le Blanc, *Letters on the English and French Nations, Containing Curious and Useful Observations* ..., two vols (London: J. Brindley, 1747), I: 37.

19 A. N. Wilson, *The Laird of Abbotsford. A View of Sir Walter Scott* (Oxford: Oxford University Press, 1980), 4.

20 James Boswell, *Life of Johnson*, ed. G. Birkbeck Hill, rev. L. F. Powell, 6 vols (Oxford: Clarendon Press, 1934-50), III: 36.

21 *Letters*, XII: 47-8, WS to Arthur Schopenhauer, Mainz, [3 June] 1832. This draft letter is endorsed by Scott's son Charles thus: 'I think the last words my poor father ever wrote.' Scott misdated the letter 3 May 1834 [*sic*]. Charles Scott's (unpaginated) travel diary records the Scott party at Mainz on 6 June: NLS, MS. 1614.

22 *Journal*, 208.

23 *Literature of Travel and Exploration. An Encyclopedia*, ed. Jennifer Speake, 3 vols (New York and London: Fitzroy Dearborn, 2003).

24 Lockhart, VII: 249.

25 A significant study, the importance of which is belied by its title, is Richard Mullen and James Munson, *The Smell of the Continent. The British Discover Europe 1814-1914* (London: Macmillan, 2009). For the rush to the Continent, see xii-xii; and for the new kind of travel begun in 1814, see Mullen and Munson, 131.

26 See *The Italian Journal of Samuel Rogers*, ed. and with an Account of Rogers' Life and of Travel in Italy in 1814-21 by J. R. Hale (London: Faber and Faber, 1956), 9.

27 James Buzard, *The Beaten Track. European Tourism, Literature and the Ways to Culture 1800-1918* (Oxford: Clarendon Press, 1993), 110, 121-2.

28 John Urry, *The Tourist Gaze. Leisure and Travel in Contemporary Societies* (London: Sage Publications, 1990), 4.

29 *The Making of Modern Tourism. The Cultural History of the British Experience, 1600-2000*, ed. Hartmut Berghoff, Barbara Korte, Ralf Schneider and Christopher Harvie (Basingstoke: Palgrave, 2002): essays by Hartmut Berghoff and Barbara Korte, 'Britain and the Making of Modern Tourism. An Interdisciplinary Approach', 5; and by Chloe Chard, 'From the Sublime to the Ridiculous: The Anxieties of Sightseeing', 60.

30 John Towner, 'The Grand Tour: a Key Phase in the History of Tourism', *Annals of Tourism Research*, 12, no 3 (1985), 297-333, especially 313-5.

31 Michèle Cohen, *Fashioning Masculinity: national identity and language in the*

eighteenth century (London: Routledge, 1996), 60, 62-63.

32 William Edward Mead's fundamental study, *The Grand Tour in the Eighteenth Century* (Boston and New York: Houghton Mifflin & Co., 1914; reissued by Benjamin Blom, New York, 1972), is still unsurpassed as an introduction—and one both elegant and readable—to the topic. However, it specifically omits the European 'fringes' of the customary Grand Tour itinerary. Christopher Hibbert, *The Grand Tour* (London: Thames Methuen, 1987) is an admirable work that revisits ground already very well tilled in the same author's earlier book of the same subject published with the same title by Weidenfeld and Nicolson in 1969. Together and separately these volumes constitute perhaps the best single recent surveys of the Grand Tour. Jeremy Black's personal bibliographical history of Grand Tour scholarship is even more complex. His *The British and the Grand Tour* (London: Croom Helm, 1985) has been effectively replaced by the much superior *The British Abroad. The Grand Tour in the Eighteenth Century* (Stroud: Alan Sutton, 1992) which is the product of a remarkable harvest of primary source material. The latter book has since been again recast and yet further expanded, and divided into two further titles: Black's *Italy and the Grand Tour* (New Haven and London: Yale University Press, 2003) and his *France and the Grand Tour* (Basingstoke: Palgrave Macmillan, 2003). These last two books should, however, be read in conjunction with the review article by Iain Gordon Brown, 'Eighteenth-Century British Antiquaries and Grand Tourists', *Scottish Archives*, 11 (2005), 129-41. John Pemble, *The Mediterranean Passion. Victorians and Edwardians in the South* (Oxford: Clarendon Press, 1987) is an important and stimulating work, which is now excellently supplemented by Robert Holland, *The Warm South. How the Mediterranean Shaped the British Imagination* (New Haven and London: Yale University Press, 2018). Rosemary Sweet, *Cities and the Grand Tour. The British in Italy, c. 1690-1820* (Cambridge: Cambridge University Press, 2012) is, despite its resolutely 'urban' focus, an excellent and remarkably comprehensive analysis.

33 Sweet, *Cities and the Grand Tour*, 9-10.

34 Viccy Coltman, *Art and Identity in Scotland. A Cultural History from the Jacobite Rising of 1745 to Walter Scott* (Cambridge: Cambridge University Press, 2019), 233.

35 Cecilia Powell, *Italy in the Age of Turner: "The Garden of the World"* (London: Merrell Holberton, 1998), 72. On the questionable benefits of Italy as destination for the sick in search of a cure, and specifically Rome in this respect, see Richard Wrigley, *Roman Fever. Influence, Infection and the Image of Rome, 1700-1870* (New Haven and London: Yale University Press, 2013), *passim*, but especially Chapter 4, 'Confronting *Mal' Aria*'. Perhaps surprisingly, Wrigley takes no account of Scott's or indeed of J. G. Lockhart's later experience. On Rome as an inappropriate place to seek a health cure, see also Harriet Harvey Wood, *Lockhart of the Quarterly* ([London]: Sciennes Press, 2018), 309-10.

36 See Pemble, *Mediterranean Passion*, 22-24, v, 9 for these various points and the relevant quotations.

37 Holland, *The Warm South*, 86.

38 The quotations are taken from Chloe Chard, 'Introduction', in *Transports: Travel, Pleasure and Imaginative Geography 1660-1830*, ed. Chloe Chard and Helen Langdon (New Haven and London: Yale University Press, 1996), 20.

39 *Ibid.*, 26-27.

2 *Milordi Scozzesi* and Home-Keeping Youth

1 *Journal*, 486; 252.

2 Karl Miller, *Cockburn's Millennium* (London: Gerald Duckworth, 1975), 81; *Lord Cockburn: Selected Letters,* ed. Alan Bell (Edinburgh: John Donald, 2005), 55.

3 Scott retailed the splendid anecdote of Melville and Ellis in a letter to William Brockedon which is quoted in Lockhart, II: 57-58 n. Scott refers to the original episode again when writing to Henry Mackenzie on 2 Apr. 1825: *Letters*, IX: 59.

4 William Stewart Rose, *Letters from the North of Italy. Addressed to Henry Hallam, Esq.,* two vols (London: John Murray, 1819), I: v-vi. The Abbotsford copy is unfortunately bound with the title 'Hallam's North of Italy'—which, one hopes, Rose did not notice when he visited Scott's country house.

5 Walter Scott, *The Fair Maid of Perth*, ed. A. D. Hook and Donald Mackenzie, Edinburgh Edition of the Waverley Novels (Edinburgh: Edinburgh University Press, 1999), 11, 13.

6 *Letters*, IV: 263, WS to Joanna Baillie, 12 July 1816.

7 *Letters*, II: 357, WS to John Richardson, 3 July 1810.

8 Christopher Smout, 'Tours in the Scottish Highlands from the eighteenth to the twentieth centuries', *Northern Scotland*, 5, no 2 (1983), 100.

9 Richard W. Butler, 'Evolution of Tourism in the Scottish Highlands', *Annals of Tourism Research*, 12, no 3 (1985), 374-6, places Scott and his impact in context.

10 Krystyn Lach-Szyrma, *From Charlotte Square to Fingal's Cave. Reminiscences of a Journey through Scotland 1820-1824*, ed. Mona Kedslie McLeod (East Linton: Tuckwell Press, 2004), 200.

11 Alastair Durie, 'Scotland is Scott-land: Scott and the Development of Tourism', in *The Reception of Sir Walter Scott in Europe*, ed. Murray Pittock (London: Continuum, 2006), 314.

12 Smout, 'Tours in the Scottish Highlands', 117.

13 John R. Gold and Margaret M. Gold, *Imagining Scotland: Tradition, Representation and Promotion in Scottish Tourism since 1750* (Aldershot: Scolar Press, 1995), 193, and Chapter 4, 'Sir Walter Scott and the propagation of the Highland myth', 60-85. See also Lynne Withey, *Grand Tours and Cook's Tours. A History of Leisure Travel, 1750 to 1915*, British edn (London: Aurum Press, 1998), 55-7.

14 Allison Lockwood, *Passionate Pilgrims: The American Traveler in Great Britain 1800-1914* (East Brunswick, NJ: Cornwall Books and Associated University Presses, 1981), 70, quoting Bayard Taylor. The soubriquet has been taken up by Stuart Kelly in the title of his *Scott-land. The Man Who Invented a Nation* (Edinburgh; Polygon, 2010).

15 William Howitt, *Visits to Remarkable Places: Old Halls, Battle Fields and Scenes Illustrative of Striking Passages in English History and Poetry*, second edn., (London: Longman, 1840), 173, 200.

16 *Letters*, II: 383, WS to Miss [Sarah]Smith, 4 Oct [as in Grierson—but actually datable to Nov., according to J. C. Corson] 1810.

17 *Letters*, I: 26-7, WS to Patrick Murray of Simprim, 13 Sept. 1793.

18 *Letters*, XII: 207, WS to George Ellis, 7 Dec. 1801.

19 John Pemble, *The Rome We Have Lost* (Oxford: Oxford University Press, 2017), 24.

20 Mary Shelley, 'The English in Italy', 326.

21 Joseph Forsyth, *Remarks on Antiquities, Arts, and Letters During an Excursion in Italy in the Years 1802 and 1803*, ed Keith Crook (Newark, NJ, and London: University of Delaware Press and Associated University Presses, 2001), Introduction, xi-xii. The first edition bears the note that the book was written during Forsyth's 'long captivity'.

22 *Letters*, III: 141, WS to Byron, 16 July 1812.

23 NLS, MS 926, no. 72.

24 *Letters*, XII: 102, 104, WS to Charlotte Scott, 10 Apr. 1807.

25 Bodleian Library, Oxford, MS. Top. Gen. e. 61, 'Iter Oxoniense' (1710), f. 85v.

26 Lockhart, VIII: 7-8.

27 [J. G. Lockhart], *Peter's Letters to his Kinsfolk*, three vols (Edinburgh: William Blackwood, 1819), II: 318, 320.

28 See the significant line in James Hogg, *The Private Memoirs and Confessions of a Justified Sinner*, ed. P. D. Garside (Edinburgh: Edinburgh University Press, 2002), 169. Ian Duncan has drawn attention to this passage in his *Scott's Shadow. The Novel in Romantic Edinburgh* (Princeton and Oxford: Princeton University Press, 2007), 173.

29 *Letters*, II: 89, WS to Sarah Smith, 17 Sept. 1808; II: 94, WS to Lady Abercorn, 14 Oct. 1808, but corrected from the text in *Scott on Himself. A Selection of the Autobiographical Writings of Sir Walter Scott*, ed. David Hewitt (Edinburgh: Scottish Academic Press, 1981), 74; *Letters*, II: 92, WS to Joanna Baillie, 18 Sept. 1808.

30 *Journal*, 243, 484, 243, 245.

31 See Iain Gordon Brown, 'Griffins, Nabobs and a Seasoning of Curry Powder: Walter Scott and the Indian Theme in Life and Literature', in Anne Buddle, Pauline Rohatgi and Iain Gordon Brown, *The Tiger and the Thistle. Tipu Sultan and the Scots in India 1760-1800* (Edinburgh: National Galleries of Scotland, 1999), 71-79 with 91-92.

3 Ideas of Iberia

1 John Towner, 'The Grand Tour: a Key Phase in the History of Tourism', includes two excellent and ingenious maps (302-3) which are based on a statistical analysis of journeys undertaken by travellers in what Towner sees (313-5) as the two distinct periods of the Grand Tour as a whole. Withey, *Grand Tours and Cook's Tours*, 20 and 64-5 is helpful on the Alpine passes. She observes that the Mont Cenis pass was difficult and not suitable for wheeled transport, and that the newer Simplon route was much easier. It also made accessible to the traveller a remarkably beautiful stretch of Alpine scenery.

2 Mead, *The Grand Tour*, 252, 254. Black gives an admirable assessment of the place of Spain and Portugal in the Grand Tour in *The British Abroad*, 76-79. See also Holland, *The Warm South*, 56. See also *Spain in British Romanticism 1800-1840*, ed. Diego Saglia and Ian Haywood (London: Palgrave Macmillan, 2018), 'Introduction: Spain and British Romanticism', 5-6.

3 David Howarth, 'The Quest for Spain, c. 1625-1825', in Christopher Baker, David Howarth and Paul Stirton, *The Discovery of Spain*, ed. David Howarth (Edinburgh: National Galleries of Scotland, 2009), 13. 15.

4 [Walter Scott], Art. IX. '*Childe Harold's Pilgrimage. Canto IV. By Lord Byron*', *The Quarterly Review*, XIX, no. xxxvii (April 1818), 222.

5 Christopher Baker, 'Introduction' to *The Discovery of Spain*, 9.

6 Boswell, *Life of Johnson*, I: 365.

7 Pemble, *The Mediterranean Passion*, 48.

8 Henry Fielding, *The Journal of a Voyage to Lisbon* (London: A. Millar, 1755), Preface, x.

9 *Letters*, VII: 422-3, WS to Thomas Scott, 28 Aug. 1808.

10 *Letters*, II: 95, 14 Oct. 1808.

11 *Letters*, II: 111, WS to Lady Abercorn, 27 Oct. 1808, but corrected from the text in *Scott on Himself*, ed. Hewitt, 77. Peter Garside has drawn attention to the fact of Scott's familiarity with European languages and has observed that he felt more at home with them that he did with the Classics. See <www.walterscottclub.com/blog/prof-peter-garside-scotts-shorter-verse-versatility-in-an-edinburgh-and-european-poet>, 2, 9.

12 *Letters*, II: 95, WS to Lady Abercorn, 14 Oct. 1808; *Letters*, II: 111, to Lady Abercorn, 27 Oct. 1808.

13 *Letters*, II: 76, WS to Thomas Scott, 20 June 1808.

14 Lockhart, X: 165.

15 Scott, 'Prefatory Memoir to Le Sage': *Lives of the Novelists*, 81,75, 88, 92.

16 These remarks are found in Scott's anonymous review of *Childe Harold's Pilgrimage. Canto IV*, in *The Quarterly Review* (see note 4 above), 222.

17 *Letters*, II: 117, WS to Joanna Baillie, 31 Oct. 1808. Although Scott wrote 'Castalian'—and thus alluded to the Castalian spring at Delphi, with its many classical literary associations, and had doubtless become confused also with notions of the so-called 'Castalian Band' of Scottish 'makars' at the court of King James VI—in the Spanish context of which he was thinking he should actually have written 'Castilian'.

18 This phrase was written by Scott on the flyleaf of a copy of Walter Scot [of Satchells], *A True History of Several Honourable Families of the Right Honourable Name of Scot*. The book is in the library of Abbotsford. See Lockhart I: 67.

19 *Letters*, II: 404-5, WS to Joanna Baillie, 23 Nov. 1810.

20 *Lockhart*, III: 273.

21 *Letters*, II: 464, WS to Miss [Sarah] Smith, 12 Mar. 1811.

22 *Letters*, II: 432, to Lady Abercorn, 11 Jan 1811.

23 *Edinburgh Annual Register*, II (1809), but in fact published only in 1811. See Kenneth Curry, *Sir Walter Scott's Edinburgh Annual Register* (Knoxville, TN: University of Tennessee Press, 1977), 99-118.

24 For publication details see William B. Todd and Ann Bowden, *Sir Walter Scott. A Bibliographical History 1796-1832* (New Castle, DE: Oak Knoll Press, 1998), 246, 255.

25 *Letters*, II: 482, WS to Morritt, 30 Apr. 1811.

26 *Letters*, II: 513, WS to William Hayley, 2 July 1811.

27 Lockhart, III: 286-7.

28 *Letters*, II: 478, WS to Lady Abercorn, 30 Apr. 1811.

29 W. M. Thackeray, *Notes of a Journey from Cornhill to Grand Cairo*, new introduction by Sarah Searight; illustrations compiled by Briony Llewellyn (Heathfield: Cockbird Press, 1991), 41. Thackeray's book was originally published in 1846.

30 Pemble, *Mediterranean Passion*, 48.

31 The anecdote was retailed by Lockhart (X. 142) on the basis of a conversation recorded by Sir William Gell, who had attempted to reproduce Scott's pronunciation of 'beat' as 'bet'. See Gell, *Reminiscences of Sir Walter Scott's Residence in Italy, 1832*, ed. James C. Corson (London and Edinburgh:

Thomas Nelson, 1957), 13: '... he bet me out of the field in the description of the strong passions, and in deep-seated knowledge of the human heart; so I gave up poetry for the time.'

32 Byron, *Childe Harold's Pilgrimage*, Canto I, line 387.

33 Byron, *The Complete Poetical Works*, ed. Jerome J. McGann, two vols (Oxford: Clarendon Press, 1980), I: 41. These lines in fact allude to Sir John Carr and his *Descriptive Travels in Spain* of 1811. But in the aftermath of the publication of Scott's *Vision of Don Roderick* it seems very possible that Byron was also thinking of his fellow poet as an object of satire: an author who knew Spain in books—'cooped within one Quarto's brink'—but not in actuality. Paternoster Row was the centre of the London book-trade.

34 'Memoirs' in *Scott on Himself*, ed. Hewitt, 36; see *Scott on Himself*, xxiv-v, for Hewitt's argument for the dating of this passage.

35 Walter Scott, *Redgauntlet*, ed. G. A. M. Wood with David Hewitt, Edinburgh Edition of the Waverley Novels (Edinburgh: Edinburgh University Press, 1997), 10.

36 *Letters*, V: 253, n. 1, printing extracts from a letter of Buccleuch to WS, 4 Dec. 1818; *Letters*, V: 276, WS to Adam Ferguson, 31 Dec. 1818.

37 *Letters*, V: 291-2, WS to Adam Ferguson, 15 Jan. [1819].

38 *Letters*, V: 352, WS to Buccleuch, 15 Apr. [1819]. In this letter Scott refers to Giuseppe Marc' Antonio Baretti's *Journey from London to Genoa through England, Portugal, Spain and France*, published in four volumes in 1770: an example of Scott's wide reading which guaranteed him a familiarity with Europe even if he had never been to the countries described.

39 *Letters*, V: 354, WS to Adam Ferguson, [16 Apr.] 1819. Scott will have known of Cintra and Mafra, from (among other sources) the evocations of them in *Childe Harold's Pilgrimage*, Canto I, stanzas 18-21 and 29-30.

40 Thomas Constable, *Archibald Constable and his Literary Correspondents*, three vols (Edinburgh: Edmonston and Douglas, 1873), III: 114-15; 119.

41 Scott, *Lives of the Novelists*, 25, 65-66.

42 Edgar Johnson, *Sir Walter Scott. The Great Unknown*, two vols (London: Hamish Hamilton, 1970), II: 1249 states that, in Frankfurt in June 1832, Scott bought a copy of the newly published *Alhambra*. Unfortunately Johnson's alleged source is suspect, and there is no copy of the book at Abbotsford.

43 Washington Irving, *The Alhambra* (London: Darf Publishers, 1986), 10, 14.

4 A Sudden Frisk to Paris

1 Mary Shelley, 'The English in Italy', 325.

2 Wilfred Partington, *Sir Walter's Post-Bag. More stories and sidelights from his unpublished Letter-Books* (London: John Murray, 1932), 105: Morritt to WS, 13 May 1814.

3 *Letters*, III: 456, WS to Morritt, 9 July 1814.

4 Shelley, 'The English in Italy', 326.

5 WS to Morritt, 11 Nov. 1814, quoted in Lockhart, V: 10-11; *Letters*, III: 514, WS to Daniel Terry, 10 Nov. 1814.

6 *Letters*, III: 477 and III: 498, WS to Morritt, 28 July and 14 Sept. 1814.

7 *Letters*, III: 486, WS to Ballantyne, 13 Aug. 1814.

8 *The Pirate*, Waverley Novels, Vol XXIV (Edinburgh: Cadell & Company, 1831), iv-v.

9   On this subject see Iain Gordon Brown, 'Curious on Continent and Isle:
    William Daniell, Walter Scott and the Vision of the Scottish Coastal Voyage',
    in *Daniell's Scotland. A Voyage Round the Coast of Scotland and the
    Adjacent Isles 1815-1822*, (Edinburgh: Birlinn, 2006), xvi-xxv. See also John
    Garvey, *William Daniell's Inverness & The Moray Firth. An Artist's Journey
    in 1815* (Kibworth Beauchamp: Matador, 2014), Foreword by Iain Gordon
    Brown, ix-xii, and Chapters 1-2.

10 On Hakewill and Turner see Cecilia Powell, *Turner in the South: Rome,
    Naples and Florence* (New Haven and London: Yale University Press, 1987),
    18, 34.

11 Lockhart, IV: 339 note, quoting Byron to Moore, 3 Aug. 1814. It is surprising
    that Lockhart should have printed this less than flattering comment on his
    father-in-law; but the second part of the extract shows, at least, how Scott
    differed morally—for the better—from Byron.

12 *Letters*, III: 495-6, WS to Morritt, 14 Sept. 1814. Nova Zembla and Thule are
    cited as emblematic of places so remote as almost to be at the world's end,
    even though Thule was also identified with the Northern Isles. Barnard Castle,
    County Durham, is close to Morritt's seat of Rokeby, near Greta Bridge;
    Cauldshiels Loch is on the Abbotsford estate.

13 Mary Shelley, 'The English in Italy', 327, here adopting (and slightly altering)
    the spoof medical condition first 'identified' by Thomas Love Peacock in
    his novella *Maid Marian* (London: Hookham and Longman, 1822) where
    the word was used in Chapter 1, 15: '... domesticity, or, as learned doctors
    call it, the faculty of stayathomeitiveness...'. Peacock had written most of
    Maid Marian in 1818, but publication was delayed until 1822 because it
    was thought to be, in part, an imitation of Scott's *Ivanhoe* (1820). Peacock's
    novella, in fact, opens with an epigraph taken from Scott's
    'Young Lochinvar'.

14 For Scott's reference see *Journal*, 257. In 1827 Spurzheim was in Edinburgh.
    Scott wrote to Maria Edgeworth of how he was 'out of charity at present
    with the fair sex for a party of them actually went to see that German
    quack Spurzeim [sic] dissect a human head, so I am not able to look at an
    Edinburgh belle without thinking of raw head and bloody bone.' (*Letters*, X:
    312, 14-15 Nov. 1827).

15 *Letters*, III: 389, WS to Joanna Baillie, [10 Dec. 1813].

16 *Letters*, III: 456, WS to William Hayley, 20 June 1814.

17 *Letters*, IV: 6, WS to Lady Abercorn, 10 Jan. 1815.

18 James Simpson, *A Visit to Flanders, in July, 1815, Being Chiefly an Account of
    the Field of Waterloo*, fourth edition (Edinburgh: William Blackwood, 1816),
    54.

19 *Letters*, IV: 7, to Daniel Terry, 15 [July] 1815. Grierson mistakenly read the
    date as 'January', and published the letter in sequence as if it were of that
    date; but content and context make it clear that the date must actually be
    July.

20 *Letters*, IV: 74, WS to John Richardson, 15 July 1815.

21 Lockhart, V: 49.

22 *Letters*, IV: 76, WS to Matthew Weld Hartstonge, 26 July 1815. Although
    Scott admitted to Hartstonge that Paris might in future be easily accessible,
    now was the time to see the city. This being so, his desire to make the visit
    'has predominated over my wish to see green Erin'. Another putative Irish trip
    had been shelved.

23 Lockhart, V: 52.

24 [Constantine Henry Phipps, Viscount Normanby], *The English in Italy*, three vols (London: Saunders & Otley, 1825), I: 12,118, 234, 256; II: 1, 221. For Scott's evaluation of Normanby's book, see *Journal*, 82.

25 Philip Mansel, *Paris Between Empires 1814-1852* (London: John Murray, 2001), 41. Mansel quotes from Scott's *Paul's Letters to his Kinsfolk* once only, and then extremely briefly: see *Paris Between Empires*, 91.

26 Andrew Lang, *The Life and Letters of John Gibson Lockhart*, two vols (London: John C. Nimmo, 1897), I: 96, Lockhart to Jonathan H. Christie, 29 Nov. 1815.

27 *Paul's Letters to his Kinsfolk* (Edinburgh: Archibald Constable, 1816), 5.

28 NLS, Acc. 12244. See Iain Gordon Brown, 'A Grand Tour Letterbook of Roger Robertson, Younger of Ladykirk, Berwickshire, 1750-1753', *Friends of the National Libraries Annual Report* (2003): 24-27.

29 *Paul's Letters*, 462-3.

30 Walter Scott came to change his opinion of John Scott (1783-1821) in the most dramatic of ways. The latter, an Aberdonian, was a radical London journalist. As editor of *The London Magazine* he began a heated dispute with J. G. Lockhart over some very strong articles by Lockhart in *Blackwood's Magazine*. Mutual abuse on paper nearly progressed to actual physical violence between the two men in 1820. Lockhart avoided a challenge and counter-challenge. But Lockhart's London barrister friend Jonathan Christie provoked a further quarrel, and this was the immediate cause of the duel on 16 February 1821 at Chalk Farm between Christie and John Scott. In a second, unnecessary, round Scott was wounded and subsequently died as a result of his injuries. By this time, Walter Scott had come to regard John Scott as a scoundrel. The matter was not so simple. Lockhart's satirical and abusive journalism was key to what had followed. His father-in-law took his part, but urged him to moderate his satire in future, and to sever his connection with *Blackwood's Magazine*. See Harriet Harvey Wood, *Lockhart of the Quarterly*, Chapter 5, *passim*; and, on John Scott's fascinating career in general, Patrick O'Leary, *Regency Editor. Life of John Scott* (Aberdeen: Aberdeen University Press, 1983).

31 Patrick Fraser Tytler [with Archibald Alison], *Travels in France during the Years 1814-15, Comprising a Residence at Paris During the Stay of the Allied Armies, and at Aix, at the Period of the Landing of Bonaparte*, 2 vols (Edinburgh: Macredie, Skelly and Muckersy, 1815).

32 *A Visit to Flanders, in July, 1815, Being Chiefly an Account of the Field of Waterloo.*

33 *Letters*, X: 159, WS to Lockhart, 15 Feb. 1827.

34 *Letters*, IV: 214, WS to Robert Southey, 17 Apr. 1816.

35 John Scott [of Gala], *Journal of a Tour to Waterloo and Paris in Company with Sir Walter Scott in 1815* (London: Saunders and Otley, 1842), 46.

36 *Narrative of a Residence in Belgium during the Campaign of 1815; and of a Visit to the Field of Waterloo* (London: John Murray, 1817).

37 *Ibid.*, v-vi; 326.

38 *Ibid.*, 122, 238, 294, 292, 313, 285.

39 Philip Shaw, '"Shocking Sights of War": Charles Bell and the Battle of Waterloo', in *Conflicting Visions: War and Visual Culture in Britain and France c. 1700-1830* , ed. John Bonehill and Geoff Quilley (Aldershot: Ashgate, 2005), 193. Shaw does not appear to know of Charlotte Waldie's 1817 *Narrative of a Residence*, but relies rather on a work of hers published much later in the century, as well as on her (unacknowledged) authorship of Booth's *Battle of Waterloo*.

40 John Scott, *Paris Revisited in 1815, By Way of Brussels: Including a Walk over the Field of Battle at Waterloo*, third edn (London: Longman, 1816), 202, 219, 221.

41 *The Field of Waterloo*, Stanza VI; see Paul O'Keeffe's Introduction to the reprint of the poem in the compilation *Scott on Waterloo*, ed. Paul O'Keeffe (London: Vintage, 2015), 360.

42 Philip Shaw, *Waterloo and the Romantic Imagination* (Basingstoke: Palgrave Macmillan, 2002), 45. Shaw alludes, I think, to a passage in *Paul's Letters* (156) which he misinterprets.

43 *Paul's Letters*, 198.

44 Shaw, *Waterloo and the Romantic Imagination*, 45.

45 *Paul's Letters*, 198-9.

46 Simpson, *A Visit to Flanders in July 1815*, 82, 124.

47 *A Visit to Flanders*, 99. Simpson and his friends misquoted three lines from Stanza XI of the Conclusion to *Don Roderick*.

48 Shaw, *Waterloo and the Romantic Imagination*, 36.

49 *Letters*, XII: 136-7, WS to Charlotte Scott, 8 Aug. 1815.

50 *Letters*, VII: 483, WS to Thomas Scott, a retrospective letter of 29 May 1816.

51 *Paul's Letters*, 318-21. Lenoir's museum was closed in 1816 and its contents redistributed to the places whence the works had come in the first place. The seed of an idea had been sown, however; and the museum was reconstituted, with casts replacing the now-dispersed originals that Scott had seen. Today the Musée national des Monuments Français is located at the Palais de Chaillot.

52 *Paul's Letters*, 323.

53 Pemble, *The Rome We Have Lost*, 21-26.

54 *The Poetical Works of Sir Walter Scott, Bart.*, Author's Edn, ed. J. G. Lockhart (Edinburgh: A. & C. Black, 1869), 604.

55 *Paul's Letters*, 324.

56 *Letters*, XII: 142, WS to Charlotte Scott [Aug. 1815].

57 John Scott, *Paris Revisited in 1815*, 265, 279, 324-5.

58 The Ardizzone drawing is conveniently reproduced in Patricia R. Andrew, *A Chasm in Time: Scottish War Art and Artists in the Twentieth Century* (Edinburgh: Birlinn, 2014), 147.

59 J. B. S. Morritt, *A Grand Tour. Letters and Journeys 1794-96*, ed. G. E. Marindin (London: John Murray, 1914), 309.

60 Stendhal [Marie-Henri Beyle], *Rome, Naples et Florence*, (Paris: Michel Levy, 1854), 270.

61 *Letters*, IV.108-9, WS to Lady Compton, 25 Oct. 1815.

62 *Paul's Letters*, 330-41.

63 *Paul's Letters*, 338, 340-41.

64 In his retrospective memoir, John Scott of Gala recorded the indebtedness of Scott and his friends to Le Chevalier for his role as guide and mentor: see *Journal of a Tour to Waterloo and Paris*, 111-2, 200, 217. Le Chevalier's paper was read to the Royal Society of Edinburgh, in French, at three meetings in February and March 1791. It was translated by Andrew Dalzel and published both in the Society's *Transactions* and as a monograph with the title *Description of the Plain of Troy: With a Map of that Region…* (Edinburgh: T. Cadell, 1791): see Preface by Dalzel, [v].

65 *Letters*, IV: 88, WS to James Ballantyne, 30 Aug. 1815.

66 *Paul's Letters*, 339.

67 *Letters*, VIII: 53, WS to Joanna Baillie, 18 July 1823.

68 On this see Mansel, *Paris Between Empires*, 93-96; also Paul O'Keeffe, *Waterloo. The Aftermath* (London: The Bodley Head, 2014), 224.

69 Simpson, *Paris After Waterloo. Notes Taken at the Time and Hitherto Unpublished* (Edinburgh: William Blackwood, 1853), 268.

70 Scott, *Paris Revisited in 1815*, 317, 328.

71 *Ibid.*, 349-51.

72 *Ibid.*, 371, 383.

73 *Paul's Letters*, 337.

74 *Ibid.*, 413, 416-7.

75 Edward Planta, *A New Picture of Paris; or, a Stranger's Guide to the French Metropolis* (London: Samuel Leigh, 1814), 55-56.

76 John Scott, *Paris Revisited in 1815*, 278.

77 Patrick Fraser Tytler [with Archibald Alison], *Travels in France during the Years 1814-15...*, 134.

78 James Simpson, *Paris After Waterloo*, 112-13.

79 Gregor Dallas, *1815. The Roads to Waterloo* (London: Pimlico, 2001), 98.

80 Mansel, *Paris Between Empires*, 41-44, 91, 92.

81 Simpson, *Paris After Waterloo*, 114.

82 *Picturesque Views of the City of Paris and its Environs ...; The Original Drawings by Mr Frederick Nash; the Literary Department by Mr John Scott* (London: Longman, 1820). The work is unpaginated.

83 David Carey, *Life in Paris; Comprising the Rambles, Sprees, and Amours, of Dick Wildfire ... and his Bang-up Companion, Squire Jenkins, and Captain O'Shuffleton; with the Whimsical Adventures of the Halibut Family ... in the French Metropolis.* (London: John Fairbairn, 1822), 200.

84 *Letters*, XII: 145, 147, WS to Charlotte Scott, [late Aug. 1815].

85 *Poetical Works of Sir Walter Scott*, Author's Edn, 648. When discussing the appeal of Saint-Cloud, in *Paris Between Empires*, 224, Philip Mansel might profitably have quoted from Scott's short poem. It seems unjustly overlooked.

86 *Letters*, XII: 145, 147, WS to Charlotte Scott, [late Aug. 1815].

87 *Letters*, IV: 108, WS to Lady Compton, 25 Oct. 1815.

88 See *Scott on Waterloo*, ed. O'Keeffe, 6, where the advertisement is reproduced; also O'Keeffe, *Waterloo: The Aftermath* 101.

89 [Thomas Moore], *The Fudge Family in Paris, edited by Thomas Brown, the Younger,* eighth edn, (London: Longman, 1818), 87. Later collected editions of Moore's works spell 'Gauffrier' with only one 'f'.

90 John Hughes, *Itinerary of Provence and the Rhone Made During the Year 1819* (London: James Cawthorn, 1822), 3.

91 *Paul's Letters*, 314, 288; cf. *Letters*, IV: 263. WS to Joanna Baillie, 12 July 1816 for a further, retrospective assessment of Paris, couched in similar terms.

92 Walter Scott, *Quentin Durward*, ed. J. H. Alexander and G. A. M. Wood, Edinburgh Edition of the Waverley Novels (Edinburgh: Edinburgh University Press, 2006), 4, 6.

93 Lockhart, VII: 117.

94 Lockhart, VII: 118-19.

95 *Letters*, VII: 322, WS to Archibald Constable, 23 Jan. 1823.

96 *Letters*, IV: 263, WS to Joanna Baillie, 12 July 1816.

97 *Letters*, X: 113, WS to John Gibson, 8 Oct. 1826.

98 *Letters*, X: 117, WS to Lord Melville, 10 Oct. 1826.

99 *Journal*, 226.

100 *Journal*, 228, 230.

101 Mansel, *Paris Between Empires*, 160-61.

102 *Journal*, 226, 233, 229-30.

103 *Journal*, 227. On Madame de Souza see Mansel, *Paris Between Empires*, 23, 61, 153-6.

104 *Journal*, 233-4.

105 *Correspondence of James Fenimore-Cooper*, ed. James Fenimore Cooper, two vols (New Haven, Conn., 1922), I: 111-12, extract of letter of Susan Augusta de Lancey Cooper, 28 Nov. 1826.

106 *Soirées de Walter Scott à Paris, recueillies et publiées par M. P. L. Jacob, Bibliophile* (Paris: Eugène Renduel, 1829), 13, 19, 21, 29. There is no copy at Abbotsford, despite the author's specious claim of a *dédicace* to the proprietor.

107 *Journal*, 226, 228, 231, 232, 239.

5 'To Roll a Little About'

1 *Letters*, V: 291-2, WS to Adam Ferguson, 15 Jan. [1819].

2 <www.walterscottclub.com/blog/prof-peter-garside-scotts-shorter-verse-versatility-in-an-edinburgh-and-european-poet>, 9.

3 On the growth of interest in Switzerland see W. E. Mead, *The Grand Tour*, 255-68. The maps included by John Towner in 'The Grand Tour: a Key Phase in the History of Tourism', 302-3, make this point effectively. See also Mullen and Munson, *The Smell of the Continent*, 4, 75, 76-7, 81.

4 Miller, *Cockburn's Millennium*, 87.

5 *Letters*, XII: 144, WS to Charlotte Scott, [28 Aug. 1815]. He also wrote to Charlotte in similar terms about the same time of how she must 'certainly come to France & proceed as far as Switzerland—the journey would be delightful in this fine weather.' See *Letters*, XII: 147, WS to Charlotte Scott, [late Aug. 1815].

6 *Letters*, IV: 164-5, WS to James Skene, 7 Jan. 1816. Scott showed great interest in the possible publication of Skene's journals and, though the matter was really out of his area of expertise, concerned himself in their illustration. He wrote, in the letter cited above: 'But the most difficult thing is to arrange the mode in which the engravings are to be executed... Stroke engraving is intolerably expensive, and one is by no means sure of having it executed well even by employing the best engravers and paying the highest price. These gentlemen's temptation to make money is so great that they do not hesitate to employ their pupils on works to which they give their own name. [Archibald] Constable seems to incline to a sort of etching or aqua tinta affair, which looks showy enough and can be executed, he says, for five or six guineas a plate. As I wish you to judge for yourself, I caused him to send you a copy of Sir George Mackenzie's Travels as a specimen of the style in which he thinks your journal should be published. He... would prefer the Tour through Sicily and Malta...'. Scott confessed that he himself considered the 'style of etching slight and a little too sketchy', but added the qualification: 'I could take it upon me to act for you in matters of literary concern, yet I am by no means qualified to do so in point of vertu.'

7 *Letters*, IV: 164-5, WS to James Skene, 7 Jan. 1816.

8 James Skene, *[The Skene Papers:] Memories of Sir Walter Scott*, ed. Basil Thomson (London: John Murray, 1909), 45.

9 On these points see Maura O'Connor, *The Romance of Italy and the English Imagination* (Basingstoke: Macmillan, 1998), 19-20, 54, who does not, however, cite Scott as illustration or example.

10 Mary Shelley, 'The English in Italy', 333.

11 *Letters*, IV: 263, WS to Joanna Baillie, 12 July 1816.

12 *The Collected Letters of Joanna Baillie*, ed. Judith Bailey Slagle, two vols (Madison, NJ: Farleigh Dickinson University Press, 1999), I: 353-4, to WS, 2 July 1816; I: 357-9, to WS, 13 Sept. 1816. *Letters*, IV: 263, WS to Joanna Baillie, 12 July 1816.

13 *Letters*, IV:165, WS to Joanna Baillie, 12 July 1816; *Collected Letters of Joanna Baillie*, I: 357-9, Baillie to WS, 13 Sept. 1816.

14 *Letters*, IV: 299-303, WS to Joanna Baillie, 26 Nov. 1816.

15 *Peter's Letters to his Kinsfolk*, II: 178.

16 On the *Provincial Antiquites...* project see Gerald Finley, *Landscapes of Memory: Turner as Illustrator to Scott* (London; Scolar Press), 49-68; and Katrina Thomson, *Turner and Sir Walter Scott. The Provincial Antiquities and Picturesque Scenery of Scotland* (Edinburgh: National Galleries of Scotland, 1999).

17 *Letters*, V. 145, WS to Maria Edgeworth, 10/15 May 1818.

18 *Letters*, V: 244, WS to Lady Compton, 2 Dec. 1818.

19 *Letters*, VI: 19 and 41-42, WS to Walter Scott, 18 Nov and 3 Dec. 1819.

20 The phrase 'German-mad' occurs in a letter of Scott to Mrs Thomas Hughes, 13 Dec. 1827: *Letters*, X: 331. Scott was looking back on his intense interest in German literature in the 1790s. The strongly Italophile Mary Shelley unburdened herself, in 1826, of the opinion that 'The name of Germany is sufficient in itself to inspire a kind of metaphysical gloom...': see 'The English in Italy', 326.

21 *Letters*, V: 408, WS to Morritt, 8 July 1819; V: 405, WS to Mrs Clephane, 15 July 1819.

22 *Letters*, XII: 449-50, WS to J. H. Voss, [Mar.–Apr. 1822].

23 *Letters*, VII: 91, WS to Walter Scott, ?March 1822.

24 *The Private Letter-books of Sir Walter Scott*, ed. Wilfred Partington (London: Hodder and Stoughton, 1930), 34.

25 *Journal*, 302.

26 *Letters*, VII: 167, WS to Walter Scott, 15 May 1822.

27 *Letters*, VII: 243, WS to Lady Abercorn, 13 Sept. 1822.

28 *Letters*, VII: 199, WS to Byron, 26 June 1822.

29 *Letters*, IX: 135, WS to Charles Scott, 12 June 1825.

30 *Letters*, IX: 153, WS to Lord Montagu, 26 June 1825.

31 Charles Tennant, *A Tour through Parts of the Netherlands, Holland, Germany, Switzerland, Savoy and France in the Years 1821-2, Including a Description of the Rhine Voyage in the Middle of Autumn, and the Stupendous Scenery of the Alps in the Depth of Winter*, two vols (London: Longman, 1824).

32 Planché's dedication is dated 1 Jan. 1827. The London publishers were Goulding, D'Almaine, & Co. See also *The Recollections and Reflections of J. R. Planché: a Professional Biography*, 2 vols (London: Tinsley Brothers, 1872), I: Chapter VII, for Planché's German trip; and 115 for the circumstances of the book's dedication to Scott.

33 *Letters*, X: 476-7, WS to Charles Scott [late July 1828]. Lockhart's letter to WS is quoted *Letters*, X: 476.

6   Irish Interlude: a 'Grand Tour' in Microcosm

1   *Letters*, II: 32 and 95, WS to Lady Abercorn, 13 Mar. and 14 Oct. 1808; II: 74, WS to Lady Lousia Stuart, 16 June 1808; II: 154, WS to J. B. S. Morritt, 14 Jan. 1809.
2   *Letters*, II: 216, WS to Lady Abercorn, 8 Aug. 1809; II: 201.
3   *Letters*, II: 201, WS to the Revd Edward Berwick, [July] 1809.
4   *Letters*, II: 384, WS to Miss [Sarah] Smith, 4 [Nov.] 1810.
5   *Letters*, II: 511, WS to Edgeworth, 2 July 1811; II: 485, to Matthew Weld Hartstonge, 1 May 1811; III: 57, to the Revd Edward Berwick, 16 Jan. 1812.
6   *Letters*, IV: 32, WS to Maria Edgeworth, 17 Feb. 1815.
7   *Letters*, IX: 178, WS to Lady Louisa Stuart, 7 July 1815.
8   *Letters*, IX: 24, WS to Morritt, 5 Mar. 1825.
9   *Letters*, IX: 79, WS to Maria Edgeworth, [mid-Apr.] 1825.
10   *Letters*, IX: 178, WS to Lady Louisa Stuart, 7 July 1825.
11   *Letters*, IX: 171-2, 4 July 1825.
12   *Letters*, IX: 179-80, 7 July 1815.
13   For 'steam kettle' references, see *Letters*, VII: 385, WS to Daniel Terry, 2 May 1823; and IX: 162, WS to Walter Scott, 1 July 1825, where Scott writes of starting 'in the steam kettle' for Dublin.
14   *Letters*, VI: 487, 1 July 1821. In the eighteenth century, and indeed still in Walter Scott's lifetime, Scots went 'up' to London and, from there, 'down' to Edinburgh. A 'po-chay' is a colloquial contraction of 'post-chaise'.
15   *Letters*, IX: 187, to Sir Adam Ferguson, 18 July 1825; IX: 190, to Maria Edgeworth, 18 July 1825.
16   *Letters*, IX: 195, 31 July 1815.
17   *Letters*, IX: 240, WS to Joanna Baillie, 12 Oct. 1825; IX: 195, to Morritt, 31 July 1825; IX: 210, to Morritt, 25 Aug. 1825; IX: 214, to Sir George Beaumont, 28 Aug. 1825; IX: 265-6, to Lady Abercorn.
18   Lockhart, VIII: 33.
19   *Letters*, IX: 265-6, WS to Lady Abercorn, 26 Oct. 1825; IX: 192, to James Ballantyne, 27 July 1825; XI: 199-200, to Thomas Moore, 5 Aug. 1825; IX: 225, to the Duke of Buccleuch, 28 Sept. 1825. Lockhart's letter to his wife, Sophia Scott, is quoted in D. J. O'Donoghue, *Sir Walter Scott's Tour in Ireland in 1825* (Glasgow: Gowans & Gray; Dublin: O'Donoghue & Co., 1905), 44.
20   Patrick Brydone, *A Tour through Sicily and Malta, in a Series of Letters to William Beckford, Esq.*, two vols (London: Strahan and Cadell, 1773), I: 56-57.
21   *Letters*, IX: 240, to Joanna Baillie, 12 Oct. 1825.
22   O'Donoghue, *Scott's Tour in Ireland*, 89, quoting the *Dublin Penny Journal* (1832), 199.
23   *Letters*, IX: 193, WS to Maria Edgeworth, 27 July 1825.
24   O'Donoghue, *Scott's Tour in Ireland*, 46, 48, 49-50. Although Lockhart refers to 'the Royal Society of Dublin' and the 'Dublin Society', the Royal Irish Academy rather than the Royal Dublin Society may actually be the institution meant. This seems more probable, given the collection of Itish antiquities inspected.
25   O'Donoghue, *Scott's Tour in Ireland*, 81.
26   Sir George Otto Trevelyan, *The Life and Letters of Lord Macaulay*, two vols (London: Longmans, 1876), II: 265-6 (24 August 1849).
27   Lockhart, VIII: 21, 32-33.

7 Painting Scenery in Words; or, Travels in the Library

1 Skene, *Memories of Sir Walter Scott*, 90-91.
2 Iain Gordon Brown, 'Scott, Literature and Abbotsford', in *Abbotsford and Sir Walter Scott: The Image and the Influence*, ed. Iain Gordon Brown (Edinburgh: Society of Antiquaries of Scotland, 2003), 4-36, *passim*.
3 Skene, *Memories of Sir Walter Scott*, 90-91.
4 *Letters*, VI: 263-4, WS to James Skene, 29 Aug. 1820.
5 *Letters*, VI: 110, WS to Constable, 12 Jan. 1820.
6 Terence Bowers, 'Reconstituting the National Body in Smollett's *Travels through France and Italy, Eighteenth Century Life*, 21, no 1 (Feb. 1997), 4-5. Bowers provides a good, concise analysis of the purpose of the Grand Tour on page 6.
7 Lockhart, X: 96. The anecdote was taken by Lockhart from a letter of John Scott of Gala, who had met his kinsman in London. O'Connor, *The Romance of Italy and the English Imagination*, 16, has suggested that Brydone's book combined 'two essential qualities associated with the best travel literature: the curiosity to see and the ingenuity to describe'; and she points out that the work was still widely read by early nineteenth-century travellers and Romantic poets.
8 Sweet, *Cities and the Grand Tour*, 12.
9 [Walter Scott], Art. IX. '*Childe Harold's Pilgrimage. Canto IV.* By Lord Byron', *The Quarterly Review*, XIX, no. xxxvii (April 1818), 215-32: see specifically 225, 223-4.
10 O'Connor, *The Romance of Italy and the English Imagination*, 23.
11 *Letters*, III: 391, WS to Joanna Baillie, 10 Dec. 1813; III: 420, WS to Morritt, ?March 1814.
12 See Mullen and Munson, *The Smell of the Continent*, 152. This British-built vessel was very quickly sold to the French Postal Administration and re-named the *Henri IV*. See <https://medium.com/@DariaSWhites/dover-to-calais-ferry-history-24cdf085f56>.
13 Maria Graham, *Three Months Passed in the Mountains East of Rome During the Year 1819* (London: Longman; and Edinburgh: Archibald Constable, 1820), 144.
14 Leslie A. Marchand, *Byron: a Portrait* (London: John Murray 1971), 331-2.
15 Fiona MacCarthy, *Byron: Life and Legend* (London: John Murray 2002), 473.
16 Hughes, *Itinerary of Provence and the Rhone*, 216. Scott had clearly described the Tower of Westburnflat as small and square and situated on boggy ground: *The Black Dwarf*, ed. P. D. Garside, Edinburgh Edition of theWaverley Novels (Edinburgh: Edinburgh University Press, 1993), 59.
17 William Hazlitt, *Notes of a Journey through France and Italy* (London: Hunt and Clarke, 1826), 200.
18 James Pope-Hennessy, *Monckton Milnes. The Years of Promise 1809-1851* (London: Constable, 1949), 44.
19 *Life in the South. The Naples Journal of Marianne Talbot*, ed. Michael Heafford (Cambridge: Postillion Books, 2012), 25, 131, 27.
20 'A Last Memory of Sir Walter Scott', from the 'Memorial of a Tour' by Owen Blayney Cole, *The Cornhill Magazine*, LV, no 327 (September 1923), 257-67.
21 *The Journal of the Hon. Henry Edward Fox (later 4th and last Lord Holland)*, ed. The Earl of Ilchester (London: Thornton Butterworth, 1923), 309.

22 *Life in the South*, 105.

23 [Jane Waldie], *Sketches Descriptive of Italy in the Years 1816 and 1817 with a Brief Account of Travels in Various Parts of France and Switzerland in the same Years*, four vols (London: John Murray, 1820), III: 110.

24 Henry Matthews, *Diary of an Invalid*, new edn (Stroud: Nonsuch Publishing, 2005), 123. The full title of Matthews's book is *Diary of an Invalid. Being the Journal of a Tour in Pursuit of Health in Portugal, Italy, Switzerland and France in the Years 1817, 1818 and 1819*. John Murray was the British publisher, in 1820. A popular edition, the third—and one no doubt frequently purchased by British travellers on the Continent—was that reprinted and published by Galignani in Paris, 1825. This reference equates to pages 126-6 of the Galignani edition.

25 *The English in Italy*, III: 211.

26 *Journal*, 82.

27 See Iain Gordon Brown, 'The illustrated "Grand Tour" alphabets of George Tytler, 1820-1825', *The British Art Journal*, XIX, No 3 (Winter 2018/2019), 56-63.

28 *Journal*, 82, 303, 425. On some intriguing connections between Scott, William Scrope and Hugh William Williams, see Iain Gordon Brown, 'Setting Scott in Stone. Abbotsford and Melrose in Miniature', *Discover NLS*, 1 (Spring 2006), 23-24.

29 Walter Scott, *Count Robert of Paris*, ed. J. H. Alexander, Edinburgh Edition of the Waverley Novels (Edinburgh: Edinburgh University Press, 2006), 127.

30 *Letters*, XII: 44, WS to Harriet Scott, 6 Mar. 1831 [but actually 1832].

31 *Letters*, IV: 164, WS to James Skene, 7 Jan. 1816.

32 *Letters*, VI: 264, WS to James Skene, 29 Aug. 1820; and *Journal*, 521.

33 *Letters*, IX: 164, WS to Mary Hughes, [2 July 1815]; VIII: 59, WS to Mary Hughes, 26 July [1825]. John Hughes's prints appeared in book form in 1825 as *Views in the South of France, Chiefly on the Rhone, Engraved by W.B. Cooke, from Drawings by P. de Wint, after Original Sketches by J[ohn] H[ughes]*.

34 *Letters*, VII: 283, WS to Mary Hughes, 11 Dec. 1822.

35 *Journal*, 500. Simond's book is *Switzerland; or a Journal of a Tour and Residence in that Country in 1817, 1818 and 1819; Followed by an Historical Sketch on the Manners and Customs of Ancient and Modern Helvetia*, second edn (London: John Murray, 1823).

36 Tennant, *Tour through Parts of the Netherlands, Holland, Germany, Switzerland, Savoy and France … Including a Description of the … the Stupendous Scenery of the Alps in the Depth of Winter*. A reading of Tennant's book (published 1824) may possibly have influenced Scott's decision to employ a particular metaphor in *Redgauntlet* (1824). This, of adventurous travellers who explore the summit of Mont Blanc, is used to illustrate the process of constructing a novel partly from supposed correspondence, partly from connecting narrative, and the 'interface' between the two methods of writing. Scott writes of slow progress through 'the crumbling snow drift' being assisted by the 'springing over… intervening chasms' with the aid of 'pilgrim-staves'. See *Redgauntlet*, ed. Wood with Hewitt, 125.

37 'The English in Italy', 337. Mary Shelley complimented Charlotte Eaton fulsomely for her descriptions of mountains, glaciers, crevasses and precipices, and quoted extensively from her excellent description (Vol. II:134) of the landscape. Shelley went as far as to praise *Continental Adventures*, which she

did not rate highly as a *novel*, as 'the best guide to Switzerland'.

38   The book, containing 96 engravings, was printed in parts and then issued in two volumes for the author-artist in London, 1828-29.

39   WS to William Brockedon, 12 Feb. 1830, quoted in Lockhart, II: 58.

40   Skene, *Memories of Sir Walter Scott*, 4, 155-6.

41   'Mrs Ann Radcliffe', 314.

42   C. R. Leslie, *Autobiographical Recollections*, ed. Tom Taylor, two vols (London: John Murray, 1860), I: 93.

43   *The Quarterly Review*, III, no. vi (May 1810), 512-3.

44   *Letters*, V: 182-3.

45   See, for example, Catherine Gordon, 'The Illustration of Sir Walter Scott: Nineteenth-Century Enthusiasm and Adaptation', *Journal of the Warburg and Courtauld Institutes*, 34 (1971), 297-317; and Richard J. Hill, *Picturing Scotland through the Waverley Novels: Walter Scott and the Origins of the Victorian Illustrated Novel* (Farnham: Ashgate, 2010).

46   Edward Chaney, 'Milton's Visit to Vallombrosa: A Literary Tradition', in *The Evolution of the Grand Tour. Anglo-Italian Cultural Relations Since the Renaissance* (London: Frank Cass, 1998), 280-81.

47   Frances Trollope, *A Visit to Italy*, two vols (London: Richard Bentley, 1842), I: 222.

48   For these ideas see Alastair Durie, 'Scotland is Scott-land: Scott and the Development of Tourism', in *The Reception of Sir Walter Scott in Europe*, ed. Pittock, 320-21.

8   'Methinks I Will Not Die Quite Happy...'

1   *Letters*, IV: 224, WS to M. W. Hartstonge, 30 Apr. 1816.

2   *Ibid.*

3   *Letters*, IV: 306, WS to M. W. Hartstonge, 28 Nov. 1816.

4   William Congreve, *The Way of the World*, Act III, line 548; Act I, lines 196-200.

5   *Letters*, IV: 306, WS to M. W. Hartstonge, 28 Nov. 1816.

6   *Letters*, IV: 477, WS to Joanna Baillie, 24 July 1817.

7   *Letters*, IV: 332, WS to Miss [Anna Jane] Clephane, 26 Dec. 1816.

8   *Sketches Descriptive of Italy...*, I: Preface, xi, xii-xiii.

9   *Rome in the Nineteenth Century*, I: 328-9, 340.

10   *Letters*, IV: 420, WS to Mrs Marianne Maclean Clephane, 23 Mar. 1817. Mrs Clephane was Lady Compton's mother.

11   *Diary of an Invalid*, 59, 127-8 (Galignani third edn., 52, 132-3).

12   Anna Jameson, *Diary of an Ennuyée*, new edn (London: Henry Colburn, 1826), 155.

13   *Letters*, I: 23, WS to William Clerk, 30 Sept. 1792.

14   The lines come from Scott's poem 'To a Lady, with Flowers from a Roman Wall', 1797: *Poetical Works*, 624.

15   Iain Gordon Brown, *The Hobby-Horsical Antiquary: a Scottish Character 1640-1830* (Edinburgh: National Library of Scotland, 1980), 6. See further Iain Gordon Brown, 'Introduction: A Flibbertigibbet of a House to Suit an Antiquary', in *Abbotsford and Sir Walter Scott: The Image and the Influence*, ed. Iain Gordon Brown (Edinburgh: Society of Antiquaries of Scotland, 2003), xiv-xv.

16   Iain Gordon Brown, 'The Advocates' Library as National Museum', in *For the Encouragement of Learning. Scotland's National Library 1689-1989*, ed. Patrick Cadell and Ann Matheson (Edinburgh: Her Majesty's Stationery

Office, 1989), 172.

17   *Letters*, XII: 153, WS to Charlotte Scott, 11 Nov. 1815.

18   *Journal*, 90. The prints in question cannot have been as Scott described them, as if Charles-Louis Clérisseau had somehow engraved drawings by Piranesi. They are likely to be the set of fourteen prints after Clérisseau published by J. Brett in 1766. Scott promised them to Charles Kirkpatrick Sharpe, and wrote of them thus, with mockery all round: 'I believe they were once in some esteem though now so detestably smoked that they will only suit your suburban villa in the Cowgate when you retire to that Classical residence.' See *Letters*, IX. 438, WS to Charles Kirkpatrick Sharpe, [? Mar. 1826].

19   *Letters*, XI: 445, WS to Charles Scott, 22 Dec. 1830. On Scott's collection in general see Mary Monica Maxwell-Scott, *Abbotsford: The Personal Relics and Antiquarian Treasures of Sir Walter Scott* (London; A. & C. Black, 1893); and Walter Scott, *Reliquiæ Trotcosienses or the Gabions of the Late Jonathan Oldbuck Esq. of Monkbarns*, ed. Gerard Carruthers and Alison Lumsden, with an Introduction by David Hewitt (Edinburgh: Edinburgh University Press in association with The Abbotsford Library Project Trust, 2004).

20   For the Montfaucon reference see Scott, *Reliquæ Trotcosienses...*, 48.

21   *Journal*, 692. Gilbert Laing Meason's book, of which a copy remains at Abbotsford, is *On the Landscape Architecture of the Great Painters of Italy* (London: Hullmandel, 1828). The title-page bears only the author's initials.

22   *Letters*, VII: 243, WS to Lady Abercorn, 13 Sept. 1822.

23   Lockhart, X: 96. The statement is derived from a letter to Lockhart from John Scott of Gala, who met Sir Walter Scott in London on the eve of his departure for the Mediterranean.

24   *Journal*, 367, with reference to Miss Barbara Haig's performances, October 1827.

25   ['M.B. A. A.' = Marie-Henri Beyle = Stendhal], *Histoire de la pienture en Italie*, 2 vols (Paris: Didot, 1817).

26   Paris: P. Mongie, two vols, 1822. The presentation copy is at Abbotsford.

27   Walter Scott, *Waverley*, ed. P. D. Garside, Edinburgh Edition of the Waverley Novels, (Edinburgh: Edinburgh University Press, 2007), 15.

28   NLS, MS. 1752, f. 428, WS to Robert Cadell, 23 Nov. 1831.

29   Iain Gordon Brown, 'Prelude and Pattern: The Remarkable Grand Tour of Sir John Clerk of Penicuik in the 1690s', in *The Grand Tour and its Influence on Architecture, Artistic Taste and Patronage*, ed. Lester Borley ([Edinburgh]: Europa Nostra, 2008), 45-71, esp. 67-8; John Fleming, *Robert Adam and his Circle in Edinburgh and Rome* (London: John Murray 1962), 145.

30   Sir William Gell, *Reminiscences of Walter Scott's Residence in Italy, 1832*, ed. James C. Corson (Edinburgh and London: Thomas Nelson, 1957), 4; *Letters*, IV: 360-1, WS to James Bailey, 4 Jan. 1817. In his dealings with Bailey, a young and precocious Cambridge classical prizeman, and feeling somewhat in awe of a learned, if penurious prodigy, Scott had described himself in these terms—not just in playful self-deprecation but in genuine admiration for the talents of a young scholar whom he felt merited his interest. Bailey's admirably intelligent linguistic speculations had both prompted Scott's respect and stimulated his own thoughts.

31   *Sir William Gell in Italy. Letters to the Society of Dilettanti, 1831-1835*, ed. Edith Clay in collaboration with Martin Frederiksen (London: Hamish Hamilton, 1976), 99, 69, 117.

32   R. R. Madden, *The Literary Life and Correspondence of the Countess of Blessington*, second edn, three vols (London: T. C. Newby, 1855), II: 77-8.

33 *Letters*, IV: 224, 30 April 1816.

34 *Letters*, III: 453, WS to Hartstonge, 30 June [1814: thus dated by Grierson, but the date in fact must be 1812].

35 See, for example, *Letters*, IV: 139, to the classicist James Bailey of Trinity College, Cambridge, 30 Nov. 1815; IV: 148, to William Erskine in [1815]; VI: 149, to James Gray of Edinburgh High School, 11 Mar. 1820; and finally XI: 469, to Jean Baptiste Le Chevalier, 17 Feb. 1831. Scott showed great kindness to Bailey and took exceptional trouble to try to help him in his career. In the course of a scholarly interchange, which ranged from classical literature to Bailey's theories of Egyptian hieroglyphics—in which Scott took a great interest, and to which he responded with admirable perspicacity—Scott made the confession: 'I am however (to my shame be it spoken) no Grecian having in my youth neglected the language which I now bitterly regret.' He added the self-deprecating observation that he was 'one of the unlearned', in contrast with those he called the 'Aristarchs' of the *Edinburgh* and *Quarterly* Reviews, namely Francis Jeffrey and William Gifford. This term is derived from the name of a severe ancient Greek literary critic. So, in using it, Scott actually shows his own learning. (*Letters*, IV: 139)

36 *Letters*, VIII: 148, WS to Constable, 6 Jan. 1824; Scott, *Reliquiæ Trotcosienses...*, 49.

37 Lockhart, V: 37-8.

38 [Walter Scott], Art. IX. '*Childe Harold's Pilgrimage. Canto IV.* By Lord Byron', *The Quarterly Review*, XIX, no. xxxvii (April 1818), 221.

39 The Abbotsford copy of Dodwell's *A Classical and Topographical Tour through Greece in the Years 1801, 1805 and 1806* (London 1819) bears a presentation inscription from the publishers, Rodwell and Martin.

40 *Letters*, VIII: 436, WS to John Carne, 23 Nov. 1824. The presentation copy of John Carne's *Letters from the East* (London: Henry Colburn,1826) remains at Abbotsford. Carne's lively narrative takes him from Constantinople through Syria, Egypt and Sinai, back to Acre, Tyre and Beirut; through Palestine to Jerusalem and then to Damascus and Baalbek; thence to Cyprus, Rhodes and, ultimately, through the more unexpected parts of mainland Greece. So his travels were much more wide-ranging than the purely 'Grecian' Scott's letter implies.

41 I quote from the six-volume English (eighth) edition of 1817, *Travels of Anacharsis the Younger in Greece* (London: J. Mawman, 1817), I: Preface (by W. Beaumont), i-ii; II: 173; III: 61. 'Anacharsis' happened to be one of several pseudonyms that Sir William Gell adopted in his sometimes arch correspondence with literary contemporaries.

42 *Byron's Letters and Journals*, ed. Leslie A. Marchand, 13 vols (London: John Murray, 1973-82), 9: 87, Byron to WS, 12 Jan. 1822.

43 *The Private Letter-Books of Sir Walter Scott*, 266-7.

44 *Ibid.*

45 *Letters*, VIII: 396, WS to Maria Edgeworth, 15 Oct. 1824. Grierson reads 'John Bally'. The manuscript (NLS MS. 23130, f. 41) is ambiguous, but surely Scott intends John *Bully*. The allusion was to James Wyatt's magnificent Pantheon, Oxford Street, London. First built 1769-72, it was altered by the architect in 1790-91 only to be destroyed by fire the next year and rebuilt 1794-95 as a 'Winter Ranelagh'. It was subsequently reconstructed, remodelled and reused before its ultimate demolition in 1937. The London Pantheon was one of the great buildings of its age. Scott's second-hand reminiscence contributes tellingly to the literature of the mockery of the

Cockney as a 'type' in the new age of travel after 1814/15. Had they but been aware of it, the anecdote would doubtless have added much to the argument in Mullen and Munson, *The Smell of the Continent*, 28, 33-34, 133-5. For a similar anecdote of an English traveller encountered in Venice, see Anna Jameson, *Diary of an Ennuyée*, 80. He knew nothing of 'them things', viz. the buildings and paintings of Venice; and when told that there was a great gallery of pictures to be seen in Florence replied, 'Nothing else?'.

46   Paul Langford, *A Polite and Commercial People. England 1727-1783* (Oxford: Oxford University Press, 1989), 321.

47   *The Complete Letters of Lady Mary Wortley Montagu*, ed. Robert Halsband, three vols (Oxford: Clarendon Press, 1965-7), III: 148; Tobias Smollett, *Travels Through France and Italy*, ed. Frank Felsenstein (Oxford: Oxford University Press, 1981), 241.

48   Simpson, *Paris After Waterloo*, 109.

49   David Carey, *Life in Paris ...*, 200.

50   'The English in Italy', 327.

51   Thackeray, *Notes of a Journey from Cornhill to Grand Cairo*, 61.

52   *Letters*, II: 357, WS to John Richardson, 3 July 1810.

53   [Lockhart], *Peter's Letters to his Kinsfolk*, II: 329.

54   Duncan, *Scott's Shadow*, 67,96, citing, *inter alia*, the *Edinburgh Magazine*, 2 (1818), 149.

55   Newman, *Rise of English Nationalism*, 43; cf. 42-45.

56   Iain Gordon Brown, '"Tre Volte Terra Classica". La Spedizione Siciliana di James Hall', in James Hall, *Diario Siciliano (Febbraio–Marzio 1822)*, ed. Rosario Portale (Lugano: Agorà, 2013), 1-15. See also Iain Gordon Brown, 'Intimacy & Immediacy: James Hall's Journals in Italy and Germany, 1821-1822', in *Britannia Italia Germania: Taste & Travel in the Nineteenth Century*, ed. Carol Richardson and Graham Smith (Edinburgh: VARIE, 2001), 23-42; and Iain Gordon Brown, 'James Hall's Paris Day', *Scottish Archives*, 17 (2011), 13-25.

57   *Letters*, X: 348, WS to Mary Hughes, 25 Dec. 1827.

58   *Letters*, VIII: 462, WS to Lady Compton, 21 Dec. 1824.

59   Lockhart, I: 101-02; Arthur Melville Clark, *Sir Walter Scott: the formative years* (Edinburgh: William Blackwood, 1969), 21.

60   *Italian Journey. Being Excerpts from the Pre-Victorian Diary of James Skene of Rubislaw*, with a Preface by Sir H.J.C. Grierson (London: International Publishing Co., 1937), 209.

61   NLS, MS. 3896, ff. 65-86, Margaret Compton, later Marchioness of Northampton, to WS, 14 Mar. 1823. She also gave Scott 'an admirable account of Rome' in September 1827: see *Journal*, 348.

62   NLS, MS. 3907, ff. 3-4, Lady Northampton to WS, 2 July 1828. She wrote from Paris.

63   *Letters*, X: 474, WS to Lady Northampton, 16 July 1828.

64   Scott, *Redgauntlet*, ed. Wood with Hewitt, 33. Elizabeth Wheeler Manwaring discusses the use of Claude glasses by, for example, Thomas Gray, William Gilpin and Charles Gough. She observes that *two* kinds of glass were available: one with dark foil for sunny days, and one with silver foil for cloudy skies: see her pioneering *Italian Landscape in Eighteenth Century England. A Study Chiefly of the Influence of Claude Lorrain and Salvator Rosa on English Taste* (New York: Oxford University Press, 1925), 182, 186, 194. For a good recent discussion of the use of the Claude glass, with many interesting quotations from contemporary literature and some excellent

illustrations, see Adrian Tinniswood, *The Polite Tourist. A History of Country House Visiting* (London: The National Trust, 1998), 114-8. For James Skene and the use of the camera obscura, see Richard Stoneman, *A Luminous Land. Artists Discover Greece* (Los Angeles: J. Paul Getty Museum, 1998), 118 and plate 71. Karl Miller neatly defines the Claude glass as 'an aesthete's mirror for securing suitable views', and, possibly following the earlier observation of Manwaring, notes that the unfortunate Charles Gough had been carrying not one but two of these devices—hence possibly (though Miller does not say this) those for alternative weather conditions— when he met his fate in searching for The Picturesque on Helvellyn. See Miller, *Cockburn's Millennium*, 89. The artist, who had fallen to his death on the mountain, fell subsequently into a famous poem of Scott's.

9 A Cast in a King's Ship

1 See Anderson's narrative filling a gap in Scott's text: *Journal*, 658.
2 *Letters*, XI: 433, WS to Robert Cadell, [8 Dec. 1830].
3 *Journal*, 616.
4 *Letters*, XI: 432, WS to James Ballantyne, [8 Dec. 1830]. John Sutherland, *The Life of Walter Scott* (Oxford: Blackwell, 1995), 340, renders this statement about Scott's novelist predecessors more poignant even than it actually is by silently inserting the word 'for' into the quoted text and running up against this the signature on the letter, 'Walter Scott'.
5 *Journal*, 616.
6 NLS, MS 3915, ff. 158-158v, Cadell to WS, 10 Dec. 1830.
7 *The Fair Maid of Perth*, Magnum Edition, vol. XLII (Edinburgh: Robert Cadell, 1832), 18. Reference may be made back to the whimsical letter of September 1793 to Murray of Simprim (Chapter 2 above, note 17) on Border rivers holding their own against Italian streams.
8 NLS, MS. 3009, f. 10b, WS to Walter Scott, [*c.* 3 to17] July 1831.
9 *Letters*, XI. 444, WS to Charles Scott, 22 Dec. 1830.
10 *Letters*, XI: 228, WS to Walter Scott, 15 Aug. 1829.
11 NLS, MS. 917, Charles Scott's Neapolitan letter-book, ff. 4v-7v, Charles Scott to WS, 24 June and 29 Aug. 1831.
12 *Letters*, XI: 469, WS to Le Chevalier, 17 Feb. 1831.
13 Scott, *Quentin Durward*, ed. Alexander and Wood (2006), 15.
14 NLS, MS. 140, f. 54, WS to Walter Scott, 9 Sept. 1831; MS 3009, f. 10b, WS to Walter Scott, [*c.* 3-17 Jul] 1831. WS writes of the city as 'Mayenz'.
15 Mullen and Munson, *The Smell of the Continent*, 68-70.
16 Karl Miller, *Cockburn's Millennium*, 87.
17 Iain Gordon Brown, 'Intimacy & Immediacy: James Hall's Journals in Italy and Germany, 1821-1822', 39.
18 NLS, MS. 141, ff. 109-10, WS to Charles Scott, 17 July 1831, cf. MS. 1752, f. 335.
19 *Letters*, XII: 28, WS to Charles Scott, 8 Aug. 1831. When Charles was first posted to Naples, Sir Walter encouraged him to 'pay particular attention' to studying the region's history: '... you may take it for gospel that nothing makes history read with so much interest as the history of the country in which you reside for the time.' See *Letters*, XI: 444, WS to Charles Scott, 22 Dec. 1830.
20 NLS MS. 1752 (Grierson rejected transcripts), f. 380, WS to Buccleuch,

15 Sept. 1831. The 'Grierson Rejects' is the soubriquet given to the very
large quantity of Scott letters, transcribed by Sir Herbert Grierson and his
assistants, but ultimately not included in the twelve-volume edition of 1932-7.
The typed transcripts are preserved in the National Library of Scotland.

21 *Journal*, 397.

22 *Letters*, XII: 20, WS to Charlotte Eaton, 8 June 1831.

23 *Letters*, XI: 459-61, WS to Samuel Rogers, 15 Jan.[1831].

24 NLS, MS. 3916, f. 224, Rogers to WS, 4 Feb. 1831.

25 *Letters*, XI: 493-4, WS to Cadell, 24 Mar. 1831.

26 Samuel Rogers, *Italy, A Poem* (London: Cadell and Moxon, 1830), 171,
    172-3; cf. James Buzard, *The Beaten Track. European Tourism, Literature and
    Culture*, 101.

27 *Letters*, XII: 28, WS to Charles Scott, 8 Aug. 1831.

28 *Memoirs, Journal and Correspondence of Thomas Moore*, ed. Lord John
    Russell, 8 vols (London: Longman, 1853-56), VI: 227.

29 NLS, MS. 1752, f. 416, WS to Robert Cadell, 18 Oct. 1831.

30 *Journal*, 668.

31 Basil Hall, *Fragments of Voyages and Travels*, third series, three vols (Edinburgh:
    Robert Cadell, 1833), III: Chapter IX: 'Sir Walter Scott's Embarkation at
    Portsmouth in the Autumn of 1831', 280-32, specifically here 282.

32 NLS, MS. 1752, f. 378, Croker to Lockhart, 9 Sept. 1831; Hall, *Fragments of
    Voyages and Travels*, III: 283-6: Lockhart, X: 78-9.

33 Hall, *Fragments of Voyages and Travels...*, III: 284.

34 HMS *Barham* was originally a 74-gun ship-of-the-line but razeed and reduced
    to a 50-gun (32 pdr), fourth-rate frigate. (Some sources state that she carried
    52 guns.) See David Lyon, *The Sailing Navy List. All the Ships of the Royal
    Navy 1688-1860* (London: Conway Maritime Press, 1993), 114; *Conway's
    History of the Ship. The Line of Battle. The Sailing Warship 1650-1840*, ed.
    Robert Gardiner (London: Conway Maritime Press, 1992), 45. She was a
    relatively large and powerful ship, which makes the fact of her being placed
    at Scott's service all the more noteworthy. Scott himself called her 'a beautiful
    ship', and understood the facts of her reduction in rating: see *Journal*, 673.
    Barham's captain, Hugh Pigot CB, was a very senior captain with a great
    deal of distinguished service behind him. Everything was done to make
    Scott's passage as comfortable as possible, even to the extent of boarding
    over the grating steps of some of the ship's ladders lest Scott's stick catch in
    the apertures. *Barham* was not deployed, with the Channel fleet, as part of a
    deterrent force against the Dutch and in defence of Belgian independence in
    October 1831, Scott's arranged passage in her apparently being given priority:
    see *Journal*, 671. For the background, see Eric J. Grove, *The Royal Navy Since
    1815. A New Short History* (Basingstoke: Palgrave Macmillan, 2005), 10.

35 NLS, MS. 5317, f. 150, Sir James Graham, Bt., to WS, 15 Sept. 1831.

36 Hall, *Fragments of Voyages and Travels...*, III: 288.

37 NLS, MS. 1752, f. 382, WS to J. E. Shortreed (son of Scott's friend Robert
    Shortreed, Sheriff-Substitute of Roxburghshire), 15 Sept. 1831; ff. 383-4, WS
    to Robert Cadell, 16 Sept. 1831.

38 *Scott on Himself*, ed. Hewitt, 34 and n. 83. If 'teens' seems a rather modern
    expression, Scott himself did use it of his own youth.

39 *Sir Walter Scott. The Great Unknown*, II: 1191.

40 NLS, MS. 921, ff. 67-67v, 'To His Majesty's Ship *Barham*, Appointed by the
    King to Convey Sir Walter Scott to Naples'. A printed broadsheet is among
    the Abbotsford Papers. It is signed, oddly enough, 'W.S'; is written from

Epping Forest; and is dated 18 Nov. 1831.

41 *The Laird of Abbotsford*, 1-2.
42 *Letters*, IV: 419, WS to Mrs Clephane, 23 Mar. 1817.
43 *Letters*, XII: 29-30, WS to C. K. Sharpe, Sept. 1831.
44 Lockhart, X: 104-05. The endnote, or postscript, appears as a conclusion to the text of *Castle Dangerous* on pages 145-6 of vol. XLVIII (1833) of the Magnum Edition.
45 *The Border Magazine*, I, no. ii (December 1831), 90.
46 Basil Hall's own account is given at length in his *Fragments of Voyages and Travels...*, III: 280-328.
47 Matthews, *Diary of an Invalid*, 29 (20 in the Galignani third edn.); Semple, *Observations on a Journey Through Spain and Italy*, I: 10; Matthews, *Diary of an Invalid*, 13 (Galignani third edn, 1). Fielding's grave is now marked by a grandiloquent monument.
48 *Life in the South. The Naples Journal of Marianne Talbot*, 149, 162.
49 NLS, MS. 917, Charles Scott's Neapolitan letter-book, ff. 9v and 15, Charles Scott to Paley, n.d., and 23 Nov. 1831.
50 NLS, MS. 917, f. 13, to Sophia Lockhart, 10 Oct. 1831.
51 NLS, MS. 1614, Charles Scott's (unpaginated) Naples diary, 26 Dec. 1831.
52 *Journal*, 671.
53 NLS MS. 5317, ff. 170-71, John Gibson to WS, 26 Sept. 1831, with annexed copy letter from the Norwich Union; cf. Robert G. Alloo, *In the Warmth of the Limelight: The Untold Story of the Unlikely Partnership of Sir Walter Scott and His Lawyer, John Gibson, WS* ([Parker, Colorado]: Outskirts Press, 2019), 197-8. The Edinburgh Life Assurance Company added a premium of 10 shillings per cent [*sic*] 'for the risk of the voyage'. His passage in *Barham* (52 guns; Captain Arthur [*sic*: he was in fact Hugh] Pigot) is referred to, the destination being specified as 'Malta or Naples'. The endorsement to Scott's policy document, a facsimile of which is in my possession, is dated 5 Oct. 1831.

10 'The Glory of Scotland, Sent to Visit Strangers'

1 *Journal*, 677.
2 Forsyth, *Remarks on Antiquities, Arts, and Letters ... in Italy*, 71.
3 Lockhart, X: 96. The remark was made to John Scott of Gala.
4 *Journal*, 682.
5 Basil Hall, *Patchwork*, second edn, three vols (London: Edward Moxon, 1841), II: 172-81. Hall was dragged up Vesuvius by rope; heard the volcano 'bellow in a most terrific style'; then witnessed it 'vomit forth a mass of fiery materials', projectiles larger than a man's head falling like cannon-shot. His guide told him how Professor John Playfair, of Edinburgh, a friend of Scott, had spent six hours on the edge of the crater in similar conditions, and could not be persuaded to descend for his own or the guide's safety.
6 Iain Gordon Brown, 'Intimacy & Immediacy: James Hall's Journals in Italy and Germany 1821-22', 36.
7 Lockhart, X: 112, where a letter of Scott to Skene, 25 Nov. 1831, is printed. For Scott's two letters to Cadell see NLS, MS. 1752, ff. 443 and 453, 25 Dec. 1831 and c. 7 Jan. 1832. For a concise summary of the island's many names and changing international status, see <https://blog.geolsoc. org.uk/2016/12/20/door-20-corrao-hotham-graham-ferdinandea-julia-

neritasciacca-island-december>. For an early publication see 'On the new
Insular Volcano, named Hotham Island, which has just appeared off Sicily;
with a view of the Volcano, by one of the Officers of the *Philomel*', *The New
Edinburgh Philosophical Journal* (Edinburgh: Adam Black), 11 (April-October
1831), Art. XXI, 365-73, with an engraving of the volcano in eruption.

8 Lockhart, X: 112.
9 NLS, MS. 5317, ff. 212-212v, Skene to WS, 26 Dec. 1831.
10 *Letters*, XII: 39-40, 23 Nov. 1831.
11 Lockhart, X: 118.
12 NLS, MS. 5317, f. 207v, Stoddart to WS, 21 Nov. 1831.
13 Lockhart, X: 115.
14 *Letters*, XII: 45, 6 Mar 1832.
15 *Journal*, 684.
16 *Journal*, 689-90, 698.
17 *Journal*, 685. Donald Sultana's two important and very detailed studies are
   relevant here, and I seek neither to emulate nor to expand upon them. *The
   Siege of Malta Rediscovered. An Account of Sir Walter Scott's Mediterranean
   Journey and his Last Novel* (Edinburgh: Scottish Academic Press, 1977) sets
   the unpublished work in context; and the reconstructed text of the book is
   prefaced by an extended narrative (pages 1-121) of the whole voyage and of
   Scott's periods in Malta, Naples, Rome and of the journey home. *The Journey
   of Sir Walter Scott to Malta* (Gloucester: Alan Sutton, 1986) contains an even
   more detailed narrative and analysis of the voyage up to and including Malta,
   but not beyond.
18 NLS, MS. 1752, f. 493, WS to James Skene, 5 Mar. 1832. See also Skene,
   Memories of Sir Walter Scott, 202.
19 NLS, MS. 5317, f. 213, Skene to WS, 26 Dec. 1831.
20 Lockhart, X: 96.
21 NLS, MS. 1752, f. 428, WS to Cadell, 23 Nov. 1831.
22 *Information and Directions for Travellers on the Continent*, sixth edn
   (London: John Murray 1828), 298-9,.
23 *Remarks on Antiquities, Arts, and Letters … in Italy*, 148.
24 *Diary of an Invalid*, 139 (Galignani third edn., 143-4).
25 *Sketches Descriptive of Italy*, III: 209.
26 *Diary of an Ennuyée*, 272-3.
27 *Remarks on Antiquities, Arts, and Letters … in Italy*, 223, 225.
28 *Diary of an Ennuyée*, 272.
29 *Remarks on Antiquities, Arts, and Letters … in Italy*, 151.
30 *Remarks on Antiquities, Arts, and Letters … in Italy*, 151-2.
31 NLS. MS. 5317, f. 212-3.
32 For the balls, see *Life in the South. The Naples Journal of Marianne Talbot*,
   151; and NLS, MS. 917, Charles Scott's Naples letter-book, f. 29, copy letter
   20 Jan. 1832 to Delmé. Ann Rigney refers to this (second) masquerade ball
   as 'an "embodied" form of remediation' which involved 'people acting out
   stories and getting dressed up as their favourite characters'; it was 'part of
   a fashion in the 1820s and1830s for tableaux vivants and masquerades on
   the Waverley themes': see her *The Afterlives of Walter Scott: Memory on the
   Move* (Oxford: Oxford University Press, 2012), 106.
33 NLS, MS. 5317, f. 219, Mathias to WS, 2 Jan. 1832. Marianne Talbot wrote
   unflatteringly of Mathias who 'at 82 spends all his time & money in printing
   his poems & distributing them to his friends. 30 Latin Lines to Sir W. Scott on
   his visiting Naples came yes'y [yesterday]. Mr Mathias is not a pleasant man,

eager & irritable, but a wonderful person at 82.' (*Life in the South*, 168.)

34 NLS, MS. 5317, f. 224, Mathias to WS, 8 Feb. 1832.

35 NLS, Acc. 11136, WS to Charles Scott, 1 Feb. 1832.

36 *Letters*, XII: 45, WS to Harriet Brühl, Mrs Scott of Harden (later Lady Polwarth), 6 Mar. 1832.

37 NLS, MS. 1752, ff. 502 and 523, WS to Willam Laidlaw, 8 and 29 Mar. 1832.

38 'A Last Memory of Sir Walter Scott', 260, 258-9. The designation of his outfit as his 'Caledonian Club' dress is not quite correct: the 'Celtic Society' is more likely, though it could equally well have been—and more probably was—his Royal Company of Archers uniform. By Palazzo Garnier, Cole must mean the splendid accommodation rented by Mr and Mrs Garnier, a rich and somewhat vulgar couple, about whom Marianne Talbot was usually cutting.

39 Edgar Johnson, *Sir Walter Scott*, II: 1233. See Peter Garside's observations in <www.walterscottclub.com/blog/prof-peter-garside-scotts-shorter-verse-versatility-in-an-edinburgh-and-european-poet>, 9-10. The allusion is to Matthew 7:6, 'Do men gather grapes of thorns, or figs of thistles?' A surviving manuscript of the poem is NLS, MS. 2208, f. 41. There has been some confusion between this episode and one that Sir William Gell suggests took place later in Rome. However, I think that James Corson was wrong to interpret a cryptic remark by Gell as implying that Scott found the Princess's request in any way either disagreeable or irksome, or indeed to link this mysterious later occasion with the one in Naples that resulted in Scott's composition of the verses. On this see Gell, *Reminiscences*, 28 and particularly Corson's note 64. It is further to be noted that Gell, in a supplementary passage that he requested Lady Blessington to add to his memoir of Scott, stated that: 'His amiable feeling on every occasion, led him to assist and encourage all younger authors, and he seemed totally devoid of every spark of that littleness and jealousy which sometimes activates even the most illustrious and established literati.' See Madden, *Literary Life and Correspondence of the Countess of Blessington*, II: 84.

40 *Journal*, 695.

41 NLS, MS. 1752, f. 493, WS To James Skene, 5 Mar. 1832.

42 *Life in the South*, 147-8.

43 *Ibid.*, 155-7.

44 *Ibid.*, 151-2.

45 *Ibid.*, 157.

46 *Memoirs, Journal and Correspondence of Thomas Moore*, VI: 226-7.

47 Madden took this anecdote from Willis's book and reprinted it verbatim in his own: *Literary Life and Correspondence of the Countess of Blessington*, II: 12-14.

48 See the letters of Gell to Lady Blessington in Madden, II: 70-80.

49 N. P. Willis, *Pencillings by the Way*, three vols (London: John Macrone, 1835), III: 97-100; Gell, *Reminiscences*, n. 40.

50 Gell, *Reminiscences*, 15. See also *Life in the South*, 157, for Marianne Talbot's account of Scott's visit to the '[National] Library [of Naples] at the Studio [*sic*]', 'where all the learned were in great array to do him honor, but the only thing he took much interest in was a neapolitan version of Mother Goose of great antiquity.'

51 Willis, *Pencillings by the Way*, III: 97-99.

52 NLS, MS. 1752, f. 505, WS to Lockhart, 15 Mar. 1832.

53 *Journal*, 702. Anderson was mistaken in making the assumption that Sorrento is the place referred to. Scott may well have been looking at a map and have

become muddled between names and actual places.

54 *Journal*, 701; NLS, MS. 1752, f. 452, WS to Cadell, c. 7 Jan. 1832.

55 NLS, MS. 1752, f. 481, WS to William Laidlaw, 27 Feb. 1832; *Life in the South*, 159, 162, 160.

56 *Ibid.*, 152.

57 *Journal*, 699. The travelling tutor or 'bear-leader' was a stock figure in Grand Tour literature and imagery: a character half-revered and half-mocked. Scott had suggested to his protégé James Bailey that he might like to seek such a position and accompany some intelligent young man round Europe. 'It is an employment which has often [been] the foundation of independence to men of letters.' (*Letters*, IV: 139, WS to Bailey, [30 Nov. 1815].) A later letter to Bailey shows that Scott was not so ignorant of classical literature, its history and criticism as his comments on his own indifferent abilities might suggest. He mentions the essays on Greek drama by Richard Cumberland, collected in Cumberland's *The Observer* in 1785, and dredged up in Scott's prodigious memory over thirty years later: *Letters*, IV: 358, WS to Bailey, 4 Jan. 1817.

58 *Literary Life and Correspondence of the Countess of Blessington*, II: 83-4. The Stones of Stenness, which Scott called 'the Orcadian Stonehenge... this stupendous monument of antiquity', feature several times in Scott's *The Pirate* (1822): 'that remarkable semi-circle of huge upright stones, which has no rival in Britain, excepting the inimitable monument at Stonehenge...'. He had seen them for himself in 1814, on his 'Lighthouse cruise'. In his description of an ancient site endowed with a definite spirit of place, Scott actually seems to conflate in his mind the Stones of Stenness and the nearby Ring of Brodgar. See *The Pirate*, ed. Mark Weinstein and Alison Lumsden, Edinburgh Edition of the Waverley Novels (Edinburgh: Edinburgh University Press, 2001), 214, 308, 359, 369, 371-2 and 552.

59 Karl Miller, *Cockburn's Millennium*, 82, 85, 100.

60 Gell, *Reminiscences*, 2.

61 *Sir William Gell in Italy*, 73.

62 Gell, *Reminiscences*, 22-23.

63 Lang, *Life and Letters of John Gibson Lockhart*, II: 208, Lockhart to Jonathan Christie, 13 Sept. 1843.

64 Gell, *Reminiscences*. 8.

65 *Ibid.*, 8.

66 Laurence Goldstein, 'The Impact of Pompeii on the Literary Imagination', *The Centennial Review*, 23, no. 3 (Summer 1979), 227-8. Goldstein quotes lines from a poem by Thomas Gold Appleton. Dickens wrote memorably in Chapter XI of *Pictures from Italy* of 'The Destroyed and the Destroyer making this quiet picture in the sun.' Dickens also alluded to Scott's 'City of the Dead' phrase, which he will have known from Lockhart's biography, where it is quoted from Gell's memoranda.

67 Victoria C. Gardner Coates and Jon L. Seydl, 'Introduction', in *Antiquity Recorded. The Legacy of Pompeii and Herculaneum*, eds. Victoria C. Gardner Coates and Jon L. Seydl (J. Paul Getty Museum: Los Angeles, 2007), 4-6;10.

68 *Ibid.*, 10. On the story and significance of Fiorelli's remarkable casts see Eugene Dwyer, *Pompeii's Living Statues. Ancient Roman Lives Stolen from Death* (Ann Arbor, MI: University of Michigan Press, 2013). The subtitle adapts the words used by Fiorelli himself to describe what his casts had contrived to do for the Pompeiians so preserved.

69 Mrs Frank Russell [P. A. M. B. Russell], *Fragments of Auld Lang Syne*

(London: Hutchinson & Co., n.d. [but 1925], 35.

70 For Cockburn's *Delineations of Pompeii* project, see Powell, *Turner in the South*, 81 and 204, notes 48-54.

71 A second work, in two volumes, entitled *Pompeiana: The Topography, Edifices and Ornaments of Pompeii, the Result of Excavations since 1819*, was to appear in London, published by Jennings & Chaplin, in 1832. Scott, of course, may well not have known that this was to be published. Lockhart, a classicist, noted his own surprise, in 1843, that (as he put it) 'none of the books or prints had given us the least notion of the place, nor even of the minutest discoveries.' See Lang, *Life and Letters of John Gibson Lockhart*, II: 208.

72 NLS, MS. 1752, f. 455, WS to Robert Cadell, 18 Jan. 1832.

73 Sumner Lincoln Fairfield, *The Last Night of Pompeii: A Poem* (New York: Elliott & Palmer, 1832), Preface [iii].

74 Cf. Holland, *The Warm South*, 114-5.

75 Michael Heafford, 'The history of the Auldjo Jug 1830-60—a review and critique: was Sir Walter Scott the real benefactor?', *Proceedings of the Society of Antiquaries of Scotland*, 148 (2018), 276. This interesting but rather speculative article suggests that the fragments of the famous Roman glass jug, now in the British Museum, once belonged to Scott, having been presented to him by Neapolitan royal command. The fact that those who accompanied Scott to Pompeii never mention his having received any such present, and that no one else in Naples did so either, seems to undermine the thesis; the oddity of the object/s apparently selected as a gift for Scott also poses a problem for the credibility of this idea. However, it cannot be dismissed as entirely fanciful, and it at least makes more sense than the alternative provenance history of the object.

76 *Life and Correspondence of the Countess of Blessington*, II: 209-11, which prints a letter of Auldjo to Lady Blessington from Naples, 25 Sept. 1835. I have been unable to identify 'Bonnucci' conclusively. He may or may not be one and the same as Carlo Bonucci [*sic*] (1799-1870), 'architetto-direttore' of the Pompeii excavations and author of a popular—and somewhat romanticised—guidebook to the site as well as of a guide to the Real Museo Borbonico. Scott obtained a copy of Bonucci's *Pompei* in its second French translation from the third Italian edition (Naples, 1830): this remains at Abbotsford. Susan Matoff, *Marguerite, Countess of Blessington. The Turbulent Life of a Salonnière and Author* (Madison, DE: University of Delaware Press, 2015), 177-8 calls the Neapolitan author 'Bonuccio' but does not attempt an identification. This is the spelling given in the first edition of Madden's *Life and Correspondence*.

77 Gell, *Reminiscences*, 21.

78 *Letters*, XII: 43, WS to Lockhart, [January 1832]; Lang, *Life and Letters of John Gibson Lockhart*, II: 208.

79 MS. 1752, f. 481, to Laidlaw, 27 Feb. 1832; *Life in the South*, 160-61, 163.

80 *Sir Willam Gell in Italy*, 68-9, 20/22 Feb. 1832.

81 *Literary Life and Correspondence of the Countess of Blessington*, II: 63, 20 Mar. 1832.

82 *Ibid.*, 70, 80.

83 *Journal*, 699; NLS, MS. 1752, ff. 455, 457, 472 and 476-7, WS to Robert Cadell, 18 Jan., 26 Jan., 13 Feb., and 16 Feb. 1832.

84 Matthews, *Diary of an Invalid*, 60 (Galignani third edn, 53-54).

85 Stephen Cheeke, '"What so Many have Told, Who Would Tell Again": Romanticism and the Commonplaces of Rome', *European Romantic Review*,

17, no. 5 (December 2006), 525-6.

86 The corrected proofs of *The Talisman* are in the Beinecke Library, Yale University, Gen. MSS. 266, Box 39. Bound in with the proofs are some letters relating to the progress of the novel to the press. From one of these comes the passage quoted. See Walter Scott, *The Talisman*, ed. J. B. Ellis, with J. H. Alexander, P. D. Garside and David Hewitt, Edinburgh Edition of the Waverley Novels (Edinburgh: Edinburgh University Press, 2009, 'Essay on the Text', Section 2: Composition of *The Talisman*: The Proofs, 302.

87 *The Talisman*, Magnum Edition, vol. XXXVIII (Edinburgh: Robert Cadell, 1832), Introduction, iii-iv.

88 *The English in Italy*, II: 239-42.

89 *Continental Adventures*, III: 395-6.

90 *The Warm South*, 67.

91 Basil Hall, *Fragments of Voyages and Travels*, 312.

92 *Journal*, 667.

93 *Letters*, XII: 43, WS to Lockhart, [Jan. 1832]; NLS. MS. 1752, f. 470, to Cadell, 5 Feb. 1832.

94 NLS, MS. 1752, f. 529, WS to Cadell, Mar.-Apr. 1832.

95 NLS, MS. 1752, ff. 457,472, 476-7, 520 and 533, WS to Robert Cadell, 26 Jan., 13 Feb., 16 Feb., 23 Mar., and 14 Apr. 1832; NLS, MS. 1554, f. 8, Anne Scott to Sophia Lockhart, 17 Feb. 1832.

96 NLS, MS. 5317, f. 230, Sir Frederick Adam to WS, 28 Mar. 1832.

97 On Sir John Franklin in the Mediterranean and Aegean, see Andrew Lambert, *Franklin: Tragic Hero of Polar Exploration* (London: Faber & Faber, 2009), 46, 49. (It is ironic that HMS *Barham* had actually sailed on from Naples to Constantinople in order to collect the British Ambassador to the Sublime Porte, Sir Stratford Canning, and bring him home. Scott might, just possibly, have had his Aegean cruise that way.)

98 NLS, MS. 1752, f. 533, WS to Robert Cadell, 14 April 1832; f. 536, to Lockhart, 17 Apr. 1832.

99 Gell, *Reminiscences*, 23, 14.

100 Thackeray, *Notes of a Journey from Cornhill to Grand Cairo*, 82-4.

101 It is interesting to note that Thackeray had gone to the Mediterranean, like Scott before him, on a free passage. Scott was the Admiralty's guest; Thackeray, in 1844, travelled at the expense of the Peninsular & Oriental line, on the understanding that he would publicise the shipping company with his resulting narrative.

102 *Sir William Gell in Italy*, 69.

103 *Ibid.*, 74. In the library at Abbotsford is a bound manuscript entitled 'Notes to save Sir Walter the trouble of looking out for information about Rhodes. By W. Gell 1832.' This bears out Gell's suggestion that he could tell Scott all he needed to know.

104 John Sutherland, *Life of Walter Scott* , 353; cf. Edgar Johnson, *Sir Walter Scott*, II: 1240.

105 NLS, MS. 1752, f. 531, WS to Robert Cadell, [Mar.-Apr. 1832].

106 NLS, MS. 5317, f. 228, Sophia Lockhart to Anne Scott: date cut away; postmark illegible, but Feb. 1832. The most pernickety of the life assurance companies had endorsed only a voyage to Malta or Naples: see above, Chapter 9, note 50. See also NLS. MS. 917, Neapolitan letter-book of Charles Scott, f. 37v., to Lockhart, 23 Mar. 1832.

107 NLS, MS. 1752, ff. 477 and 529-30, WS to Robert Cadell, 16 Feb. and [Mar.-Apr.],1832.

108 *Journal*, 704; NLS, MS. 1752, f. 505, WS to Lockhart, 15 Mar. 1832.
109 *Journal*, 708.
110 NLS. MS. 1752, ff. 522, WS to William Laidlaw, 29 Mar. 1832, and f. 533, to Robert Cadell, 14 Apr. 1832.
111 The presentation copy of Auldjo's *Narrative of an Ascent to the Summit of Mont Blanc in 1827*, second edn (London: Longman, 1830) is at Abbotsford. Gell refers to Scott's meetings with Auldjo in *Reminiscences*, 9-10.
112 *Letters*, IV: 477, WS to Joanna Baillie, 24 July 1817.
113 *Sketches Descriptive of Italy*, III. 207.
114 *Diary of an Ennuyée*, 209.
115 *Remarks on Antiquities, Arts, and Letters ... in Italy*, 104, 97-8.
116 *Rome in the Nineteenth Century*, III: 286-7.
117 *The Journal of the Hon. Henry Edward Fox*, 295.
118 See Frank Salmon, *Building on Ruins: The Rediscovery of Rome and English Architecture* (Aldershot: Ashgate, 2000), 78. Gell himself was oddly mistaken when he recorded, in his *Reminiscences of Sir Walter Scott's Residence in Italy*, 28, that his villa was on the Quirinal.
119 See *Sir William Gell in Italy*, 81, note 1; and H. V. Morton, *A Traveller in Rome*, (London: Methuen, 1957), Appendix, 419.
120 *Rome in the Nineteenth Century*, I: 219-20.
121 *Reminiscences of Sir Walter Scott's Residence in Italy*, 28.
122 *Reminiscences*, 26; *Sir William Gell in Italy*, 78.
123 Sweet, *Cities and the Grand Tour*, 21 and Chapter 6 *passim*, with 'Conclusion'.
124 Angus Davidson, *Miss Douglas of New York* (London: Sidgwick and Jackson, 1952), 205-6.
125 *Sketches Descriptive of Italy*, II: 345.
126 Lockhart, X: 173-4.
127 On Murdo and his work see P. Macgregor Chalmers, *A Scots Mediaeval Architect* (Glasgow: William Hodge, 1895.
128 A version of this text appeared in a note to Samuel Rogers's *Italy*, in its 1836 edition (London: Thomas Cadell and Edward Moxon), 264, with reference to a passage (page 100, line 6) in the 'Bologna' section of Rogers's poem. Rogers states that Scott had repeated this 'ancient inscription' from Melrose Abbey to him years before. The lines worked their way into the consciousness of a wider circle. Mrs Fanny Bury Palliser included them, as Scott's, in the section on 'Time' in her *The Modern Poetical Speaker; or a Collection of Pieces Adapted for Recitation, Carefully Selected from the Poets of the Nineteenth Century* (London: Longman, 1845), 410.
129 *Life in the South*, 181.
130 *Sir William Gell in Italy*, 78.
131 This fascinating and evocative painting now seems likely to be the work of three different minor artists. Various attributions had earlier been suggested. On the picture in general and in in context see Edward Corp, *The King Over the Water. Portraits of the Stuarts in Exile after 1689* (Edinburgh: National Galleries of Scotland, 2001), 83-5 and Fig. 78; Edward Corp, 'The Stuart Court and the Patronage of Portrait-Painters in Rome, 1715-57', in *Roma Britannica. Art Patronage and Cultural Exchange in Eighteenth-Century Rome*, ed. David R. Marshall, Susan Russell and Karin Wolfe (London: The British School at Rome, 2011), esp. 40-4, 47-9; and David R. Marshall, 'The Cardinal's Clothes: The Temporary Façade for the Investiture Celebration of Cardinal York in 1747', in *Roma Britannica...*, 55-69, esp. 55-59 and 62-6.

132 James Lees-Milne, *St Peter's* (London: Hamish Hamilton, 1967), 313.

133 Richard Monckton Milnes, *Memorials of Many Scenes* (London: Edward Moxon, 1844), Preface [vii]; 131-3.

134 It is misinterpreted and seriously misdated by John Varriano, *Rome. A Literary Companion* (London: John Murray, 1991), 225. Varriano further implies that the record of Scott's visit was Lockhart's own, whereas, in fact, Lockhart was quoting Gell's account. The Milnes poem is misdated simply on the basis that it was reprinted and included in Milnes's *Collected Poetical Works* of 1876.

135 James Pope-Hennessy, *Monckton Milnes. The Years of Promise 1809-1851* (London: Constable, 1949), 41, 51; *Monckton Milnes. The Flight of Youth 1851-1885* (London: Constable, 1951), 251.

136 Hakewill claimed that such interior views had never before been included in a book on Italy: see Powell, *Turner in the South*, 18. On the significance of Hakewill's book see further O'Connor, *The Romance of Italy and the English Imagination*, 23. In fact, two series of interior views of the new Museo Pio-Clementino in the Vatican had been produced at the end of the eighteenth century: those by Louis Ducros and Giovanni Volpato, and by Vincenzo Feoli. On these see *Grand Tour. The Lure of Italy in the Eighteenth Century*, ed. Andrew Wilton and Ilaria Bignamini (London: Tate Gallery Publishing, 1996), 241-9.

137 Maria Fairweather, *The Pilgrim Princess. A Life of Princess Zinaida Volkonsky* (London; Constable, 1999), 229. Lady Fairweather was not aware that Scott and the Princess had met in Naples, nor that he had composed verses there for her at her request.

138 *Ibid.*

139 On Bryullov and his picture, see Ingrid D. Rowland, *From Pompeii. The Afterlife of a Roman Town* (Cambridge, Mass. and London, 2014), 129-36.

140 Judith Harris, *Pompeii Awakened. A Story of Rediscovery* (London and New York: I. B. Tauris, 2007), 164.

141 On the phenomenon see, for example, Iain Bamforth, 'Stendhal's Syndrome', *British Journal of General Practice*, 60, no. 581 (2010), 945-6, which unites Stendhal, the Grand Tour, Italy and being overcome by emotion in the context of too much art.

142 Fairweather, *The Pilgrim Princess*, 229-30. The Volkonsky 'essay' is here quoted and presumably (?badly) translated from *Oeuvres Choisies de la Princesse Zénéide Volkonsky* (Paris, 1865), no page being cited.

143 Anthony Blunt, *Guide to Baroque Rome* (London: Granada, 1982), 8-10; Varriano, *Rome. A Literary Companion*, 146-7; Georgina Masson, *The Companion Guide to Rome*, eighth edition, rev. by John Frost (Woodbridge: Boydell & Brewer, 2003), 231-2.

144 Iain Gordon Brown, 'Canova, Thorvaldsen and the Ancients. A Scottish View of Sculpture in Rome, 1821-1822', in *The Three Graces. Antonia Canova*, ed. Hugh Honour and Aidan Weston-Lewis (Edinburgh: National Galleries of Scotland, 1995), 73-80.

145 Skene, *Memories of Sir Walter Scott*, 207.

146 See Francis Russell, *Portraits of Sir Walter Scott, a Study of Romantic Portraiture* (London: Printed for the Author, 1987), 85. For a more recent discussion of Thorvaldsen's images of Scott, see Tim Knox and Todd Longstaffe-Gowan, 'Thorvaldsen's "Valdrescot": a lost bust of Sir Walter Scott discovered', *Apollo*, CXXVII, no. 372, (February 1993), 75-81. The sculpture is now in the Scottish National Portrait Gallery. Thorvaldsen also made a profile 'medallion' of Scott, perhaps from the bust. Lockhart was

anxious about this medallion in 1848: see Lang, *Life and Letters of John Gibson Lockhart*, II: 311 for a letter mentioning a cast of the medallion portrait which should be handled carefully by Scott's grand-daughter Charlotte. Francis Russell suggests that this is to be identified with the plaque over an archway in the Hope-Scott wing at Abbotsford. Although the scale of the latter seems very different, the work does bear the character of a 'Thorvaldsen' medallion portrait.

147 Mullen and Munson, *The Smell of the Continent*, 59.

148 See, for example, *Journal*, 294 where Scott writes of showing 'the lions' of Melrose.

149 Eugenia Stanhope, *Letters Written by the Late Right Honourable Philip Dormer Stanhope, Earl of Chesterfield, to his Son, Philip Stanhope, Esq.* seventh edn, four vols (London, J, Dodsley, 1776), II: 313, Letter CLXXXI, 11 Jan. 1750.

150 *Journal*, 498-9.

151 *Letters*, XI: 124, WS to Maria Edgeworth, 4 Feb. 1819.

152 *Journal*, 708. Scott told his daughter Sophia that he had encountered Miss Douglas in Naples 'to our no real confusion': NLS, MS. 138, f. 101v, n.d. He further wrote to Lockhart of 'the truly detestable Miss Douglas': NLS, MS. 1752, f. 509, 23 Mar. 1832. Charles Scott also added his pennyworth of venom, expressing a similar wish to his father that the cholera might carry off 'an inundation of horrible people', Miss Douglas especially: see NLS, MS. 917, f. 36v, to J. G. Lockhart, 19-23 Mar. 1832.

153 *Life in the South*, 180-81.

154 *The Letters of Charles Dickens*, three vols, ed. Walter Dexter (London: Nonesuch Press, 1938), I: 544-6, Dickens to Forster, 1 and 2 Nov. 1843.

155 Charles Dickens, *Pictures of Italy*, with an introduction and notes by David Paroissien (London: André Deutch, 1973), 12.

156 *Reminiscences of Sir Walter Scott's Residence in Italy*, 1, 36-7.

157 *Sir William Gell in Italy*, 117.

158 *Ibid.*, 50.

159 Holland, *The Warm South*, 87.

160 Knox and Longstaffe-Gowan, '"Valdrescot": a lost bust of Sir Walter Scott discovered', 79.

161 [W. M. Thackeray], *The Paris Sketchbook* (London: George Routledge, 1885), 67-8.

162 Lang, *Life and Letters of John Gibson Lockhart*, II: 380.

163 *Ibid.*, 377, 16 Jan. 1854. I had written the passage about Grand Tours often failing to deliver hoped-for health benefits before I had read in any detail Richard Wrigley's *Roman Fever: Influence, Infection and the Image of Rome, 1700-1870*, also cited above at Chapter 1, note 35. I find that Wrigley had considered entitling his book 'The Dark Side of the Grand Tour': see *Roman Fever*, 4. As I had already hit on similar phrasing here, I let it stand as symbolic of how similar views—and sometimes similar wording—can be arrived at entirely independently.

164 Lang, *Life and Letters of John Gibson Lockhart*, II: 384.

165 On Allan Massie's *The Ragged Lion*, at the time and in the context of the presentation of the manuscript to the National Library of Scotland, see Iain Gordon Brown, 'Collecting Scott for Scotland: 1850-2000', *The Book Collector*, 49, no 4 (Winter 2000), 520-22.

166 Allan Massie, *The Ragged Lion*, Sceptre edition (London: Hodder and Stoughton, 1995), 273-6, 286-7. For Scott's admiration of Cunningham's

song, see *Letters*, VI: 319, WS to Allan Cunningham, 12 Dec. 1820,.

11 'Let Us to Abbotsford'

1   Eric Quayle, *The Ruin of Sir Walter Scott* (London: Rupert Hart-Davis, 1968), 264; Sutherland, *Life of Walter Scott*, 353. For a short but good account of Scott's journey, published on the occasion of the centenary of his starting from Naples on 16 April 1832, see W. M. Parker, 'The Return of the Native: Scott's Last Journey, *The Scotsman*, 16 April 1932, 15. Charles Scott's (unpaginated) travel diary, recording the journey home in some detail, is NLS, MS. 1614.

2   NLS, MS. 138, no. 51 (f. 103), n.d [but ?12 May 1832].

3   Davidson, *Miss Douglas of New York*, 207-9.

4   *Journal*, 697.

5   *Diary of an Ennuyée*, 79.

6   This phrase is quoted by Hesketh Pearson in *Sir Walter Scott: His Life and Personality* (London: Methuen, 1954), 149. The manuscript of 'Sylva' remains at Abbotsford, and Scott was still working on it in a desultory way in the period before his departure for Italy.

7   'A Last Memory of Sir Walter Scott', 264.

8   Sweet, *Cities and the Grand Tour*, 263-4.

9   'A Last Memory of Sir Walter Scott', 267.

10 The silver-mounted rummer is illustrated in Angus Davidson's *Miss Douglas of New York*. Through Harriet Douglas's care, the Augsburg rummer was not to suffer the fate of King George IV's glass used to toast Scott at Leith in August 1822. That, taken home in Scott's tail pocket, had been crushed when he sat on it inadvertently. Surely this parallel would not have been lost on Scott, who would probably also have recollected his own father's action in seeing to it that no-one would drink afterwards from the tea-cup used by John Murray of Broughton—a man seen by some as a traitor to the Jacobite cause—by throwing it from the window of the family house in George Square. See Lockhart's accounts of both episodes: I: 201, and VII: 49.

11 See Gifford's short survey article 'Scott, Opera and the Italian Journey' in the online journal *The Bottle Imp* (issue 9, May 2011) which offers a brief overview of the Mediterranean trip of 1831-32. <https://www.thebottleimp. org.uk/2011/05/scott-opera-and-the-italian-journey/>.

12 Richard Hurd, *Dialogues on the Uses of Foreign Travel; Considered as a Part of An English Gentleman's Education* (London: A. Millar, 1764), 8. This work, which Scott had in his library, purports to be a conversation between John Locke and the Earl of Shaftesbury.

13 NLS, MS. 917, ff. 31 and 36, Charles Scott to Lockhart, 10 Feb. and 19-23 Mar. 1832; Parker, 'The Return of the Native'.

14 Miller, *Cockburn's Millennium*, 98.

15 On the Alpine passes see Lynne Withey, *Grand Tours and Cook's Tours*, (above, Chapter 3, note 1), 20-21 and 64-65.

16 *Sir Willam Gell in Italy*, 78.

17 'Mrs Ann Radcliffe', 338; Lockhart, X: 155.

18 Lockhart, X: 176-77. The idea has been adapted in Iain Gordon Brown, 'A Flibbertigibbet of a House to Suit an Antiquary', xiii. See also Iain Gordon Brown, 'Setting Scott in Stone', 24.

19 Sutherland, *Life of Walter Scott*, 354.

20 NLS, Acc. 11975, 6 July 1832. Pigot received this letter on 17 September and answered it on the 22nd, ironically the day after Scott died.

21 Gell, *Reminiscences*, 1. In April 1833 Gell, who considered himself to have been 'the last of [Scott's] friends', complained to Lady Blessington that the set of Scott's works 'which he ordered for me with almost the last sentence he uttered that was intelligible' had either not been sent or had not arrived: *Literary Life and Correspondence of the Countess of Blessington*, II: 70, 74.
22 G. O. Trevelyan, *Life and Letters of Lord Macaulay*, I: 258.
23 *The Collected Letters of Thomas and Jane Welsh Carlyle*, Duke-Edinburgh Edition, ed. C.R. Sanders and K. J. Fielding [and others subsequently], in progress, 45 vols to date, 6: 193, 31 July; 220, 31 Aug.; 185, 2 July; 197, 31 July 1832.

Index

There are no index entries for 'Sir Walter Scott', 'travel', 'Europe' or 'Grand Tour'